Jamaica Kincaid

Jamaica Kincaid

Writing Memory, Writing Back to the Mother

J. Brooks Bouson

State University of New York Press

Published by
State University of New York Press, Albany

For information, address State University of New York Press,
194 Washington Avenue, Suite 305, Albany, NY 12210-2365

Production by Judith Block
Marketing by Michael Campochiaro

Library of Congress Cataloging-in-Publication Data

Bouson, J. Brooks.
  Jamaica Kincaid : writing memory, writing back to the mother / J. Brooks Bouson.
    p. cm.
  Includes bibliographical references and index.
  ISBN 0-7914-6523-3 (alk. paper) — ISBN 0-7914-6524-1 (pbk. : alk. paper)
  1. Kincaid, Jamaica—Criticism and interpretation. 2. Women and literature—Antigua—
History—20th century. 3. Mothers and daughters in literature. 4. Antigua—In
literature. 5. Memory in literature. I. Title.

PR9275.A583K564 2005
813'.54—dc22

                                                                        2004027305

10 9 8 7 6 5 4 3 2 1

Contents

Part III. Family Portraits

❦ *For Roberts* ❦

Acknowledgments

During the time I have spent working on this project, I have been heartened by the good will, enthusiasm, and support of others. I would like to express my appreciation to the many students that I have had the good fortune to teach in my Women in Literature and Studies in Women Writers classes at Loyola University of Chicago. Their spirited and at times combative responses to Kincaid and their eagerness to think and talk about—and indeed, talk back to—Kincaid inspired me to investigate the emotionally charged world of Kincaid's writings and sustained me as I labored on this book. I am also grateful to Frank Fennell, the chair of Loyola's English department, for encouraging and cheering me on; to the administration of Loyola University, for granting me a research leave during the early stages of my work on this project and for providing Research Services funds as I was preparing the book for publication; to Jon Weidler, my graduate assistant, for aiding me in the arduous task of checking sources in the final stages of my work; and to Shelly Jarenski, for assisting me in the equally arduous tasks of proofreading and indexing. Special thanks are due to Joseph Adamson, whose scholarship on shame in literature has been a continuing source of inspiration to me, and to James Peltz, the editor-in-chief of State University of New York Press, and Judith Block, the production editor, for their good-natured and generous support of my project. And finally, I want to thank my husband, Roberts, a true friend of my mind, for his abiding and affectionate interest in my work.

❧ *1* ❧

Introduction:
"When You Think of Me,
Think of My Life"

In the eyes of her many interviewers, Jamaica Kincaid is an unusual and forceful individual: she is described as a woman with a "dramatic" look and as a "tall, striking, clear-eyed" woman who turns heads and "projects a natural authority that attracts attention" (Garis, Garner). Kincaid's interviewers also often make note of the Antiguan-born writer's "proper British accent" or comment that she sounds "like a genteel Englishwoman with a mysterious background that puts music in her speech" (Kreilkamp 54, Garis). "Even when she's denouncing the world's many evil-doers, her voice is gentle and engaging. The effect is not so much a softening of her anger but an intensification of it by contrast. She makes anger and outrage completely compatible with good humor," writes one of her interviewers (Kreilkamp 55). To another, she is a "highly opinionated" woman who is "steadfast in her beliefs" and "fiercely determined" about those things she believes to be social injustices (Vorda 80).

A memory-haunted woman who continually remembers and tries to make sense of her Caribbean upbringing on the island of Antigua, Kincaid is a writer out of necessity. Speaking openly about her life and work in her many interviews, Kincaid emphasizes the autobiographical and psychological origins of her writing. "[F]or me, writing is like going to a psychiatrist. I just discover things about myself," Kincaid has revealingly remarked (Perry, "Interview" 498). When she writes, she is not Caribbean, not black;[1] instead, she is "just this sort of unhappy person struggling to make something, struggling to be free. Yet the freedom isn't a political one or a public one: it's a personal one. It's a struggle I realize that will go on until the day that I die" (Vorda 82). Kincaid, who has always asserted that for her writing is a personal act, says that she is "trying to discover the secret" of herself in her writing (Kennedy).

"When you think of me, think of my life" (Vorda 83). In Kincaid's works, whether it be her short story collection, *At the Bottom of the River* (1983), her avowedly autobiographical fiction, *Annie John* (1985) and *Lucy* (1990), her fictionalized *The Autobiography of My Mother* (1996), her factual account of her brother's death from AIDS in *My Brother* (1997), or her fictional memoir of her biological father in *Mr. Potter* (2002), she insistently, if not obsessively, focuses on her relationship with her family, especially her powerful, and to Kincaid, tyrannical mother. And she similarly draws on her personal life in her angry attack on the tourist industry in Antigua in *A Small Place* (1988) and in her essays on gardening collected in *My Garden (Book):* (1999). My aim is to investigate the ongoing construction of Kincaid's autobiographical self and writer's identity as I examine the aspect of her writings that many critics find so enigmatic—what has been called the "mother mystery"[2] that lies at the heart of her work.

"I hate tyranny," Kincaid states. "It's better to be dead than to have people forcing you to do things that are a violation" (Garner). Well-known for her fierce self-assertiveness and her frank expression of her feelings, Kincaid considers anger "a badge of honor," and she also insists on the power of shamelessness—whatever causes shame "you should just wear brazenly," she comments (Perry, "Interview" 497, Garner). Yet while Kincaid openly expresses her anger and defiant shamelessness in her writings, she deals with intensely painful, even frightening, experiences and feelings as she describes, through her daughter characters, her intensely ambivalent love-hate relationship with her mother, her episodic experiences of profound depression and subjective emptiness, her injured pride and intense rage, and her feelings of exposure and bodily shame. Behind the intense idealization of the daughter's attachment to the perfectly attuned mother and the often accusatory depictions of the withdrawn and rejecting mother lie not only feelings of sadness and betrayal and injury but also a profound sense of shame and dread.

Providing an absorbing account of the often conflicting needs and fantasies that animate psychic life and family relationships, Kincaid conveys, through her hallmark style, the ambivalences and uncertainties that drive her work. The classic Kincaidian sentence, in Derek Walcott's often quoted description, "heads toward its own contradiction" (Garis). Through her associative but also highly controlled narrative style, Kincaid makes her readers privy to a deeply conflicted consciousness, an inner voice in open conflict with others and in deep self-conflict. Focusing more on individual experience than on the Caribbean collective experience, Kincaid's narrative style, as Caribbean writer Merle Hodge has aptly remarked, is one in which "the main speaking voice is the voice of the protagonist/narrator, and the main dialogue is with her own, searching self" (52). Driven by the need for self-rescue and self-repair, Kincaid, through her self-searching style, writes not only to relieve the mental torment caused by her obsessive ruminations about the past but also to make a kind of literary sense of her life experiences and to construct a meaningful and livable autobiographical and writer's identity. Describing her writing as "very autobiographical," Kincaid insists that when she began to write, the act of writing "was really an act of saving" her life (Ferguson, "Interview" 176). For Kincaid, the writing process is "always full of pain," but it also is "a way of being" (Snell). She writes because she does not know "how else to live," and writing also allows her to live "in the deepest way" (Ferguson, "Interview" 169).

An author who has commented that she must "find the emotion somewhere inside" herself to write (Perry, "Interview" 495), Kincaid taps into what Nancy Chodorow calls "the power of feelings" in her writings. "A particular feeling condenses and expresses an unconscious fantasy about self, body, other, other's body, or self and other," writes Chodorow in her analysis of the psychoanalytic contribution to the study of feelings. "Through the power of feelings, unconscious fantasy recasts the subject—emotions and stories about different aspects of self in relation to one another and about the self and body in relation to an inner and outer object world" (*Power* 239–40).[3] Countering contemporary cultural theorists who focus on how cultural forms give rise to a culturally determined psyche, Chodorow argues that cultural meanings are kept alive for the individual and culture because they are "emotionally charged and continually invested with fantasy, conflict, and shifting private meaning" (*Power* 201). Chodorow, who takes issue with the cultural determinism of antipsychological theorists,[4] states that "the psychological is just as irreducible as the cultural and has as much force and power in shaping and constituting human life and society" (*Power* 217).

No more a seamless whole than culture is, psychological life, as Chodorow aptly comments, is a "multiplicity of unconscious fantasies and conflicts and the complex internal worlds that characterize psychic life for the individual" (*Power* 217). While individuals are products of their culture, they also "create cultural selves and emotions and animate cultural meanings and interpretations individually" (*Power* 225). In her both-and approach, Chodorow argues that meaning is at once cultural and personal: that is, it is an "inextricable mixture of the sociocultural and historically contextualized on the one hand and the personally psychodynamic and psychobiographically contextualized on the other" (*Power* 2). Moreover, "There is no simple internalization of culture, no single way in which psyches hook onto culture" (*Power* 197). Thus, "people avail themselves of cultural meanings and images, but they experience them emotionally and through fantasy, as well as in particular interpersonal contexts. Emotional meaning, affective tone, and unconscious fantasies that arise from within and are not experienced linguistically interact with and give individual animation and nuance to cultural categories, stories, and language (that is, make them subjectively meaningful)" (*Power* 71–72). "That thoughts and feelings are entangled and that thoughts are thought in culturally specific languages—these ideas do not mean that there is no private feeling or that any particular thought has only a public cultural meaning" (*Power* 166). For Chodorow, "if cultural meanings matter, they matter personally. . . . Psychological force drives the experience of culturally recognized emotions just as cultures help to shape emotional life" (*Power* 170–71).

That cultural meanings are "emotionally charged and continually invested with fantasy, conflict, and shifting private meaning" is apparent in Kincaid's representation of the private and cultural lives of her protagonists. Yet in the scholarly responses to Kincaid's writings, critics, while they typically concur that mother-daughter and family relations are central to her work, also tend to shun the psychological and instead allegorize and politicize the personal and relational in her writings. Thus, as Kincaid critics have frequently argued, Kincaid's troubled relationship with her mother is a metaphor for her troubled relation with her colonial Antiguan culture and the colonial motherland. "There is a clear correlation established throughout Kincaid's work between motherhood and the colonial metropolis as motherland," remarks one critic (Paravisini-Gebert 27). Although the relations between Kincaid's female characters and their mothers "are crucially formative," they are also "always mediated by intimations of life as colonized subjects" so that "[c]ultural location becomes paramount" in Kincaid's art, writes another (Ferguson, *Jamaica Kincaid* 1). For yet another critic, in Kincaid's novels "the alienation from the mother becomes a metaphor for the young woman's alienation from an island culture that has been completely dominated by the imperialist power of England" (de Abruna 173).

Despite the argument that it is "narrow and prescriptive" to read postcolonial works featuring mothers and daughters as "uniformly allegorical of colonizer/colonized relationships" (Curry 100), one can find evidence of this tendency in studies of Kincaid's works. Indeed, Kincaid herself, over time, has come to make a conscious connection between her fierce hatred of maternal domination and her colonial upbringing as she, in her own description, has developed a political consciousness.

But if the psychosocial development of Kincaid's characters can—and indeed should—be read in the context of the colonial situation, it is nevertheless reductive to read the mother/daughter relationship in Kincaid as "metonymic of the colonial condition" (Ledent 59) or to ignore or minimize the importance of the psychological and familial in Kincaid's art. In a similar way, the handful of psychological readings of Kincaid's writings by critics have focused largely on the regressive pre-oedipal dynamics of Kincaid's art[5] to the exclusion of a broader understanding of the autobiographical origins and persistence of the mother-daughter conflict in her work. My aim is to draw on Kincaid's many remarks on the autobiographical sources of her writings as I read her works through the lens of contemporary shame and trauma theory. If there is a politics to Kincaid's psychology, there also is a psychology to Kincaid's politics, as I will show as I provide a sustained analysis of the psychological and affective dynamics of Kincaid's works, including her openly political writings.

From Elaine Potter Richardson to Jamaica Kincaid

Kincaid was born Elaine Potter Richardson in 1949 and grew up in the West Indies on the island of Antigua in the shadow of her mother, Annie Drew, née Richardson. Characterizing her mother as an impressive and powerful woman but also as someone who should never have had children, Kincaid insists that the way she is "is solely owing" to her mother, and that, indeed, her mother is the "fertile soil" of her "creative life" (Cudjoe 219, 222). The same mother who "gave" her daughter words by teaching her how to read when she was three-and-one-half years old and giving her a *Concise Oxford Dictionary* when she was seven later became a source of intense pain, Kincaid recalls, yet because of her mother, she is "able to articulate the pain" (Mendelsohn). Although admired by her mother for her reading when she was young, later, when Kincaid read obsessively as an adolescent and consequently ignored her household duties at times, her mother became annoyed with her reading habits. When the fifteen-year-old Kincaid, who had been asked to babysit her two-year-old brother, Devon, became so absorbed in a book that she failed to notice that his diaper needed to be changed, Annie Drew, in a state of fury, gathered up all of her daughter's treasured books and burned them. As an adolescent, Kincaid came to identify with the bookish—and to her idealized—world of literature, a world, as she would later speculate, she tried to recreate in her writing as she attempted to bring back into her life all the books her mother had burned.

Kincaid was an only child until age nine, and from ages nine to thirteen her life was disrupted by the birth of her three brothers: Joseph, Dalma, and Devon. For Kincaid one of the great betrayals of her life was her family's interruption of her education after the birth of her brothers. "My brothers were going to be gentlemen of achievement, one was going to be Prime Minister, one a doctor, one a Minister, things like that. I never heard anybody say that I was going to be anything except maybe a nurse. There was no huge future for me, nothing planned. In fact my education was so casually interrupted, my life might very well have been destroyed by that casual act . . . if I hadn't intervened in my own life and pulled myself out of the water" (BBC). Kincaid was educated in British colonial schools in Antigua, which became self-governing in 1967 and an independent nation within the British Commonwealth in 1981. Although she was a bright student, her teachers considered her difficult. "I was always being accused of being rude, because I gave some back chat," Kincaid recalls (Garis). Not only did she refuse to stand at the refrain of "God Save Our King," but she also hated "Rule, Britannia" with its refrain, "'Rule Britannia, Britannia rule the waves, Britons never ever shall be slaves.' I thought that we weren't Britons and that we were slaves" (Cudjoe 217).

Kincaid, who had hoped to stay in school and then go on to the University of the West Indies in Jamaica, remembers with great bitterness how her mother removed her from high school in Antigua, claiming that she needed help caring for her three sons after her husband—Kincaid's stepfather, David Drew—became ill. Kincaid wanted to go to the university so she could become one of those "very respected women who come back from the university and just sort of push everyone around" (Vorda 91). Instead, in 1965 the sixteen-year-old Kincaid was sent to America to work as an au pair, so she could help support her family. "I dutifully sent my paychecks home, and then one day it dawned on me that I was being asked to support someone else's mistake," she recalls. "I was a brilliant young girl who should have gone on to a university. Nothing was dependent on the sacrifice of my life. . . . I stopped sending them money and stopped writing to them and began to send myself to school. I became the parents I didn't have for myself" ("Portraits: Jamaica Kincaid" 20).

After breaking off all contact with her family, Kincaid set about, as she tells her story, reinventing herself. In an act of self-creation that also served as a self-protective disguise, she changed her name to *Jamaica Kincaid* in 1973. "I was with friends and we were all calling ourselves different names and I thought of that name, and I said, 'That's my name'" (Wachtel 64). Kincaid, who is "part African, part Carib Indian" and "a very small part . . . Scot" (Vorda 81), called herself "Jamaica" because of her Caribbean origins. When she decided to change her name, the Caribbean had become "very remote" to her. "It was a kind of invention: I wouldn't go home to visit that part of the world, so I decided to recreate it. 'Jamaica' was symbolic of that place" (Cudjoe 220). Despite her explanation that she chose "Kincaid" simply because it "seemed to go with" the name "Jamaica" and she "liked the sound" (Cudjoe 220, J. Kaufman), the name "Kincaid," as one commentator has observed, does, in fact, sound Scottish,[6] so it, too, points to Kincaid's origins (see J. King 885). In changing her name when she began to write, Kincaid was also attempting to disguise herself so that her family would not know she was writing, for she was afraid that she would fail, and they would laugh at her. Despite her fears of failure, Kincaid became an almost overnight success as a writer. After being befriended by *New Yorker* writer George Trow, who began to quote her in his "Talk of the Town" pieces, calling her "our sassy black friend" (Garis), she was hired as a staff writer for *The New Yorker* by the editor, William Shawn, who also published her stories in the magazine, and she later married his son. In 1983, with the publication of her first book of stories, *At the Bottom of the River*, Kincaid caught the attention of the critical establishment, and she has since become a widely acclaimed and often studied author, celebrated as an important voice in literature for both her fiction and nonfiction works.

In the composite portrait of Kincaid that emerges from her many interviews, she is identified, if not mythologized, as a classic American type: the self-created and successful individual. "She is an Elaine turned a Jamaica," writes one commentator. "She is a former servant—as she describes herself—who is now one of the more remarkable voices in contemporary literature." Moreover, "'Jamaica herself may be Jamaica's greatest work of art. She is totally self-created. . . . She came here and she picked and chose and built a life'" (Jacobs). To another commentator, Kincaid's story "sounds a bit like a cross between Charlotte Brontë's *Jane Eyre* and Jean Rhys's *Wide Sargasso Sea*, except in this version, the woman from the West Indies triumphs, working her way through governess jobs to become a renowned author" (Kreilkamp 54). If in describing the trajectory of Kincaid's literary career and life in America, interviewers often invoke the discourse of the American success story and the self-made individual—and Kincaid's story does indeed follow such a script, as she tells it—embedded in Kincaid's literary success story is another story that she tells and retells in her interviews as she recounts her abiding struggle to make sense of her painful past and free herself from her obsessive love-hate relationship with her mother and also to understand the external cultural forces that have helped make her what she is.

"I've come to see that I've worked through the relationship of the mother and the girl to a relationship between Europe and the place that I'm from, which is to say a relationship between the powerful and the powerless. The girl is powerless, and the mother is powerful" (Vorda 86). But even as Kincaid recognizes that she must have "consciously viewed" her relationship with her mother as "a sort of prototype" for the larger social relationship between Antiguans and the British, she also insists that for her writing is "an act of self-rescue, self-rehabilitation, self-curiosity: about my mind, about myself, what I think, what happened to me in the personal way, in the public way, what things mean. It's so much a personal act that I have no real understanding of it" (Birbalsingh 144, 149). Stating that she has "never really written about anyone" except herself and her mother, Kincaid describes herself as "one of those pathetic people for whom writing is therapy" (Listfield). "It's still a mystery to me, and it's still an awe-inspiring thing to me, that I came to discover that I can write. . . . I could be dead or in jail. If you don't know how to make sense of what's happened to you, if you see things but can't express them—it's so painful" (Kennedy). Kincaid's work, which has often been read as a political allegory, is political, but it is also highly personal.

Memory, Narrative, Identity

"[M]y mother wrote my life for me and told it to me," Kincaid has said of her writing (O'Conner). Kincaid's well-known remark on the origins of her autobiographical self-representation in the stories her mother, Annie Drew, told her about herself when she was a child recalls Paul Eakin's account of the origins of the autobiographical impulse in the developmental process of "memory talk." Beginning in early childhood when the child learns to share memories with others, "memory talk" leads to "the establishment of a store of memories that are shareable and ultimately reviewable by the individual, forming a personal history" (Nelson, cited by Eakin 109). As part of her "memory talk" training, "the child learns that she is expected to be able to display to others autobiographical memories arranged in narrative form" (111). Parents not only play an important role in the "continuous, lifelong trajectory of self-narration," which starts in childhood as the child learns to narrativize her experiences, but "parental styles of engagement can exert an enormous influence, transmitting both models of self and story" (Eakin 113, 115). Serving as "the 'vicar of the culture,'" the family indoctrinates the child in "the received 'genres of life-accounting,'" and, indeed, the child's very sense of self emerges "within a crucible of family stories and cultural scripts" (Eakin 117). Explaining the connections among memory, narrative, and identity, Eakin comments that narrative is "not merely one form among many in which to express identity, but rather [is] an integral part of a primary mode of identity experience, that of the extended self, the self in time" (137). Moreover, "the writing of autobiography is properly understood as an integral part of a lifelong process of identity formation in which acts of self-narration play a major part" (101).

Even as Kincaid finds the origins of her writing in her mother's storytelling, she also, as we shall see in the course of this study, finds it necessary to talk and write back to the mother who incessantly shamed her daughter in the stories she told about her. Kincaid also insists on the importance of memory and truth-telling in her writing, recalling that as a young child she was praised for her memory but over time was chastised for remembering things her mother wanted to forget. Indeed, in her adult relationship with her mother described in *My Brother* and in her interviews, Kincaid complains that her mother plays with memory and with the "truth" about the past. Remarking that she "grew up in a place where the truth is in the shadows—which is to say there is none," Kincaid recalls, "When I was a child, I was much praised for my memory because it was very precocious. I could remember everything I saw and heard, and I would complete people's stories—everyone thought it was so charming. And then when I kept it up and told people things they didn't want to remember, everyone grew annoyed with me. I have often overheard my mother describing some incident that I was directly involved in as a child, and it just enrages me, because her telling of it is always so different from how I remember it. . . . [S]he plays with memory" (Goldfarb 98). For Kincaid, "if something really happened, it *really happened*," and while she does not "mind so much that it happened," she does mind "not knowing the truth of it" (Goldfarb 98, Hansen). "'What a memory you have!'" Annie Drew says of the trait she so dislikes in her daughter (*My Brother* 6). "This is what my family, the people I grew up with, hate about me. I always say, Do you remember?" (*My Brother* 19).

For Kincaid, the memory process[7] involves the recovery of events—and not necessarily buried or repressed events[8]—and also the continual mental processing of the past in light of later knowledge as she attempts to make sense of her relationship with her mother. "I go over my life all the time—events in my life—and suddenly I remember that I was with my mother somewhere," as Kincaid describes this process. "Over and over again, I remember my mother and I went somewhere and only now it has dawned on me what was happening" (Ferguson, "Interview" 183). As Kincaid continually reviews events from her past, she gains expanded awareness of "what was happening," allowing her to elaborate on or even revise her ongoing self-narration. In *My Brother*, Kincaid remarks on the process of memory and self-narration: "[A]t this moment that I am sitting and contemplating (though I am not sure that I am capable of contemplation), I am remembering the life of my brother, I am remembering my own life, or at least a part of my own life, for my own life is still ongoing, I hope, and each moment of its present shapes its past and each moment of its present will shape its future and even so influence the way I see its future" (167).

In Kincaid's work, memory is central to the process of self-narration and thus the making of what Eakin calls the "storied self" (see 99–141). But Kincaid also insists that she writes fiction and not pure autobiography because she manipulates facts to bring out the connections between events, arranging "things in a way" so that she can "understand them." Yet in everything she says "there is the truth" (Perry, "Interview" 507). Even though Kincaid has remarked that "it is fair" for her mother to say, "'This is not me,'" of the mother characters in novels such as *Annie John* and *Lucy*, insisting that "[i]t is only the mother as the person I used to be perceived her," she also says of her mother, "I don't think anyone could destroy us [Kincaid and her brothers] as powerfully as she did" (Ferguson, "Interview" 176, Mehren). "I want to say, this is not a mother like your mother. This is a mother like you have never known" (Mehren). Responding to her mother's frequent remark, "'Oh, you remember all those old times stories,'" Kincaid insists, "[W]hat I remember is not an old times story: it's the truth" (Birbalsingh 146). Kincaid emphasizes the importance of memory—memory of what "really happened"—in her writing yet she also insists on the constructed nature of her autobiographical-fictional narratives of the past as she, the powerful "Jamaica Kincaid," identifies with her discarded yet remembered self, the powerless and vulnerable and deeply shamed "Elaine Potter Richardson."

"I am someone who had to make sense out of my past," Kincaid insists. "I had to write or I would have died" (Ferguson, "Interview" 176). For Kincaid writing about herself in *At the Bottom of the River*, *Annie John*, and *Lucy*, and writing about her family as a way to gain expanded insight into her own identity in *The Autobiography of My Mother*, *My Brother*, and *Mr. Potter*, are not only acts of self-narration

and the creation of a storied identity but also acts of self-preservation
and survival. Yet for all her need to "tell the truth" Kincaid, as we shall
see, is a reluctant witness to the "real story" of what happened to her.

The Mother-Daughter Relationship

Focusing attention on the mother-daughter dyadic relationship, Kincaid
evokes a well-known relational pattern in describing how characters
such as Annie John and Lucy have problems with attachment and autonomy in their intense bond with the mother. In Nancy Chodorow's well-
known description in *The Reproduction of Mothering*, the infant daughter's preoedipal attachment to her mother leads, in the developing girl
and the adult woman, to a relational mode of identification characterized by a fluidity of self-other boundaries. The recurrent division of the
mother into loved and hated parts in Kincaid's fiction is also illuminated
by relational theorists in their description of "splitting," an important
"developmental and defensive process" that arises from the daughter's
conflicting perceptions of and feelings about the mother (St. Clair 190).
In the "complex" relationship with the mother "where feelings of love
and hate, frustration and gratification coexist," splitting functions to
keep dangerous feelings separate from gratifying ones (St. Clair 40).
Through splitting, the developing girl "protects the ideal, good relationship with the mother from contamination with the frustrating and bad";
splitting also protects "the good mother image" from the child's
"destructive anger" (St. Clair 132–33; Mahler 99). Relational theorists
also show how enmeshment with the mother complicates the daughter's
differentiation from the mother in adolescence, a time of "'prolonged
and painful severence from the mother'" when the mother may wish
both to keep her daughter close and to push her into adulthood and
when the daughter may use various strategies to separate from her
mother: she may become hypercritical of her mother or try to solve her
"ambivalent dependence" through splitting, seeing her mother and
homelife as bad and the world outside the home as good; or she may try
to be as unlike her mother as possible, defining herself in opposition to
her mother; or she may idealize friends or fictional characters, contrasting her mother unfavorably to these idealized figures (Chodorow,
Reproduction 135, 137). Kincaid's characters experience difficulties in
negotiating connection and separation in their girlhood and adolescent
relationships with the mother and also feel intense ambivalence toward
the mother, splitting her into the all-giving and beneficent "good"
mother or the totally withholding and persecutory "bad" mother. And

during adolescence, they defy and denigrate the mother while forming intense attachments to girls who are initially idealized but eventually denigrated like the mother. Kincaid's characters also exhibit what Adrienne Rich calls "matrophobia"—the fear "of *becoming one's mother.*" "[W]here a mother is hated to the point of matrophobia, there may also be a deep underlying pull toward her, a dread that if one relaxes one's guard one will identify with her completely," as Rich explains this phenomenon (235).

Yet while relational theory provides useful insights into Kincaid's representation of the mother-daughter relationship in her work, it does not tell the whole story, leaving what many critics see as a kind of enigma at the heart of Kincaid's work. Remarking on the "pattern of returning to the autobiographical scene" in Kincaid's writings, Leigh Gilmore describes Kincaid's "performance of autobiography as a discourse with an, as yet, limitless capacity for repetition or reengagement" (96, 99). Yet Gilmore also asserts that the "central theme of mother-daughter conflict" in Kincaid's works is presented as "a locus of enigmatic trauma" (104). Questioning the place of the mother in *Annie John*, Gilmore remarks that while the mother character is central, "her actions seem less like the cause of Annie's unhappiness than something more like the psychic force of individuation, the incomprehensibility of some forms of emotion, and deep emotion as itself a kind of trauma" (111). Like Gilmore, critic-readers commonly find the mother-daughter conflict and the daughter's intense love/hate feelings for her mother enigmatic,[9] revealing Kincaid's early reluctance to describe in her fiction the very real hurts inflicted on her in her girlhood by her mother. The fact that Kincaid, over the years, comes to forcefully describe her abiding, even obsessive, hatred for and anger toward her mother points to a hidden drama in her early stories and novels.

Kincaid, who frequently remarks on the brutality and humiliation inflicted on children in Antigua, is generalizing from her own experiences growing up. "I don't want to use the word 'abused,' but there was a great deal of cruelty directed at me when I was a child," Kincaid states, only reluctantly admitting that she was, in fact, beaten by her mother (Cryer). Kincaid also comes to admit, but again reluctantly, that she "suffered greatly from shame" as a child, including shame about various parts of her heritage, in particular the fact that she was illegitimate, leading her to realize the necessity of saying the things she was ashamed of so that others could not have "power over" her (Wachtel 65, 64). In Kincaid's repudiation of her powerless identity as Elaine Potter Richardson and her creation of her writing identity as the powerful daughter-writer, "Jamaica Kincaid," she attempts not only to reclaim but also to take power and authority over her past as she talks and writes back to the contemptuous internalized mother,[10] the mother who wrote her life and the mother with whom she carries on incessant conversations in her head in her adult life. But the internalized voice of the mother is also part of Kincaid's writing voice and is heard in the angry, contemptuous voice of the daughter-writer who publicly exposes shameful family secrets, a process I examine in detail in the following chapters.

Writing Memory, Writing to Survive

Individuals are "motivated or driven, in order to gain a sense of a meaningful life and manage threatening conscious and unconscious affects and beliefs, to create or interpret external experiences in ways that resonate with internal experiences, preoccupations, fantasies, and senses of self-other relationships," as Chodorow observes (*Power* 14). A central organizing theme in Kincaid's writings, as she herself has often remarked, is the relationship between the powerful mother and the powerless daughter. Even though Kincaid eventually comes to attach a political meaning to this type of power-imbalanced relationship, seeing it as analogous to the relationship between the colonizer and the colonized, she remains haunted—indeed, tormented—by her memories of her powerful and, to Kincaid, powerfully destructive mother. In part I, "In the Shadow of the Mother," I analyze the mother-daughter relationship in *At the Bottom of the River*, *Annie John*, and *Lucy*, using shame and trauma theory to help explain the "enigmatic trauma" at the heart of the daughter's conflicted relationship with the mother in these works.

If in *At the Bottom of the River* Kincaid uses a densely allusive style to partially obscure her meaning as she evokes the "bookish" idealized world of literature she came to love while growing up in Antigua, in *Annie John* she recounts, in a simple way, the story of her girlhood in Antigua under the control of her mother, Annie Drew. Although Kincaid omits scenes of physical beatings in *Annie John*, the secret of Kincaid's abuse does find veiled expression in the narrative, which reveals the devastating impact of trauma and shame on Kincaid's fictional projection, as I show in my discussion of *Annie John*. Like the abused child described by trauma specialists, Annie sees her mother as a powerful woman who uses her power in an arbitrary way, and she feels deeply vulnerable and helpless in her relationship with her mother, whom she rigidly and persistently splits into loving and punishing identities; she becomes obsessed with death and indeed associates her mother with death; she has an intense need for protection and care coupled with a fear of abandonment and exploitation; she reenacts with others dramas of intense and fierce idealization followed by denigration; and she engages in revealing rituals of intimacy with others in which she acts out a classic pattern of abuse, one that combines loving and punishing behaviors. And like the deeply and chronically shamed child who is subjected repeatedly to maternal contempt, the shame-vulnerable Annie succumbs to the disorganizing experiences of shame-rage and shame-depression, and she attempts to protect herself from her mother's annihilating contempt both through avoidant behaviors and through expressions of anger, shamelessness, and the active humiliation of her mother-humiliator in an attack-other shame script.

In *Annie John* and in the continuation of Annie's story in *Lucy*, Kincaid reveals that there is a "relationship between social formations and structures of feeling" (Fox 14) as she shows that the feeling of shame and the experience of being shamed are crucial to the development not only of a colonized black identity but also a female sexual identity. If Annie, when accused by her mother of behaving like a "slut," returns maternal contempt with daughterly countercontempt, she also subsequently succumbs to feelings of profound shame-depression. In a similar way Lucy, even as she employs a classic defense against shame—shamelessness—as she flaunts her "bad" identity as a "slut" and as Lucy/Lucifer, remains a prisoner of her crippling past, existing like Annie in the shadow of her powerful, and powerfully injuring, mother even though she is physically removed from her. Behind Lucy's defiant anger and bitterness lies a deep sense of woundedness. Attempting to forge a new identity as a writer, Lucy finds the act of writing a painful process of recovering the past and confronting her abiding feelings of vulnerability and shame.

The angry, contemptuous voice that pervades *Lucy*—a voice that Kincaid identifies as her mother's voice—is also the voice Kincaid adopts to great effect in her openly political writings, as I show in part II, "A Very Personal Politics." In my discussion of *A Small Place* and "On Seeing England for the First Time," I show how Kincaid uses a classic shame-reversing attack-other script as she denounces not only the British and American tourists in Antigua but also the English people she encounters during a trip to England. Even though Kincaid claims that she identifies with the powerless Antiguans in *A Small Place*, she clearly speaks from the position of authorial power as she shames the corrupt black-ruled government in Antigua and the small-minded Antiguans. That Kincaid not only has an intense love/hate relationship with England but also is overcome with feelings of loss, betrayal, resentment, profound shame, and anger when she returns to Antigua—feelings attached to the mother-daughter relationship in her work—call attention to the highly personal nature of her politics.

Just as there is something highly personal about Kincaid's politics, so her "Family Portraits," as I show in part III, are not only self-revealing, but they are also, in part, self-portraits. In *The Autobiography of My Mother*, which derives from Kincaid's observation that her mother should not have had children, Kincaid examines her matrilineal roots even as she talks and writes back to her mother. In her fictional memoir of her mother, which includes family stories passed down by her mother, Kincaid retells the story of her own girlhood and adult relationship with her angry and contemptuous mother, and she also examines aspects of her own identity in the figure of the mother character. Just as Kincaid writes about herself in *The Autobiography of My Mother*, so in *My Brother*, her memoir of her youngest brother, Devon, who died of AIDS in Antigua, she also tells the story of the failed life she might have led had she remained in Antigua under the influence of a mother hated not only by her daughter but also, as we learn in *My Brother*, by her three sons. And in her fictional memoir of her biological father, *Mr. Potter*, Kincaid, as she imagines and writes about the life of her absentee father, also deals with the missing and yet everpresent part of her repudiated identity, "Elaine Cynthia Potter," the daughter-narrator in *Mr. Potter*. As she tells the shameful story of her illegitimacy—like her biological father, she has a "line drawn through" her—she settles old scores against her biological father. But she also uses her writing not only to give narrative—indeed novelistic—dimension to her absent father who is authored, and authorized, by the daughter-writer but also to give a kind of artistic legitimacy to Elaine Cynthia Potter, the shamed girl with the line drawn through her.

Despite the sense of open emotional revelation in Kincaid's works, there also is a sense of narrative withholding and omission as readers are forced to make emotional sense out of the pervasive depression, anger, and shame of Kincaid's characters. An author whose work shows a remarkable psychological complexity even as it describes the cultural forces that impinge on the self, Kincaid deliberately unsettles readers as she demonstrates the "power of feelings" in her writings. As she dwells on painful family relations, Kincaid sheds light on the complex ways that fantasies about the family—and especially the mother—permeate the construction of her autobiographical self and writer's identity. In the course of showing how Kincaid provides literary renderings of the complex process of creating personal and cultural meaning, my aim is also to investigate the reparative function of Kincaid's writings as I trace her search for a livable—and literary—life and her transformation of inherited feelings of shame into pride as she wins the praise of an admiring critical establishment and an evergrowing reading public. While Kincaid does not claim that she can ever forget the past or heal her shame, she does, in her domestic and gardener's life, which to her are part of her writer's life, find moments of solace, as I show in the conclusion. "I am writing for solace," Kincaid states, explaining that she writes "to make sense of" what has happened to her (Holmstrom). Even though she remains haunted by the past, she does find solace in her writing, and as the self-authored and authoritative Jamaica Kincaid, she is able to fashion for herself a literary life and writer's identity that she finds livable.

PART I

In the Shadow
of the Mother

❧ 2 ❧

"I Had Embarked on Something Called Self-Invention"

Artistic Beginnings in "Antigua Crossings" and *At the Bottom of the River*

"I was born in 1949. My twenty-sixth birthday was the birthday when I felt old and used up—I had left home when I was sixteen, and ten years in a young life is a long time," Kincaid comments as she remembers her early days as a writer in New York City ("Putting Myself Together" 93). "I changed my name, and started telling people I knew that I was a writer. This declaration went without comment" ("Putting" 94). In her third-floor, two-room apartment on West Twenty-second Street, she slept on the floor in one room, first on newspapers and then on an old mattress she had found. The other room contained a large desk, a typewriter, and books stacked on the floor. Living the spare life of the would-be artist, Kincaid spent the little money she had in used-clothing stores buying vintage clothing. "I would wear a lot of old clothes and sort of looked like people from different periods—someone from the 1920s, someone from the 1930s, someone from the 1940s," she recalls (Cudjoe 216). "Being very thin . . . I looked good in clothes. I loved the way I looked all dressed up. I bought hats, I bought shoes, I bought stockings and garter belts to hold them up, I bought handbags, I bought suits, I bought blouses, I bought dresses, I bought skirts, and I bought jackets that did not match the skirts. I used to spend hours happily buying clothes to wear." Kincaid would also spend hours getting dressed as she decided which "combination of people, inconceivably older and more prosperous" than she was that she wanted "to impersonate" on any particular day ("Putting" 98). In a similar way, she changed her hair, cutting off her long, black, tightly curled hair and making it short, blond, and tightly curled. "[S]hould I say that transforming my hair was a way of transforming myself? I had no

consciousness of such things then" ("Putting" 100). As she later came to recognize, in changing her hair and wearing various styles of once expensive and stylish vintage clothing, she was attempting to refashion not only her appearance but also her identity. "I did not know then that I had embarked on something called self-invention, the making of a type of person that did not exist in the place where I was born—a place far away from New York and with a climate quite unlike the one that existed in New York. I wanted to be a writer; I was a person with opinions, and I wanted them to matter to other people" ("Putting" 100). Unlike the well-ordered domestic life that she would eventually establish in Vermont and take pride in as a writer, Kincaid spent her early years in New York City engaged in the same kinds of risky behavior she later observed—and condemned—in her youngest brother, Devon, who died of AIDS: she drank, used drugs, and had a series of sexual partners. "My youth was exhausting, it was dangerous, and it is a miracle that I grew out of it unscathed," as she remarks ("Putting" 101).

As Kincaid recalls her early days in New York, she emphasizes not only her determined act of self-invention but also her good luck in being recognized by George Trow and William Shawn, the two white men who figure prominently in the story she tells and retells about her beginnings as a writer. With her bleached blond hair, her shaved-off eyebrows painted in with gold eye makeup, and her attention-grabbing, costume-like clothing, the almost six-foot-tall Kincaid thought of herself as "an interesting person" only to be reminded of her painful Antiguan past when she was ridiculed by young American blacks. "I had grown up in a place where many people were young and black . . . and I had been stared at and laughed at, and insulting things had been said to me: I was too tall, I was too thin, I was very smart; my clothes had never fit properly there, I was flat-chested; my hair would not stay in place" ("Introduction," *Talk Stories* 7). Unlike American blacks, who were "cruel" to her, those who were "most kind and loving" were white people (Snell). Recounting the happy set of events that led to her writing for *The New Yorker*, she recalls how a man she met on an elevator while she was doing freelance work for *Ingenue* magazine introduced her to *New Yorker* writer George Trow, who, in turn, took her to meet the editor of *The New Yorker*, William Shawn, in the spring of 1974. "It was because George loved Mr. Shawn that he wanted me to meet Mr. Shawn and introduce Mr. Shawn to someone who might write for him and in that way give Mr. Shawn some amusement, some joy," she remarks of this initial, and to her mind, providential meeting with the editor of *The New Yorker* ("Introduction," *Talk Stories* 9).

Some five months later, Kincaid turned in what she thought were merely some notes on a West Indian carnival in Brooklyn and her notes and observations were published as her first "Talk of the Town" piece (see *Talk Stories* 15–24). At that moment, she came to know herself as a writer. "[I]t was through that piece of writing and Mr. Shawn's acceptance of it that I came to know writing, the thing that I was doing, the thing I would do, that thing that I now do, writing; it was through that first experience with giving Mr. Shawn some thoughts of my own on paper that I came to be the person writing that I am now" ("Introduction," *Talk Stories* 9–10). By the time she met Trow and Shawn, as she recalls, she talked incessantly about her family "and in such an obsessive way" that she "must have seemed insane" ("Introduction," *Talk Stories* 10). Yet both men accepted her, and when Shawn published her words— "[t]he words I spoke, the thoughts in my head"—she became a writer. "In the beginning was my word and my word became the world as I ordered it to be. If it now sounds too bold, if it now sounds too made up, if it now sounds too in retrospect, all the same it is true: when I saw my words and my own thoughts, as I had put them down on paper in the pages of a magazine authorized (and that is the real word for it, 'authorized') by Mr. Shawn, I became a writer and that writer became me" ("Introduction," *Talk Stories* 11).

To Kincaid, becoming a writer was a way to take on a new, self-fashioned identity, and yet in her writings she obsessively drew on and worked—and reworked—her painful memories of her Antiguan past, intent on capturing the voice of her remembered and internalized mother and also on talking back to her mother, the mother who wrote her life. Indeed, in her early days as a writer, as Kincaid makes clear in her account, her writerly acts of self-invention were also desperate attempts at self-rescue. "[A]s far as I knew then, I wanted to be that thing in particular, a writer, I did not want to be myself . . . I wanted to be a writer" ("Introduction," *Talk Stories* 10–11). Determined to hide the fact of her writing from her family in her early years, she changed her name in 1973 to disguise herself. "I wanted to write and I was going to say brutal things about myself and my family and I did not want them to know it was me" (Wachtel 63). She also changed her name to protect herself from her family's—and especially her mother's—scorn, for she believed that she might fail when she began writing, and she did not want to be ridiculed by her family. "That I would have thought I could be a writer was laughable to my family" (Ferguson, "Interview" 179). Fearing her family's scorn, the shame-sensitive Elaine Potter Richardson resorted to classic defenses against shame—withdrawal and hiding—by disguising her identity. As "Jamaica Kincaid," Elaine Potter Richardson was attempting to find a way "to do things without being the same person who couldn't do them—the same person who had all these weights" (Garis). "I wanted to speak truthfully about what I knew about myself without being myself" (Vorda 90). "Of course they recognized me," Kincaid recalls. "But all of this in retrospect turns out to be this very American thing of self-invention that I unconsciously, without even knowing the history of really what American means, I just sort of fell into it too and invented a self that I wanted to be, which was a dissenting person" (Muirhead 44).

In an artistic anticipation of *Annie John* and *Lucy*, Kincaid spoke openly and candidly about her Antiguan family in one of her first published stories—the heavily autobiographical "Antigua Crossings," which, like her story "Girl," appeared in June 1978. And yet in her other early stories—most of which originally appeared in *The New Yorker* between 1978 and 1982 and were subsequently published as a collection, *At the Bottom of the River*, in 1983—Kincaid drew on her Antiguan past, but she also worked to halfway conceal what she had revealed. In many of these works one can find the beginnings of the story that drives and gives a kind of emotional urgency to Kincaid's later writings: the story of her troubled relationship with her contemptuous and abusive—and thereby powerfully destructive—mother. Yet as she labored word by word and image by image over these stories, perhaps in part motivated by a desire to write the kind of sophisticated, literary stories she thought would appeal to *New Yorker* readers, she produced an aestheticized, poeticized account that serves to obscure her meaning and defuse the painful emotions she describes. "In those stories," as Kincaid remarks, "I was deeply interested in words. Each word in that book is carefully weighed. I no longer do that because I'm in a big hurry to get to say something, and I don't have time for nice weighings, I just sort of want to crash through. So I just now use this slash-and-burn policy of writing, I just say what I have to say and get out" (Dilger 23).

Kincaid describes *At the Bottom of the River* as "a very unangry, decent, civilized book" that reflects her Anglo-Caribbean education. "It amazes me now that I did that then. I would never write like that again," she states (Perry, "Interview" 498–99). After writing these stories, she was freed of her "obsession" with the educated language of her youth. "I memorized Wordsworth when I was a child, Keats, all sorts of things. It was an attempt to make me into a certain kind of person, the kind of person they had no use for, anyway. An educated black person. I got stuck with a lot of things, so I ended up using them" (Bonetti 30). Recalling that she had no awareness of a West Indian or African Caribbean tradition when she started to write (see, for example, Cudjoe

221, Dilger 21), Kincaid has often commented that her literary influences are from English literature. "I'm of the English-speaking-people tradition," she insists (Ferguson, "Interview" 168). But she also traces the roots of her writing to her mother's storytelling. "I did not have any African type of storytelling traditions. I had gossip, essentially. I had my mother telling me about her life, and about my life before I knew myself, and about her mother, and her father, and her sisters. . . . I heard what the other people were doing, who was trying to kill whom through secret means or was getting brutal" (Dilger 21).

If Kincaid was deeply influenced by her mother's storytelling, books were also important to her when she was growing up. Kincaid, who began to read obsessively as an adolescent, came to identify with the bookish—and to her idealized—world of literature, finding books to be "the only thing that connected" her to "a world apart from the cesspool" of her Caribbean life (Goldfarb 98). Kincaid, in part, evokes this idealized, bookish world in *At the Bottom of the River* where she expresses, as she herself has described it, "simple" ideas in a "cloudy, difficult" style: "the ideas of someone emerging, like being born. Embryonic" (Ferguson, "Interview" 187). If as Kincaid would later say, "everything" in her writing is "autobiographical—down to the punctuation" (Kreilkamp 54), her often "cloudy, difficult" early stories mark the beginning point of Kincaid's autobiographical project, her attempt to write herself a life and to fashion her identity as Jamaica Kincaid, the powerless daughter who takes on a kind of authorial power as she writes back to the contemptuous mother who wrote her life and, in the process, seemed bent on permanently shaming her daughter and consigning her to a blighted life of failure and misery.

The Shaming Voice of the Mother

Kincaid's early stories are often opaque and puzzling, yet she also captures her mother's voice "exactly," as she has remarked, in "Girl," her first published story and probably the best-known piece in *At the Bottom of the River* (Ferguson, "Interview" 171). And in her story "Antigua Crossings," published a few days after "Girl," we find an anticipation of Kincaid's later recounting, in a straightforward and sometimes brutally frank way, stories about her family and her personal life. Indeed, "Antigua Crossings" contains family stories that recur in Kincaid's fiction: the story of how the infant Devon almost died when he was attacked by red ants; an account of Kincaid's maternal Carib Indian grandmother, who lived in Dominica, and her mother's falling out with her Dominican father and subsequent move to Antigua as a young woman; the story of Kincaid's prolonged bedwetting problem; and an account of the mother's amused response when she learned that her Dominican father was suffering from constipation—"So the great man can't shit." Even more significantly, "Antigua Crossings" focuses on the shaming relationship between the daughter character, named Mignonette in the story, and her mother, Victoria. In passages that look forward to the story of Annie John, the twelve-year-old Mignonette recounts how she has been sent to Dominica five times, beginning at age nine, because her parents think that she is "an overly troublesome child" and that her bad behavior is caused by enemies of her family who are working obeah on her, including a woman who claims that Mignonette's father has parented the woman's only child (49).

Like Annie John, Mignonette is accused by her mother of being a liar and a thief, and like Annie John she consequently takes on the identity of the bad child. When Mignonette turns nine, her mother complains that Mignonette talks so fast that she cannot understand her and then accuses her of having something to hide. "I better keep an eye on you because all fast chatters are liars," the mother tells her daughter, who, in response to her mother's shaming words, becomes a brazen liar even though she knows she will be found out. When the mother, in yet another contemptuous remark, tells her daughter, "I better keep an eye on you because where there's a liar there's a thief," Mignonette starts to steal money from her mother (49). In her rebellious embrace of her mother's shaming definitions of her badness, Mignonette anticipates the defiant behavior of Annie John and Lucy. The bad child, Mignonette is sent away for her troublesome behavior.[1] Before she is sent away to Dominica for the first time when she is nine years old, her mother tells her what to do and what not to do when visiting her grandparents. "She said that I was to try hard not to bring shame on her and my father. I said the appropriate 'Yes Mamie, No Mamie, Yes Mamie,' but if you were to ask me now exactly what it was she said to me then I couldn't say, since it all went in one ear and came out the next, just the way she always says I take her advice." As Mignonette is about to leave, she feels "very sorry for all the things" she has done and almost says, "'Oh please, don't send me away. I won't do it again and I love all of you so much.'" The mother's actions and words as she parts from her daughter—she plasters her daughter's "unruly" braids to her head, removes a "spot of dirt" from her chin, and again tells her not to "bring shame" on her family—reinforce the message that Mignonette is a shameful, that is, a dirty and bad, child (50). "Antigua Crossings," with its focus on the daughter being sent away from her Antiguan family because of her badness, anticipates the stories of Annie John and Lucy, which similarly describe the daughter's shaming at the hands of her mother and her forced departure from her homeland.

Like "Antigua Crossings," "Girl," which is strategically placed as the first story in *At the Bottom of the River*, focuses on a troubled mother-daughter relation, and it, too, anticipates the stories of Annie John and Lucy. Looking forward to the scene in which Mrs. John refers to her daughter, Annie, as a "slut" and also to Lucy's embrace of the slut's identity, the unnamed mother in "Girl" admonishes her daughter to be the good, dutiful daughter and to follow the mother's—and society's—rules of proper behavior so that she will not become the "slut" that her mother repeatedly accuses her of being "so bent on becoming." What may seem at first an innocuous list of "this-is-how-to" and "this-is-what-not-to-do" advice turns into a verbal harangue: "Wash the white clothes on Monday and put them on the stone heap; wash the color clothes on Tuesday and put them on the clothesline to dry; don't walk barehead in the hot sun; cook pumpkin fritters in very hot sweet oil; . . . always eat your food in such a way that it won't turn someone else's stomach; on Sundays try to walk like a lady and not like the slut you are so bent on becoming" (3).

As the mother's voice goes on and on, her words of motherly advice turn into hostile commands and, suddenly and unexpectedly, humiliating words of rebuke for her daughter—the verbal equivalent of a sudden slap in the face. If the mother's words serve to confine the daughter to the domestic world of cooking and setting the table and ironing and sweeping the house and yard, they also contain subversive messages as the mother explains how to abort a fetus, or bully a man, or smile at a person one dislikes, or spit up into the air. But the thrust of the mother's message is that the daughter should be a good and dutiful girl and should not bring shame on her family: "[T]his is how to hem a dress when you see the hem coming down and so to prevent yourself from looking like the slut I know you are so bent on becoming" and "this is how to behave in the presence of men who don't know you very well, and this way they won't recognize immediately the slut I have warned you against becoming" (4). As the daughter listens to the controlling, assaultive speech of her mother, she interrupts her mother only two times. When the mother accuses the daughter of singing "benna," that is, calypso songs, in Sunday school, the daughter's response—*"[B]ut I don't sing benna on Sundays at all and never in Sunday school"*—is ignored, indeed, talked over, by her mother (4). And when the mother tells the daughter to always squeeze the bread to assure its freshness, and the daughter asks, *"[B]ut what if the baker won't let me feel the bread?,"* her words are turned against her by her mother who again accuses her daughter of potential sluttishness: "[Y]ou mean to say that after all you are really going to be the kind of woman who the baker won't let near the bread?" (5). In capturing the mother's controlling and assertive—and also insulting—speech, Kincaid, in effect, uses the mother's speech to condemn her. If the mother's internalized voice is a potent force in the development of Kincaid's writing, Kincaid also finds her writing an effective way to talk back to her mother, allowing her to get the final word in her ongoing, internal dispute with her mother.

Kincaid's mother, Annie Drew, as Kincaid would later remark, had a way of humiliating all her children that was "just astonishing and harsh—very cruel and very painful" (Goldfarb 96). When, in *Annie John*, the mother accuses her daughter, Annie, of behaving like a "slut," Annie, unlike the daughter in "Girl," talks back, accusing her mother of being a slut, an accusation that halfway reveals yet also conceals the very painful and shameful fact of Kincaid's illegitimacy. Later Kincaid comes to realize that she has to verbalize the things she is ashamed of so that others will not have power over her. In her early works, she begins this process, even as she presents her fictional daughters as being at the mercy of the shaming—and thereby powerful—mother. Adding to the complexity of the mother-daughter relationship are the daughter's confused love-hate feelings for her originally loving but then rejecting and abusive mother.

Living in Utter Fear

If in Kincaid's early stories, collected in *At the Bottom of the River*, the clarity of the story "Girl" gives way to a series of, at times, "cloudy, difficult" works, the kind of literary and densely allusive writing Kincaid would later come to eschew, these fictional narratives also register Kincaid's deep ambivalence about her Antiguan homeland, the place she "love[s] most" but also is "most afraid of in the world" (Donahue). "I come from a place that's very unreal," Kincaid has said of the Antigua of her childhood (Vorda 88) where side by side with Christianity there was belief in obeah spirits so that in Antigua one could not tell whether something was real or not. In Kincaid's own family, her maternal grandfather was a pious Christian and her Carib Indian grandmother accommodated her husband's Christian beliefs while retaining her belief in obeah spirits, and Kincaid's mother, reflecting the beliefs of her parents, ended up practicing both Christianity and obeah (see Cudjoe 225–26, Birbalsingh 145).[2] In part, Kincaid relates her childhood fears to her exposure to obeah, recalling how she "lived in utter fear" for a time because she was not certain that anything she saw "was itself" (Cudjoe 226). "[A]t one point in my life I never knew whether the ground would hold, whether the thing next to me was real or not" (Cudjoe 227). Kincaid recalls how, when she spent time as a girl in Dominica with her mother's family, she would gaze in wonder at the moon in the black night sky and at the distant mountains set against the horizon. But then, when she saw a moving light in the mountains, which she knew was a *jablesse*, her feeling of "pleasure" would be "overwhelmed by fear and death." Terrified, she would run inside the house to her bed and protectively pull the sheets over her head only to be afraid that she would suffocate and die if she fell asleep that way (*My Brother* 38).

Kincaid's account of her childhood fear of the *jablesse*³—the half-woman, half-beast she-devil who, appearing as a beautiful woman, lures her victims to their deaths—is suggestive, pointing as it does to her related childhood fear of her at times beautiful and loving and at other times angry and cruel mother. Indeed the childhood world Kincaid summons up in *At the Bottom of the River* recalls descriptions of the inner world of the traumatized child. Subjected to "the exercise of parental power" that is "arbitrary, capricious, and absolute," and living in a "climate of constant danger," the traumatized child may develop a fear of death and the belief that her abuser has "absolute or even supernatural powers," and she may also develop "a kind of dissociative virtuosity" as she learns to hide her memories in "complex amnesias" or to alter her "sense of time, place, or person" (Herman 98, 99, 100, 102).⁴ As Kincaid reworks her memories of her Antiguan homeland and mother in *At the Bottom of the River* in a series of highly visual, but also detached, scenes of terror and cruelty, she evokes the "sensory and iconic" forms of dissociated memory associated with trauma—memories that "lack verbal narrative and context" but are instead "encoded in the form of vivid sensations and images" (Herman 39, 38). And these narratives also repeatedly capture the trauma victim's sense that what might otherwise seem to be a safe environment is, in fact, dangerous (see Herman 37).

Kincaid conveys her childhood sense of Antigua as both a familiar world and also a place of lurking menace and danger in the fragmentary scenes of "In the Night," which draw on her memories of the night-soil men who picked up the family's dirty outhouse tub once a week and exchanged it for a clean one (Garis). During the night—"when the night is round in some places, flat in some places, and in some places like a deep hole" (6)—the night-soil men come and go. At night, along with the scratching sound of the night-soil men's straw shoes and the sound of a church bell and of creaking houses and a woman writing, "There is the sound of a man groaning in his sleep; there is the sound of a woman disgusted at the man groaning. There is the sound of the man stabbing the woman, the sound of her blood as it hits the floor, the sound of Mr. Straffee, the undertaker, taking her body away. There is the sound of her spirit back from the dead, looking at the man who used to groan; he is running a fever forever" (7). At night while someone makes a basket or a dress for a girl or soup for her husband, someone else "is sprinkling a colorless powder outside a closed door so that someone else's child will be stillborn" (11). Antigua at night is a place haunted by the harmless spirit of Mr. Gishard, who stands under a cedar tree in his white suit with a glass of rum in his hand looking at the house in which he once lived. But it is also a place haunted by dangerous spirits, for the "bird walking in trees" seen by the night-soil men is not really a bird but a *ja-blesse*, "a woman who has removed her skin and is on her way to drink the blood of her secret enemies" (6).

"Take good care when you see a beautiful woman. A jablesse always tries to look like a beautiful woman," the mother tells the daughter-speaker of "In the Night" (9). When the daughter wets the bed—a humiliating fact about Kincaid's own past that she will also allude to in *Annie John*—her young and beautiful mother wakes her up in the middle of the night to change her nightgown and bedclothes. "My mother can change everything," the daughter remarks (8), her words taking on added meaning as she learns about the *jablesse* when she asks her mother about the lights she sees in the mountains at night. A devil woman, the *jablesse* is a menacing figure that becomes associated with the idealized—young and beautiful—mother. If in describing the *jablesse*, Kincaid introduces a disturbing image that will obsessively repeat and circulate in the text, she also reactively defends against the childhood terrors she has uncovered. For the girl fantasizes that someday she will marry her mother, live with her in a mud hut, and be perfectly happy. Yet in the hut are found three pictures that tell a progressive story in a series of snapshots: in the first picture, the mother and daughter are standing on a jetty; in the second, they are embracing; and in the third, they are waving goodbye. Embedded in this account of the perfect bond between mother and daughter are images associated in "Antigua Crossings" and later in *Annie John* with maternal rejection and consequent mother-daughter separation. Rather than openly telling the story of the rejecting mother, the narrative evokes the visual but also detached and fragmented world of dissociated memory as it refers to the painful story of the mother-daughter rift.

Like Annie John, the daughter learns of her own life by listening to her mother's stories about her. "This woman I would like to marry knows many things, but to me she will only tell about things that would never dream of making me cry; and every night, over and over, she will tell me something that begins, 'Before you were born'" (12). If the mother's storytelling appears to be a healing ritual, "In the Night" also reveals that the mother's obeah stories do in fact have the power to disturb and frighten the daughter. "At Last" elaborates on this as it presents, in the mother's voice, the kinds of stories the mother tells her daughter. "At Last" weaves into the mother-daughter dialogue actual family stories relayed to Kincaid by her mother—stories about the death of Annie Drew's brother and the near-death of the infant Devon—as it describes Antigua as a place of lurking dangers where a worm crawls out of the leg of a dying man and a newborn baby is "almost eaten, eyes first, by red ants" (16, 14). "At Last" also looks forward to *Annie John*'s account of "The Long Rain" in its description of the hurricane that shook the house and brought "the rain that time" (15). Like Annie John's mother, the mother in "At Last" tells stories about the daughter's early life that cast her as a bad child, troublesome from the beginning. "I sat in this rocking chair with you on my lap," the mother recalls. "Let me calm her, I thought, let me calm her. But in my breast my milk soured." When the daughter asks her mother if she was loved, the mother responds "Yes," but her answer contains an accusation, pointing as it does to the greediness her daughter displayed as an infant: "You wore your clothes wrapped tight around your body, keeping your warmth to yourself. What greed! But how could you know?" (16). "At Last" also points to what Kincaid would later more openly describe as the cruelty and brutality of her childhood. In passages that evoke the unsafe world of the trauma victim in which a seemingly safe environment may suddenly become dangerous, the girl recalls, alongside her memories of the sound of the noon bell or the sight of a sparrow's eggs or of a fruit-bearing tree, painful—and dissociated—memories of abuse she either witnessed or more likely experienced: "The thud of small feet running, running. A girl's shriek—snaps in two," and "A sharp blow delivered quicker than an eye blink" (17–18, 18).

To the girl in "At Last," Antigua is a place where children are "quick to laugh, quick to brand, quick to scorn" (17). To the girl in "Wingless," the world of the schoolhouse is similarly a potentially cruel place where the sound of shrieking children may indicate "pain or pleasure" (21). Beautiful in their groups of three, the same children who the night before begged their mothers to softly sing to them maim each other during the school day. Anticipating Annie John's fascination with the schoolbook picture of Columbus in chains, the girl-speaker thinks that perhaps she will make a great discovery and then "be sent home in chains" (21)—that is, humiliated. A defenseless child, she wants to grow up to be like the "tall, graceful, and altogether beautiful woman"—an amalgam of the teacher-mother figure—who imposes on others her "will" and also for her "own amusement, great pain" (22). Like Annie John and Lucy, the girl comes to see herself as bad. "Am I horrid? And if so, will I always be that way? Not getting my own way causes me to fret so, I clench my fist. . . . I am so unhappy, my face is so wet, and still I can stand up and walk and tell lies in the face of terrible punishments" (23). Schooled like Annie John in lady-like behavior, the girl tries to "tell differences" and "distinguish the subtle gradations of color in fine cloth, of fingernail length, of manners" (22). She has a "list" of things she must do. "So is my life to be like an apprenticeship in dressmaking?" she wonders (23), her question recalling that Kincaid was apprenticed to a seamstress when she was growing up, a detail of Kincaid's Antiguan life that she will also allude to in *Annie John* (see 138).[5]

"I can see the great danger in what I am—a defenseless and pitiful child," the daughter remarks, describing her vulnerability in her relation with her mother (23). Deliberately frightening her daughter by telling her not to eat the strings on bananas because they will kill her by wrapping around her heart, the mother is entertained at the sight of her terrified daughter trying to remove the banana strings with her "monkey fingernails" (24). Similarly when the mother and daughter walk arm in arm by the sea during a blinding storm, and the daughter, fearful, imagines the sea snapping at her heels all the way home, the mother asks her daughter if she is "frightened" of her and is amused when the daughter admits that she is "very frightened." Expressing her contempt, the mother replies, "Oh, you should see your face. I wish you could see your face. How you make me laugh" (26). A powerful woman, the mother—the woman the girl loves—"is so much bigger" than the girl is (27). But the girl also identifies in part with the mother's power—her ability to kill with her "red, red smile" (25) and to cause others pain for her own amusement. Just as the mother is split into good/bad parts, so the daughter, in an anticipation of Annie John's split identity, is both innocent and cruel. The same brown innocent hands that slip into a dress or are clasped together in prayer or reach up with longing are also "indiscriminately dangerous" or "cruel and careless" (27–28). The daughter in "Blackness" similarly asserts her power by treating the hunchback boy in a "pitiless" way (50).

The Daughter's Anger and Despair

In "My Mother" Kincaid repeats and elaborates on the theme that runs obsessively through *At the Bottom of the River*: the daughter's love-hate relationship with her loving and cruel mother. When the daughter states that she wishes her mother were dead and then, seeing her mother's pain, is sorry for what she has said, she is forgiven by her mother but at a terrible cost. "Placing her arms around me, she drew my head closer and closer to her bosom, until finally I suffocated." The daughter remains breathless until her mother shakes her out and places her under a tree—actions that suggest the mother's physical punishment of her daughter. Afterward, the daughter stays on guard when she is with her mother: "I cast a sharp glance at her and said to myself, 'So'" (53).

Looking forward to the story of Annie John, the mother-daughter conflict in "My Mother" intensifies when the girl, growing her own bosoms, becomes an adolescent. Publicly, the daughter acts in a loving way while remaining vigilant, and she, like Annie John, becomes aware of the dark shadowy thing within herself and her mother when they sit together in a dark, candle-lit room, a setting that suggests an obeah ceremony. This dark thing becomes manifest when the mother, *jablesse*-like, reveals her "bad" or dark side as she transforms into a reptilian creature. Removing her clothes, the mother grows scales on her back and rows of teeth, and then she flattens her head so that her blazing, spinning eyes sit atop her head as she travels along on her white underbelly. Instructed to follow her mother's example, the daughter, too, transforms and travels on her white underbelly. In her subsequent power struggle with her mother, the daughter sighs to win her mother's sympathy, yet she feels "invincible" in her anger: "My skin had just blackened and cracked and fallen away and my new impregnable carapace had taken full hold." Responding to her daughter's beautiful sighs, the mother offers her shoulder for support. But when the mother reaches out toward her daughter in a soothing gesture, the daughter steps aside. "I let out a horrible roar, then a self-pitying whine. I had grown big, but my mother was bigger, and that would always be so" (56).

In the emotional drama that unfolds, the daughter feels both anger and despair. Entering a dark, cold cave with her mother, the daughter must grow a "special lens," so she can see in the dark, and a "special coat" to keep her warm. "What a strange expression you have on your face. So cross, so miserable, as if you were living in a climate not suited to your nature," the mother remarks laughingly as she, instead of expressing concern, mocks her daughter (57). The daughter then builds a beautiful house over a deep hole and invites her mother to inspect the house in hopes that her mother will fall into the hole, allowing the daughter to assert her own emotional power over her mother, a mother-daughter drama elaborated on in Kincaid's later works. But instead the mother walks up and down the house, presumably walking on air, and emerges unscathed. Enraged when her plans fail, the daughter subsequently burns down the house.

Conflicted in her emotions, the daughter retains her feelings of attachment to and anger toward the mother. During the time she lives alone on an island, the daughter, who wants her mother to look favorably on her, adorns the faces of the eight full moons visible on the island with approving expressions she has seen on her mother's face. Then when the daughter returns to her mother, and she and her mother build houses on opposite sides of the dead pond that separates them, the daughter misses her mother, yet when her mother returns alone to her house at the end of each day after accomplishing "incredible and great deeds," the daughter glows "red with anger" (59). "My mother has grown to an enormous height. I have grown to an enormous height also, but my mother's height is three times mine," the daughter remarks of her continuing awareness of her mother's power over her (58).

"My Mother" exposes the daughter's burning anger and hatred for the all-powerful mother, potent feelings that will disrupt but also propel and give narrative focus and force to Kincaid's later works. Yet "My Mother" also halfway conceals what it has revealed as it gestures toward healing in the closing scenes, which depict the daughter's regressive merger with the mother. In her physical attachment to her mother, the daughter experiences a temporary melding of her identity with her mother's: "I fit perfectly in the crook of my mother's arm, on the curve of her back, in the hollow of her stomach. We eat from the same bowl, drink from the same cup; when we sleep, our heads rest on the same pillow. As we walk through the rooms, we merge and separate, merge and separate" (60). Sitting in the "enormous lap" of her mother, the daughter, child-like again, lives in a state of plenitude and contentment (61). In a similar way, the daughter in "At the Bottom of the River" recollects her perfect and loving relationship with her beautiful mother. "I see myself as I was as a child. . . . How much I loved myself and how much I was loved by my mother." Recalling the "wondrous beauty" of her mother's face, she remarks, "How I worshipped this beauty, and in my childish heart I would always say to it, 'Yes, yes, yes'" (73). Yet the reparative gestures found in such scenes provide only temporary moments of respite. Anticipating the stories of Annie John and Lucy, the daughter in *At the Bottom of the River* is deeply attached to but also afraid of her mother. For the beautiful and protective all-good mother, as Kincaid insists over and over in *At the Bottom of the River*, is also a persecutory and all-bad mother-monster.

If at times the daughter is all but overwhelmed by her emotions as she glows "red with anger" or feels great sadness and despair, she also endures arid states of nonfeeling. Anticipating the story of Annie John, the daughter in "Blackness" experiences the detached calm of a dissociated state as she becomes swallowed up in the soft blackness that falls "like soot" (46). Absorbed in the blackness, cut off from the real world, she feels "annihilated" and "erased," unable to point to herself "and say 'I'" (47). To exist in such a world of "blackness" is to be trapped in a dreadful inner world of disconnection, aloneness, and emptiness. "[B]eyond despair or the spiritual vacuum," the daughter "rushes from death to death, so familiar a state is it to her." Summoned by the mother "into a fleeting existence, one that is perilous and subject to the violence of chance, she embraces time as it passes in numbing sameness, bearing in its wake a multitude of great sadnesses" (51). Yet in the final section of "Blackness," Kincaid, as she does in "My Mother," gestures toward healing as the speaker-daughter shrugs off her mantles of hatred and despair and moves toward and then becomes enfolded by the silent voice. "I hear the silent voice—how softly now it falls, and all of existence is caught up in it. Living in the silent voice, I am no longer 'I.' Living in the silent voice, I am at last at peace. Living in the silent voice, I am at last erased" (52). As the troubling voices that haunt her consciousness go quiet, the speaker takes solace in the silent voice, but she is also "at last erased." Rather than experiencing a healing transcendence of self, she experiences the erasure of self that occurs in a dissociated or depressed state. To seek self-erasure, as the speaker does in "Blackness," is to protect against black feelings of rage and despair, but it is also to risk becoming completely disconnected from others.

If in "Blackness," Kincaid describes the deep isolation of the daughter, who experiences episodes of dissociation[6] in which she feels "annihilated" and "erased," she also presents a kind of reparative fantasy in the final story in the collection, "At the Bottom of the River," by indicating that the daughter's art comes from the dark and isolated world of her troubled selfhood. In an artistic anticipation of Xuela in *The Autobiography of My Mother*, the daughter-speaker in "At the Bottom of the River" perceives herself in a dead world—"Dead lay everything that had lived and dead also lay everything that would live" (68)—a description that conveys her inner sense of deadness and subjective emptiness. Asserting herself in the face of this despairing awareness, the speaker, Xuela-like, becomes powerful and willful, defeated not by life but by death. "What I regret is that in the face of death and all that it is and all that it shall be I stand powerless, that in the face of death my will, to which everything I have ever known bends, stands as if it were nothing more than a string caught in the early-morning wind" (70). And yet the daughter remains susceptible to the contemptuous voice of the mother: "'Death is natural,' you said to me, in such a flat, matter-of-fact way, and then you laughed—a laugh so piercing that I felt my eardrums shred, I felt myself mocked" (71).

The daughter, in an attempt to counteract her sense of "the death in life," envisions herself as a loved child silently sending and receiving from her mother "words of love and adoration" (73, 73–74). This image of the loving mother is reinforced in the narrator's subsequent vision of the world at the bottom of the river, a world where everything is "true to itself" (76). There she sees a statuesque, gleaming woman at the door of a one-room house that glows with a strange otherworldly light. Guided by the woman, an idealized, beneficent mother figure, the daughter-speaker sees a perfected world not of darkness and death but of light:[7] "the light fell on everything, and everything seemed transparent, as if the light went through each thing, so that nothing could be hidden" (77). Seeing herself clearly in the light, the daughter is transformed into a powerful, mythic daughter-woman as, Xuela-like, she asserts her will-to-power. Made up not of flesh and blood but of her own will over which she has "complete dominion" (79), she envisions herself first standing above land and sea and then journeying to the depths of the sea and emerging reborn. Utterly transformed, her bodily self stripped away, she stands in the light as if she were "a prism, many-sided and transparent, refracting and reflecting" the indestructible light of the perfected world she inhabits and the perfected self she has become (80).

"Yet what was that light in which I stood? How singly then will the heart desire and pursue the small glowing thing resting in the distance, surrounded by darkness?" (81). After the daughter delves within and then emerges from the depths transformed, she returns to reality. The room she enters, which contains a lamp, books, a chair, a table, and a pen, is the writer's room where she finds what she has been seeking: "I claim these things then—mine—and now feel myself grow solid and complete, my name filling up my mouth" (82). Unlike the daughter in "Blackness" who experiences the erasure of self and is unable to say "I," the daughter in "At the Bottom of the River" is able to claim herself in the writer's room. Again, Kincaid gestures toward healing as she suggests that through the artistic process the daughter can gain a sense of self-possession and discover the way to a livable writer's identity. And yet the process of recovering the past by returning to the dreadful inner world of the daughter-victim, as Kincaid shows again and again in *At the Bottom of the River*, is a painful, and indeed an emotionally risky, undertaking.

Described by Kincaid as stories written in her "youth" (Vorda 87), *At the Bottom of the River* tells the story of Kincaid's past, albeit in a cloudy and difficult way that halfway conceals her meaning. In her auto-biographical novels, *Annie John* and *Lucy*, as we shall see, Kincaid returns to the narrative simplicity and clarity of "Antigua Crossings" as she attempts to tell the "truth" about her relationship with her mother. Obsessed with the past, constantly ruminating over the hurts of her life, Kincaid writes because she must. A memory-tormented woman, Kincaid, as we shall see in our discussion of *Annie John* and *Lucy*, is driven not only to make sense of and work through her past in her writings but also to talk back to and assert some control over the voice that haunts her and that she carries on endless conversations with in her head: the contemptuous voice of the mother.

❦ *3* ❦

"The Way I Became a Writer Was That My Mother Wrote My Life for Me and Told It to Me"

Living in the Shadow of the Mother in *Annie John*

"I always say it's completely autobiographical, including the punctuation," Kincaid has remarked of her 1985 coming-of-age novel, *Annie John* (Muirhead 45). "The point wasn't the truth and yet the point was the truth," she insists, describing *Annie John* as, at once, a fictional work and as autobiographical (Perry, "Interview" 494). First published as a series of stories in *The New Yorker*, *Annie John* is a fictionalized account of Kincaid's life as she grew up in Antigua in the 1950s through the mid-1960s. Recalling that until she wrote fiction she talked "obsessively" about her family, Kincaid comments that people who knew her and who read *Annie John* said to her, "'Oh yes, you told me all about that.' . . . [I]t was not news to them at all" (Ferguson, "Interview" 170). Although Kincaid insists that her writing is "very autobiographical," she also remarks that she writes fiction and not autobiographical memoir because she wants "something more" than would fit into a "straightforward memoir" (Ferguson, "Interview" 176, Perry, "Interview" 494). While the events described in *Annie John* actually happened, although not necessarily in the order they occur in the novel— for example, Annie's illness and her washing of the family photographs are based on events that occurred when Kincaid was younger than her fictional counterpart—Kincaid also makes "a kind of psychological sense" of these disparate events in writing them down (Perry, "Interview" 494). In *Annie John* she wants to tell "the truth," so within her manipulation of facts "there is no lie," she insists (Perry, "Interview" 507). One of her

aims is "to understand how I got to be the person I am. The truth is important, but it's a certain kind of truth" (Bonetti 27). Writing out of a kind of necessity, Kincaid, who "carefully weighed" each word in *At the Bottom of the River* (Dilger 23), comes to insist that she is not interested in being a literary writer. Because she has something "urgent" to say, she explains, she does not have time for "literary largesse and experimentation"—that is, for the kind of writing found in *At the Bottom of the River* (Ferguson, "Interview" 167).

"Clearly, the way I became a writer was that my mother wrote my life for me and told it to me," Kincaid has remarked of her writing (O'Conner). Kincaid recalls feeling "at the mercy of everybody" as a child, particularly her mother, Annie Drew, a deeply contemptuous woman who had a way of humiliating her daughter that was "very cruel and very painful" (J. Kaufman, Goldfarb 96). Haunted by memories of her mother-tormented past, Kincaid was moved to write because of the "immediate oppression" of the mother-daughter relation. "I wanted to free myself of that," she states (Bonetti 32). "I once did not see my mother for twenty years," Kincaid would later write in *My Brother*, "even though I thought of her first thing in the morning and last thing at night, and almost all my thoughts of her were full of intense hatred" (154). Writing gave Kincaid a way to talk back to her internalized mother—a woman who protected her right "to verbally humiliate her children" (*My Brother* 53)—and also a way to take control of her obsessive ruminations over the hurts of her past in her ongoing inner conversation with her mother. Kincaid began to write to make sense of and gain some mastery over her past, and writing remains for her an act of self-rescue. "[I]t is a matter of saving my life. . . . It is a matter of living in the deepest way," she asserts. Without writing, "I would have been insane, and that's the truth. I would have had nervous breakdowns upon nervous breakdowns" (Ferguson, "Interview" 169).

Written "as a sort of relief-release" from *At the Bottom of the River*, *Annie John*, despite its narrative simplicity, is viewed by Kincaid as a more complex work. "My ideas have gotten more complicated, so I need to express them more clearly," she comments (Ferguson, "Interview" 186–87). In *Annie John*, which marks the continuation of the process of autobiographical self-representation begun in *At the Bottom of the River*, Kincaid presents a series of vignettes as she chronicles the early life of Annie John from ages ten to seventeen, focusing on Annie's troubled relationship with her mother; her intense girlhood friendships with Gwen and the Red Girl; her experiences as a black Antiguan who is taught in school to see life through an English point of view; her mysterious illness and obeah cure by Ma Chess; and her thoughts as she prepares to leave Antigua and travel to England. Although *Annie John* may seem, at first glance, a simple narrative in its linear but episodic account of the childhood and coming-of-age of Annie John, many readers find an emotional puzzle at the heart of the work as Kincaid describes Annie's intense love-hate relationship with her all-powerful mother. Critics have found the mother character to be one of the most problematic aspects of the novel because "the absence of convincing evidence of the mother's iniquities" makes it difficult to understand the basis of Annie's "burning anger," or they have found the "trauma surrounding the mother-daughter relationship . . . enigmatic," rendering the young girl's "crisis of boundaries with her mother . . . undecidable, even, in some ways, illegible" (Paravisini-Gebert 111, Gilmore 108). Also suggestive is the comment that Kincaid's "open-ended" project of self-representation in her "serial autobiography" raises "the specter of endless autobiography" (Gilmore 96). The sense of endless autobiography and endless repetition in Kincaid's works points not only to the obsessive and driven nature of her writings but also to her difficulty in confronting and working through the past.

If, at first glance, Kincaid seems invested in telling the unvarnished "truth" about the painful past of her fictional persona, there is suggestive evidence in Kincaid's remarks on her life that a shadow trauma story haunts her narrative. For as a child, as Kincaid has admitted on several occasions in her interviews, she was subjected to physical abuse, yet she describes this only in a veiled way in *Annie John*, pointing to the deep shame attached to her memories of being beaten not only by other children or her teachers but also by her mother. Kincaid, who remarks on the "great cruelty to children in the West Indies," says of her own situation, "I don't want to use the word 'abused,' but there was a great deal of cruelty directed at me when I was a child" (Vorda 92, Cryer). Kincaid recalls getting canings from her teachers who were "very angry people" (Garis); she remembers being beaten up once by a boy and his brother because she did better than one of them on an exam, and they believed she had cheated (Bonetti 29); she describes how, when she was a girl and was "always being beaten up" by girls from school, her mother took "advantage" of her inability to fight (Ferguson, "Interview" 178); and she remembers when, as a girl, she lied to protect her privacy, "[t]hey tried to beat it out" of her (Vorda 92). Although Kincaid never identifies the people who beat her for lying, one can assume that she is referring, at least in part, to her mother, who repeatedly accused Kincaid of lying when she was growing up. In her reluctant admission that her mother did, in fact, beat her, Kincaid partly denies what happened to her. Insisting that she was not "abused" but had "cruelty directed" at her, she describes her mother's "cruelty" in an indirect way, explaining that a woman she had met during a trip to Antigua told her that when she gave her children "a good beating" and they complained, she always said to them, "'It's not as bad as what Miss Annie used to do to Elaine'" (Cryer). Despite Kincaid's insistence on telling the "truth" about her Antiguan past, she omits scenes of physical beatings and maternal abuse in *Annie John*. Yet the secret of Kincaid's childhood physical abuse at the hands of her mother does find veiled expression in *Annie John*, particularly in the aspect of the novel that critics find so enigmatic: Annie John's intense love for and murderous hatred of her mother.

Annie John's love-hate relationship with her mother also reflects on another painful aspect of Kincaid's life: her intense shaming at the hands of her mother, Annie Drew, a woman known for subjecting all her children, as Kincaid would later describe it, to her "famous tongue-lashings" (*My Brother* 53). If Kincaid finds it difficult to openly admit in *Annie John* the intense shaming she was repeatedly subjected to at the hands of her mother, she does come to recognize that it is important for her to "say the things" she is ashamed of so other people cannot have "power over" her (Wachtel 64). "I think I must have suffered greatly from shame when I was a child," as she would later admit. "Actually, I know I did. I was very ashamed of not only the perceived loss of my family's favour, when more children came into the family, but I think that as I grew older I began to be ashamed of various parts of my heritage and my family life. It turns out that my father wasn't my father, and I must have known but I didn't know, because it was too shameful. I must have suffered a lot; it made me feel powerless" (Wachtel 65).

In *Annie John*, as Kincaid reveals the devastating impact of trauma and shame on her fictional projection, she shows how Annie John, like the abused and shamed individual described by trauma and shame specialists, becomes a prisoner of her childhood. Because, as trauma specialists explain, a "secure sense of connection with caring people is the foundation of personality development," traumatic events, in calling fundamental human relationships into question, can "shatter the construction of the self that is formed and sustained in relation to others" (Herman 52, 51). The child raised in an abusive family environment, where the "exercise of parental power is arbitrary, capricious, and absolute," may develop the belief that the abuser has "absolute" power and may also have an "omnipresent fear of death" (Herman 98, 100, 98). Even impersonally inflicted punishments can cause trauma in the child because of the caretaker's inability to protect the child from harm, and such children come to recognize "'profound vulnerability in all human beings, especially themselves'" (Waites 68).

The child growing up in an abusive family environment, in an attempt to preserve a sense of attachment to the abusive parent despite continual evidence of the parent's malice or neglect, may feel strongly attached to and may idealize the abuser. But such an idealization cannot be sustained in the face of repeated trauma, so the child victim's inner representations of the abuser will remain "contradictory and split" (Herman 106). Such a child may also develop contradictory good/bad identities as she becomes convinced of her own badness and tries to camouflage her "malignant sense of inner badness" by attempting to be good (Herman 105). In the abused child, "[f]ragmentation becomes the central principle of personality organization. . . . Fragmentation in the inner representations of the self prevents the integration of identity. Fragmentation in the inner representations of others prevents the development of a reliable sense of independence within connection" (Herman 107). Abuse also fosters "dissociative virtuosity" in some victims, who learn "to ignore severe pain, to hide their memories in complex amnesias, [and] to alter their sense of time, place, or person" (Herman 102).

Because of the interruption of the normal regulation of emotional states by "traumatic experiences that repeatedly evoke terror, rage, and grief," the abused child may experience the "dreadful" feeling referred to as "dysphoria," which is "a state of confusion, agitation, emptiness, and utter aloneness." The child victim may also suffer "annihilation panic," a feeling of "complete disconnection from others and disintegration of the self" (Herman 108). As trauma responses become "woven into [the] personality structure," the individual can be left with "a lingering sense of psychological impoverishment, a feeling of self-depletion or self-estrangement" (Waites 64). The survivor of child abuse may also develop "chronic anxiety and depression which persist into adult life" (Herman 108). As an adult, such an individual remains "a prisoner of her childhood," fated to remember her traumatic past and to enact, in her relationships, "dramas of rescue, injustice, and betrayal" as she idealizes those she becomes attached to only to face inevitable disappointment, which leads her to "furiously denigrate the same person whom she so recently adored" (Herman 110, 111). Left with "fundamental problems in basic trust, autonomy, and initiative," her intimate relationships "are driven by the hunger for protection and care and are haunted by the fear of abandonment or exploitation" (Herman 110, 111).

Like the individual physically abused as a child, the individual deeply humiliated as a child may remain a prisoner of her shaming past. That shame sensitivity, as shame theorists explain, can be induced not only by the passive unresponsiveness of a preoccupied or self-involved parent but also by the active shaming of the child by the parent (Morrison, *Culture* 60) is revealed in Kincaid's novel. A "central dysphoric affect of narcissistic phenomena," shame derives from the shame sufferer's "own vicarious experience of the other's scorn" (Morrison, *Shame* 67, Helen Lewis, "Introduction" 15). At the core of shame is the "conviction of one's *unlovability*" because of an inherent sense that the self is "weak, dirty, and defective" (Wurmser, *Mask* 92, 93).

Feeling a heightened sense of self-consciousness, the shamed individual may withdraw or hide from others in an attempt to protect against feelings of exposure. Other classic defenses against shame include expressions of arrogance and anger, which repair the feelings of weakness and insignificance that accompany shame; the defiant flaunting of one's shame in shameless behavior; and turning-the-tables, an attack-other script in which the shamed individual actively shames and humiliates others (see Goldberg 69; Wurmser, *Mask* 257–64; Nathanson, *Shame* 360–73). Shamed individuals may also become stuck in a shame-shame or shame-rage "feeling trap," a self-perpetuating chain of emotions in which "a series of loops of shame"—that is, "being ashamed of being ashamed"—lead to further shame and can continue indefinitely, or in which "unacknowledged shame" leads to anger, which, in turn, results in further shame (Scheff and Retzinger 104–05). When an individual has emotional reactions to her own emotions and those of another person, both can become mired in a feeling trap: "a *triple spiral* of shame and rage *between* and *within* interactants," which, in turn, can lead to the emotional impasse of an interminable conflict. "Shame-rage spirals may be brief, lasting a matter of minutes, or they can last for hours, days, or a lifetime, as bitter hatred or resentment" (Scheff and Retzinger 126–27).

As Kincaid explores the painful childhood of her fictional persona in *Annie John*, her narrative, in a way that is characteristic of shame and trauma narratives, both reveals and conceals as she describes the complex emotional life of her character. Thus despite Kincaid's attempt to tell the "truth" in her fictional-autobiographical reconstruction of the past, readers of *Annie John* may come away from Kincaid's novel with a sense of narrative withholding or avoidance. Because of Kincaid's reluctance to fully describe the shameful and painful secrets of her past—in particular, the secret of maternal abuse—many critic/readers may find something enigmatic in the daughter's sudden and intense hatred for her mother. Yet though Kincaid omits scenes of physical beatings in her novel, the fragmented and visual qualities of her narrative recreation of the past evoke the sensory and iconic form of memory known as traumatic memory in which there is an "intense focus on fragmentary sensation, on image without context" (Herman 38). And as Kincaid elaborates on Annie's ambiva-

lent love-hate relationship with her mother, she describes her character's profound sense of vulnerability and injury, her intense shame-
rage, her episodic dissociative experiences, and her annihilation panic.
That "[b]oth childhood psychological experience and cultural deter-
minations are filtered, and in a sense personally created, in and
through psychological activity, which is . . . contingent, historicized,
individual, and biographically specific" (Chodorow, *Power* 4) becomes
apparent in Kincaid's work. In showing how the biographically specific
roots of Annie's behavior are expressed in her experiences in the social
and cultural worlds she inhabits, Kincaid's narrative also dramatizes
the continual elaboration and transformation of interpersonal and
intrapsychic meaning in Annie's relations with others and in her developing awareness of her social and cultural identity.

In her autobiographical story, "Biography of a Dress," Kincaid, in
recounting an episode from her early childhood, also provides, as it
were, glimpses into the early childhood of Annie John, who is ten years
old when the novel begins. As Kincaid's forty-three-year-old narrator in
"Biography of a Dress" reconstructs the events surrounding a black-
and-white studio photograph taken of her on her second birthday, she
emphasizes the shame and pain of her early childhood relation with her
mother. Recalling the yellow poplin dress she wore in her birthday photograph, she thinks that perhaps her mother made the dress either
because she wanted to "have a daughter" who looked like the blond-
haired, blue-eyed English girl in the yellow dress shown in an almanac
advertisement or because she wanted to "make the daughter she already
had look like that" (96–97). In her account of both the physical pain she
endured when she had her ears pierced to mark the occasion of her second birthday and her feelings when she was dressed for the birthday
photograph, Kincaid's daughter-narrator seems to refer, albeit in a veiled
way, to maternal abuse. Suffering from what "must have been unbearable" pain from her pierced earlobes, she dissociated: "[T]hat was the
first time that I separated myself from myself, and I became two people
(two small children then, I was two years old), one having the experience, the other observing the one having the experience" (97). "[I]t is
quite possible," she remarks, that the act of being bathed and powdered
and dressed in her new yellow poplin frock "had about it the feeling of
being draped in a shroud" (98). And she recalls being hurt when her
mother placed her on a small table to have her photograph taken at the
photographer's studio. "[W]hen my mother picked me up, holding me
by the armpits with her hands, her thumb accidentally (it could have
been deliberate, how could someone who loved me inflict so much pain
just in passing?) pressed deeply into my shoulder, and I cried out and

then (and still now) looked up at her face and couldn't find any reason in it, and could find no malice in it, only that her eyes were full of something, a feeling that I thought then (and am convinced now) had nothing to do with me" (99).

Perhaps, Kincaid's daughter-narrator speculates, her mother suddenly realized that she was "exhausted by this whole process, celebrating my second birthday, commemorating an event, my birth, that she may not have wished to occur in the first place and may have tried repeatedly to prevent" (99).[1] Despite the "kind and loving words" the mother said "in a kind and loving voice" in front of the photographer (100), she inflicted pain on her daughter, and the look in her eyes communicated to her daughter that she was unwanted. In *Annie John*, similarly, Annie's mother can appear kind and loving, especially to others, even as she secretly inflicts pain on her daughter and, through her contempt, makes her daughter feel excluded and unwanted. And like the daughter in "Biography of a Dress," who associates the mother's loving gesture—making a dress—with being "draped in a shroud," Annie, similarly, associates her mother with death.

Annie John and Her Mother

Although Kincaid's fictional projection, Annie John, is ten years old in the opening chapter of the novel, her dependency needs and abandonment fears seem to belong to earlier childhood. Annie's opening remarks on dead people, especially dead children, reveal that she lives in an emotionally unpredictable—and potentially dangerous—family environment. When Annie and her family move temporarily away from their home in St. John's, the capital of Antigua, while their house is being repaired, Annie finds herself living near a cemetery. Like the physically abused child, Annie becomes obsessed with death as she sees in the distance the "sticklike figures" of the mourners and learns that when these figures appear in the morning it is probably to bury a child. "Until then," Annie remarks, "I had not known that children died" (4). After the family returns to their house in St. John's, Annie learns of the death of a girl named Nalda, who died in the arms of Annie's mother.[2] A bony, red-haired girl who did not like to eat food but instead preferred to eat mud, Nalda died of a fever. Aware that Mrs. John stroked the forehead of the dead girl, bathed and dressed her, and placed her in the coffin, Annie, for a while, cannot stand to be caressed by her mother or even stand the sight of her hands. The fact that Annie associates her mother's caring hands—hands that stroke and bathe and dress—with the death of a child reveals even as it conceals the family secret that haunts the narrative: the secret of maternal abuse.

Also suggestive is Annie's behavior with Sonia, a girl Annie "loved very much—and so used to torment until she cried" (7)—behavior that combines, as abusive parents often do, "protectiveness with brutality" (Waites 69). The class dunce—a girl looked at with contempt by other girls who "twist up their lips and make a sound to show their disdain" at the mention of her name—Sonia becomes an actor in Annie's ritualistic abusive play. After treating Sonia to a sweet, Annie pulls the hair on Sonia's arms and legs, "gently at first, and then awfully hard, holding it up taut with the tips of my fingers until she cried out" (7). If Sonia becomes an embodiment of the beloved/abused child, she also is an actor in a shame drama. For after the death of Sonia's mother, Annie shuns her friend, viewing Sonia as "a shameful thing, a girl whose mother had died and left her alone in the world" (8). In a similar way, Annie links dead children with neglectful mothers and with children who, like the dunce Sonia, are defective in some way. The dead Nalda was a mud-eating girl, and the hunchbacked girl, who suffered from a deformity, had crooked parts in her badly combed hair—a detail suggesting that she was neglected by her mother. When Annie, after attending the funeral of the hunchbacked girl,[3] arrives home late and is caught lying to her mother, she is forced to eat her supper alone as a punishment. That Mrs. John says she will not kiss Annie good night only to soften and kiss her anyway suggests a close mother-daughter bond. But the opening section, in its focus on Annie's obsession with dead children and her abusive play, which combines loving and punishing behaviors, tells another shadow story about Annie's relationship with her protective but also abusive mother.

Similarly, Kincaid's account of Annie's experiences as a twelve year old tells two contradictory stories about Annie's relationship with her mother. Within the story of Annie's harmonious relation with the idealized mother is another story recounting the psychic injuries Annie suffers in her relationship with her rejecting, and thereby shaming, mother. Even when Annie feels secure because of her close bond with her mother—when, for example, she and her mother take an obeah bath together—Annie remains aware of the potential dangers of the outside world, fearing she might be harmed by women her father had children with but never married, women who want to set bad spirits on Annie and her mother. While critics often claim that obeah is identified with female magic and empowerment in *Annie John*[4]—and, indeed, Annie is later cured by Ma Chess, her maternal grandmother who is a practitioner of obeah—the narrative also describes the fears and anxieties

Annie attaches to obeah. "For a while, I lived in utter fear when I was little, of just not being sure that anything I saw was itself," Kincaid has remarked, admitting that when she came to America she was glad "to not be afraid of God anymore" (Cudjoe 226). The obeah belief in spirits—and the belief that a thing or person can be real and unreal at the same time—adds to Annie's childhood sense of danger and vulnerability, expressed in her fear, for example, that she might be lured to her death by the dead hunchbacked girl or harmed by bad spirits set on her by the women spurned by her father.[5]

Feeling important and included when she is with her mother, Annie spends her days trailing after her mother and observing how she does things. Annie idealizes her mother, comparing her features to the English ideal. "Her head looked as if it should be on a sixpence. What a beautiful long neck, and long plaited hair, which she pinned up around the crown of her head because when her hair hung down it made her too hot. Her nose was the shape of a flower on the brink of opening. Her mouth, moving up and down as she ate and talked at the same time, was such a beautiful mouth I could have looked at it forever if I had to and not mind" (18–19). In a ritual that seems, at first glance, to suggest the mother's empathic resonance with her daughter's need to feel special and to be mirrored in the idealized mother's gaze, Mrs. John tells stories about Annie's childhood as she airs out and cleans the trunk containing mementos of Annie's childhood. But the personal and family history Mrs. John relays to Annie as she tells the story of Annie's early life is far from a positive one.

In Mrs. John's account, Annie was hard to handle from her conception. Mrs. John remarks, for example, that she was unable to correctly embroider the flowers on the chemise Annie wore just after she was born because the kicking of the foetus made her hand unsteady. Despite Annie's pleasure in this story, Mrs. John's words are hostile. "'You see, even then you were hard to manage.' It pleased me to think that, before she could see my face, my mother spoke to me in the same way she did now. On and on my mother would go. No small part of my life was so unimportant that she hadn't made a note of it, and now she would tell it to me over and over again. I would sit next to her and she would show me the very dress I wore on the day I bit another child my age with whom I was playing. 'Your biting phase,' she called it" (22). Another story describes how Annie fell into the hot coals used to heat the coal pot and burned her elbows because she refused to pay heed to her mother's warning not to play near the fire.[6] In the mother's stories, Annie is represented not as the idealized good child but as a disobedient and difficult—and biting—child.

Despite this, Annie remains physically close to her mother. Feeling a sense of security in the maternal presence, Annie sits beside her mother as she tells these stories, leaning against her, or she crouches on her knees behind her mother's back and leans over her mother's shoulder. "At times I would no longer hear what it was she was saying; I just liked to look at her mouth as it opened and closed over words, or as she laughed. How terrible it must be for all the people who had no one to love them so and no one whom they loved so, I thought" (22–23). To Annie, Mrs. John is a center of emotional energy and physical power. "As my mother went around preparing our supper, picking up clothes from the stone heap, or taking clothes off the clothesline, I would sit in a corner of our yard and watch her. She never stood still. Her powerful legs carried her from one part of the yard to the other, and in and out of the house. Sometimes she might call out to me to go and get some thyme or basil or some other herb for her. . . . Sometimes when I gave her the herbs, she might stoop down and kiss me on my lips and then on my neck. It was in such a paradise that I lived" (25). If the representation of the beneficent good mother in *Annie John* is symptomatic of the splitting of the mother into all-good and all-bad identities, it also recalls Nicola King's account of how in narratives describing childhood trauma, the evocation of memories of blissful childhood origins demonstrates "the need to find such a memory 'before' the memory of pain" (28). While Kincaid avoids direct mention in the narrative of the physical abuse she suffered while growing up, she does openly describe her extreme shame vulnerability as a girl in telling the story of her daughter-character.

Annie John, in her relationship with her mother, is extremely, if not exquisitely, sensitive to maternal rejection and slights. When Mrs. John says that Annie is "getting too old" to wear clothes made of the same fabric as her mother's, making Annie resemble a "little" version of Mrs. John, Annie is devastated. "To say that I felt the earth swept away from under me would not be going too far. It wasn't just what she said, it was the way she said it" (26). And when Annie's mother refuses to look through the trunk, saying that the two of them "don't have time for that anymore," Annie, again, feels "the ground wash out from under" her (27). That the withdrawal of love, which is often used by parents in the socialization process, produces shame (Michael Lewis 114–15) is revealed in Annie's experience. Overwhelmed by shame, Annie suddenly feels unloved and vulnerable. Her feeling that the earth has been swept out from under her voices a common response to shame conveyed in the everyday expressions that one could "'crawl through a hole' or 'sink through the floor' or 'die' with shame" (Helen Lewis, "Introduction" 19).[7]

If Kincaid again and again tells versions of this story of the painful rift between Annie and her mother and the annihilating force of maternal rejection, she also, in the passage describing the autobiographical essay Annie writes at her new school, shows how Annie, by writing about her painful separation from her mother, can win the admiring praise of others and thus overcome, temporarily, her painful sense of isolation and shame.[8] In her essay, Annie recalls how, when she was a child, she and her mother used to bathe naked in the sea. Unable to swim on her own, Annie would stay on the shore and watch her mother swim and dive, or she would clasp her arms around her mother's neck and go into the water on the back of her swimming mother. "I would place my ear against her neck, and it was as if I were listening to a giant shell, for all the sounds around me—the sea, the wind, the birds screeching— would seem as if they came from inside her, the way the sounds of the sea are in a seashell." Annie describes the oceanic bliss of her early childhood bond with her powerful and idealized mother, a maternal presence that seemed all-encompassing. But she also recalls the dread she felt the day she lost sight of her swimming mother as she watched her from the shore. "A huge black space then opened up in front of me and I fell inside it. I couldn't see what was in front of me and I couldn't hear anything around me. I couldn't think of anything except that my mother was no longer near me" (43). Subsequently aware that her mother was sitting on a rock and not paying any attention to her, Annie felt abandoned and deeply vulnerable.

In writing about her childhood experience, Annie presents what for her is an original or governing scene of shame. "The scene is the event as it is lived, experienced; affect fuses with and amplifies the scene," as Gershen Kaufman explains. The "building blocks of personality," these scenes may fuse together, thus "magnifying one another" and "creating families of scenes" (*Psychology* 60). When an individual is enmeshed in an "internal shame spiral," she may relive the shaming event over and over until the self is engulfed, paralyzed by shame. In turn, "each recurrence of the shame spiral is likely to recruit previous and even unrelated shame scenes, causing them to be relived and fused together. This process inevitably entrenches shame within the personality, spreading shame throughout the self" (Kaufman, *Psychology* 93). That original or governing scenes of shame are a kind of "psychological 'black hole,'" drawing the individual inward, transporting her back to her original scenes of shame (Kaufman, *Shame* 182), is evident in Annie's account. At the threshold of adolescence, Annie relives her shaming childhood rejection at the hands of her mother, for during the summer before Annie begins her new school, she dreams over and over that her mother is sitting on the rock and not coming back. Even as Annie exposes her shame, she also in part covers it up, for in sharing this autobiographical story with her schoolmates, Annie invents a happy ending. In her invented ending, when she tells her mother her dream, her mother becomes upset and then holds Annie in her arms and comforts her. But in real life Mrs. John turned her back on her daughter when Annie told her about the dream. "I thought, I couldn't bear to show my mother in a bad light before people who hardly knew her. But the real truth was that I couldn't bear to have anyone see how deep in disfavor I was with my mother" (45).

When Mrs. John, attempting to turn her daughter into a model young lady, sends Annie for instruction in manners and piano playing, Annie rebels. In presenting this mother-daughter drama, Kincaid also points to the mother's role as the enforcer of cultural and social rules governing the construction of a proper middle-class—and English colonial—identity.[9] Annie, who defiantly makes farting noises when told by her manners teacher to practice a curtsy, lies to her mother, telling her that the teacher found her manners perfect and thus told her that she need not attend class anymore. But when Annie is asked by her piano teacher not to come back, Mrs. John expresses her contempt for her daughter when she learns from the teacher of the misdeed that led to Annie's dismissal. "I wasn't sure that if she had been asked who I was she wouldn't have said, 'I don't know,' right then and there. What a new thing this was for me: my mother's back turned on me in disgust. . . . Now I often saw her with the corners of her mouth turned down in disapproval of me" (28). Annie's response to her mother's scorn reveals the power of contempt, a "global type of aggression" and a "'cold' affect" that treats the person as if she does not exist (Wurmser, *Mask* 80–81). Having the other person turn away in contempt can be a devastating experience for contempt "removes the right of presence and even of existence." The individual who is not loved stops loving herself and feels she is "'a nothing,'" and "'empty'" (Wurmser, *Mask* 83). "Contempt says: 'You should disappear as such a being as you have shown yourself to be—failing, weak, flawed, and dirty. Get out of my sight: Disappear!' . . . To disappear into nothing is the punishment for such failure" (Wurmser, "Shame" 67).

At once a personal and cultural drama, Annie's misdeeds with her manners and piano teachers reveal her growing defiance towards the strictures of English—and maternal—culture. Mrs. John's offended reaction to Annie's natural—but unfeminine and unladylike—behavior serves to reinforce Annie's feelings of vulnerability and abandonment, and it also deepens the rift between Annie's good/bad identities, leading to her protective lying to hide the part of her identity condemned by her mother. In telling the story of Annie, Kincaid reveals how the accommodation of parental needs can lead to an "as-if personality" in which the child reveals only what is expected of her, and Kincaid's character also suffers the outcome commonly experienced by those who try to maintain the illusion of a good childhood to protect against feelings of loneliness and desertion: such individuals are plagued with abiding feelings of emptiness and self-alienation because of the partial "killing" of their spontaneous feelings and needs (see Miller, *Prisoners of Childhood* 12–14).

Given a certificate for being the best student in her Sunday school Bible study group, Annie rushes home with the award, determined to "reconquer" her mother by winning her approval. When Annie, instead, discovers her parents in bed together having sex, she is struck by the sight of her mother's hand making a circular motion on her father's back. "But her hand! It was white and bony, as if it had long been dead and had been left out in the elements. It seemed not to be her hand, and yet it could only be her hand, so well did I know it. It went around and around in the same circular motion, and I looked at it as if I would never see anything else in my life again. If I were to forget everything else in the world, I could not forget her hand as it looked then" (30–31). As Annie witnesses her mother's loving embrace of her father, she reacts intensely to her feeling of exclusion. The fact that she, yet again, associates her mother's hand with death can be read as a veiled reference to abuse—a sign that the mother's loving hand is also the feared hand of the abuser—or, more generally, as Annie's recognition that her mother's touch is somehow lethal. After this incident, Annie determines never to allow her mother to touch her again.

"'Are you going to just stand there doing nothing all day?'" Mrs. John says to her daughter after Annie sees her parents in bed together. Talking back for the first time, Annie remarks, "'And what if I do?'" By talking back, Annie assumes, temporarily, power over her contemptuous mother.[10] For rather than shaming Annie by saying "some squelching thing" designed to put Annie back in her "place," Mrs. John suddenly appears ashamed. Assuming a classic shame posture, she drops her eyes and walks away, carrying her hands "limp at her sides" and looking "small and funny" (31). In a scene that will repeat and circulate in the text, the mother-daughter bond is depicted as a dyadic and dominant-submissive relationship in which one person's power exists at the expense of the other's. In Annie's inner world, the mother is an idealized "good" mother and the angry, persecutory "bad" mother, and she also is the powerfully shaming and scornful mother as well as an abject and shamed object of contempt. Similarly, Annie splits herself, and others, into good/bad parts and compulsively replays in her relationships with others variations on the dominant-submissive and shamer-shamed drama she enacts with her mother.

Gwen and the Red Girl

When Annie wins the admiration and friendship of Gwen at her new school, the two soon fall in love and become inseparable. In a replay of the idealized mother-daughter relationship, Annie worships Gwen. "The sun, already way up in the sky so early in the morning, shone on her, and the whole street became suddenly empty so that Gwen and everything about her were perfect, as if she were in a picture" (46–47). The two walk side by side to school, not touching each other but feeling as if they are "joined at the shoulder, hip, and ankle, not to mention heart," and they share secrets: things they have overheard their parents say; their dreams and fears; and especially their "love for each other" (48).[11] Bonded with Gwen, Annie, repeating the maternal look of disapproval often directed at her, turns down the corners of her mouth to show her scorn when speaking to Gwen of her mother. Unlike Mrs. John, who seems to push Annie away, Gwen agrees with Annie's plans that the two of them will live together in a house of their own when they grow up.

Yet despite Annie's intense bond with Gwen and her new-found power as she becomes a class leader and gains authority over the other girls, she retains her inner feelings of vulnerability. "Sometimes, seeing my old frail self in a girl, I would defend her; sometimes, seeing my old frail self in a girl, I would be heartless and cruel" (49).[12] Just as Annie acts out the split in her good/bad identities in school where she is known as the "good" student and the "bad" girl who does forbidden things outside class, so she befriends first Gwen, an embodiment of the idealized good self, and then the Red Girl, an embodiment of the bad self.

A maternally indulged and neglected child who is not forced by her mother to bathe, comb her hair, or change her dress daily, the dirty and dissmelling Red Girl represents Annie's unlovable and shameful but also defiant identity. "Her face was big and round and red, like a moon—a red moon. She had big, broad, flat feet, and they were naked to the bare ground; her dress was dirty, the skirt and blouse tearing away from each other at one side; the red hair that I had first seen standing up on her head was matted and tangled; her hands were big and fat, and her fingernails held at least ten anthills of dirt under them. And on top of that, she had such an unbelievable, wonderful smell, as if she had never taken a bath in her whole life" (57). Anything but a proper little girl like Gwen, the Red Girl climbs trees and plays marbles. Unlike Gwen, who meets with Mrs. John's approval, the Red Girl is the kind of person who would be forbidden by Annie's mother, so Annie comes to worship the ground the Red Girl's unwashed feet walk on and finds Gwen's freshly pressed uniform, clean neck, and neatly combed hair dull by comparison.

Attempting to gain active mastery over her childhood sense of maternal betrayal, Annie takes secret delight in her betrayal of her mother when she secretly meets the Red Girl at an abandoned light-house. But when Mrs. John becomes suspicious about Annie's daily walks and temporarily keeps Annie a "prisoner" under her maternal "watchful gaze," Annie is unable to meet with the Red Girl for several days (62). Punished for her absence when she returns to the secret meeting place, Annie is pinched by the Red Girl, and then, when Annie cries, the Red Girl kisses the places where she pinched Annie. "Oh, the sensation was delicious—the combination of pinches and kisses. And so wonderful we found it that, almost every time we met, pinching by her, followed by tears from me, followed by kisses from her were the order of the day. I stopped wondering why all the girls whom I had mistreated and abandoned followed me around with looks of love and adoration on their faces" (63). Yet another enactment of the classic behavior of the abuser, which mingles loving and punishing behaviors, this episode points to what is omitted in the earlier scenes describing Annie's childhood looks of love and adoration for her mother who both mistreats and rejects her daughter.

Already a "good liar," Annie becomes a thief as if to prove the truth of her mother's saying, "Where there's a liar, there's a thief" (63).[13] Annie steals from her parents to buy gifts for the Red Girl. And she hides the marbles she has won and the library books she has stolen under the house, delighting in her betrayal of her mother's trust and her ability to cast suspicion away from herself and put on an innocent look. Eventually, though, Mrs. John catches Annie coming out from her hiding place with a special marble in hand, which Annie plans to give to the Red Girl. Enraged, Annie's mother undertakes a furious but futile search for the marbles,[14] and over supper, she tells Annie's father about all the bad things Annie has done. "I could hardly recognize myself from this list— how horrible I was—though all of it was true." As the object of her mother's scorn, Annie, in a classic contempt-disappear scenario, senses that her parents want her to disappear. "They talked about me as if I weren't there sitting in front of them, as if I had boarded a boat for South America without so much as a goodbye" (67).

In an attempt to cajole Annie into telling her where the marbles are, Mrs. John tells Annie a story from her own past, describing how she once carried a bunch of green figs on her head only to discover, when she took the load from her head, that there was a long black snake in the bunch of figs.[15] Envisioning her mother as a girl as Mrs. John tells the story, Annie identifies with the tall, thin, and shy girl with the stooped back she recalls having seen in pictures of her mother at that age. "Oh, to think of a dangerous, horrible black snake on top of that beautiful head; to think of those beautifully arched, pink-soled feet (the feet of which mine were an exact replica, as hers were an exact replica of her mother's) stumbling on the stony, uneven road, the weight of snake and green figs too much for that small back. If only I had been there, I would not have hesitated for even a part of a second to take her place" (69–70). So moved by the story that she feels as if her heart might break, Annie almost gives in to her mother only to suddenly see her mother as a snake-like deceiver. "Well, Little Miss, where are your marbles?" Mrs. John says in a voice that is "warm and soft and treacherous." Imitating her mother, Annie replies in a "warm, soft, and newly acquired treacherous voice" that she does not have any marbles and that she has never played marbles (70).

Annie's subsequent dream about the Red Girl, who is sent to Anguilla to live, is self-revealing. In Annie's dream, the boat taking the Red Girl to Anguilla splinters, killing everybody but the Red Girl, whom Annie rescues—an act that dramatizes Annie's own desire for rescue. Afterward, the two of them live together on an island where, at night, they send confusing signals to the cruise ships sailing by—ships presumably carrying British tourists—and when the ships consequently crash on some nearby rocks, Annie and the Red Girl laugh as the "cries of joy" of the tourists turn into "cries of sorrow" (71). Even as it dramatizes Annie's deep-seated dependency needs and wish for rescue and her abiding shame-rage, this dream also discloses Annie's growing desire for revenge against the English colonizers.

Annie's Identification with and Resistance to Her Colonial Education

Subjected to her mother's annihilating contempt and caught up in a contest of wills with her mother, Annie becomes sensitized to the power and shame dynamics of the colonizer-colonized relationship. Kincaid, in her later remarks on the shaming effects of British colonialism on her when she was growing up, recalls not only feeling "in awe and small" whenever she heard the word *England* but also being taught to believe that she had been rescued from "a hole filled with nothing, and that was the word for everything about me, nothing" ("On Seeing England" 34, 36). In a similar way, Annie, who splits herself, and others, into good/bad identities, learns to see the English colonial culture as "good" and valuable and her native Antiguan culture as "bad" and worthless. In an anticipation of *A Small Place*'s shame-reversing attack on British colonialism, Annie comes to resist her colonial education, and, in a classic attack-other script, she returns English contempt with her own countercontempt.

When Annie John first goes to her new school as a twelve year old, she and the other girls are enjoined by the English headmistress, Miss Moore, to leave behind their "bad ways" and be "good examples for each other" (36). Annie, in part, wants to be a good student and win the approval of her teachers for her "industriousness and quickness at learning things" (37). When Annie's teacher, Miss Nelson, asks her students to spend the morning of the first day of class in reflection as they write an autobiographical essay, Annie sees this as a bookish—and prototypically English—endeavor. "A day at school spent in such a way! Of course, in most books all the good people were always contemplating and reflecting before they did anything. Perhaps in her mind's eye she could see our futures and, against all prediction, we turned out to be good people" (38–39).

If in part Annie's love of books and learning and her desire to excel in her studies point to her identification with the English ideal, she also defies her teachers. To Annie, the proud headmistress, Miss Moore, is an object of contempt: "[S]he looked like a prune left out of its jar a long time and she sounded as if she had borrowed her voice from an owl" (36). Observing Miss Moore's throat beating up and down "as if a fish fresh out of water were caught inside," Annie wonders if the headmistress smells "like a fish" (36). Echoing her mother's anti-English speech and returning English racial contempt with black Antiguan countercontempt, Annie imagines that Miss Moore, like other English people, might be a dirty and dissmelling object, for she recalls her mother's remark that the English have a fish-like smell because of their poor bathing habits.

Even though Annie excels at her studies and becomes prefect of her classmates for ranking first in the class, she refuses to set herself up as a good example. Finding her academic rival, Hilarene, to be "a disgusting model of good behavior and keen attention to scholarship" (73), Annie prefers the class dunce, Ruth. While Ruth's English cultural identity could make her proud, she is, instead, an object of public humiliation, for she is frequently forced to wear the dunce cap. Not only is Ruth the (shamed) dunce, she also is shamed because of her English heritage. Turning English pride into shame, Annie remarks, "I could see how Ruth felt from looking at her face. Her ancestors had been the masters, while ours had been the slaves. She had such a lot to be ashamed of, and by being with us every day she was always being reminded" (76).

Just as Annie, in a classic turning-the-tables shame script, takes pleasure in humiliating the English humiliator, so she refuses to revere famous European historical figures, such as Christopher Columbus, who is lauded by her teachers. Thus, when Annie sees a picture in her history textbook of the proud and triumphant Columbus degraded and dejected because his hands and feet are bound in chains, she feels pleased. "What just deserts, I thought, for I did not like Columbus. How I loved this picture—to see the usually triumphant Columbus, brought so low, seated at the bottom of a boat just watching things go by" (77–78). It is significant that the words Annie writes under the picture in her book as she, in effect, talks back to her teachers—"The Great Man Can No Longer Just Get Up and Go" (78)—repeat the scornful words her mother said of her own hated father, Pa Chess.[16] In talking back—and writing back—to the colonial authorities, Annie uses to great effect the voice she has internalized: the contemptuous voice of the mother.

As her enraged teacher, Miss Edward, bears down on Annie for not paying attention, Annie sees her as a monstrous figure. "Her whole face was on fire. Her eyes were bulging out of her head. I was sure that at any minute they would land at my feet and roll away. The small pimples on her face, already looking as if they were constantly irritated, now ballooned into huge, on-the-verge-of-exploding boils" (81–82). Not only is Miss Edward like the shaming mother, but her enraged look can be read as a mirror image of the angry look of the mother which is never described in the novel. In an act of public shaming, Miss Edward accuses Annie of impertinence, finding "a hundred words for the different forms" of Annie's rude behavior. Just as Annie is getting accustomed to Miss Edward's "amazing bellowing," her teacher is temporarily rendered speechless when she discovers that Annie has defaced her history textbook. "I had gone too far this time, defaming one of the great men in history, Christopher Columbus, discoverer of the island that was my home. And now look at me. I was not even hanging my head in remorse. Had my peers ever seen anyone so arrogant, so blasphemous?" (82).[17]

As punishment, Annie is removed from her position as prefect and ordered to copy Books I and II of John Milton's *Paradise Lost*.[18] After her terrible morning, Annie hopes that her mother will comfort her at lunch time, but instead her mother lavishes attention on Annie's father and does not notice her daughter's distressed look. And when Mrs. John tricks Annie into eating the "much hated breadfruit" (83)[19] and then laughs, the shame-sensitive Annie sees her mother as hostile and her mocking laughter as venomous. "When she laughed, her mouth opened to show off big, shiny, sharp white teeth. It was as if my mother had suddenly turned into a crocodile" (84).[20]

Annie's Response to Her Maturing Body and the Prescribed Roles of Femininity

That the female body, as Kincaid has remarked, can be an "incredible source of shame" (Garner) is revealed in Annie's experiences beginning at puberty. During the summer of her twelfth year, as Annie physically matures, she comes to associate shame with her bodily changes. "My legs had become more spindlelike, the hair on my head even more unruly than usual, small tufts of hair had appeared under my arms, and when I perspired the smell was strange, as if I had turned into a strange animal" (25). Annie's nose, which recently had been "a small thing, the size of a rosebud," suddenly seems to have spread across her face, nearly blotting out her cheeks "so that if I didn't know I was me standing there I would have wondered about that strange girl" (27). Annie's feeling of self-estrangement as she examines her maturing body recalls descriptions of the "profound estrangement from world and self" that accompanies extreme shame anxiety (Wurmser, *Mask* 53). Wanting to undo her shame, she imagines screwing herself into a set of clamps at night to curtail her growing.

If Annie is secretly ashamed of her maturing body, she also publicly rebels against the prescribed feminine roles she is enjoined to perform. Urged to participate in ladylike—and prototypically English—recreations at her school during Friday afternoon recess, such as walks and discussions of novels, Annie and her friends, instead, delight in playing "band," an uninhibited game in which the girls form lines and dance up and down the schoolyard, sometimes singing calypso songs with unladylike lyrics.[21] Afterward, on the way home from school, Annie and her friends sit on tombstones in the churchyard where they sing bad songs, use banned words, and show each other body parts. But when the hated Miss Edward discovers the students in this bodily display one day, they, shame-faced, slink home while Miss Edward accompanies Annie, the ringleader, to her home and reports Annie's offense to her mother. "It was apparently such a bad thing," Annie remarks, "that my mother couldn't bring herself to repeat my misdeed to my father in my presence" (81).

Just as Annie and her friends are made to feel ashamed of their natural sexual curiosity and bodily exhibitionism, so when Annie first begins to menstruate she feels the way "a dog must feel when it has done something wrong and is ashamed of itself and trying to get somewhere quick, where it can lie low" (52). Despite the sympathy and fascination of her friends, who ask Annie to demonstrate her new-found status as the first in their group to menstruate, Annie feels not only ashamed but also vulnerable. At school she faints when she envisions herself sitting at her desk in a pool of blood—a highly visual but also detached image that, in evoking the iconic form of dissociated memory associated with trauma, points to the shadow drama of physical abuse that haunts the narrative. That Annie responds with bitterness to her mother's outstretched arms and look of concern for her pain suggests, yet again, that Annie associates her mother's protective and nurturing behavior with pain.

Several years later, when the fifteen-year-old Annie is promoted to a class containing girls two or three years older than she is, she comes to view the once-envied older and sexually mature girls with contempt. In her interpersonal relations with her schoolmates, Annie mimics her mother's disapproving look and voice. "[H]ow vain they were! Constantly they smoothed down their hair, making sure every strand was in place. . . . They actually practiced walking with their hips swinging from side to side. They were always sticking out their bosoms. . . . [W]hat a dull bunch they were!" (90). In her new class rival, Annie sees a reflection of her disapproving mother and teachers. "I could see the kind of grownup person she would be—just the kind who would take one look at me and put every effort into making my life a hardship. Already her mouth was turned down permanently at the corners" (91). Rejecting her rejecter, Annie pronounces her rival dull and is unable to recall the girl's name.

Annie also rejects Gwen, who remains a model of proper femininity. Fated to reenact in her interpersonal relationships the mother-daughter drama in which intense idealization is followed by inevitable disappointment and even furious denigration of the once idealized person, Annie, no longer thrilled at the sight of Gwen, feels at times irritated at the sound of Gwen's voice, which once contained a kind of music, and her once-idealized friend seems "small" in Annie's eyes: "a bundle of who said what and who did what" (92). Annie is also fated to reexperience with Gwen her deep-seated fears of exploitation and abandonment. When Gwen says that she wants Annie to marry her brother so that the two friends can be together always, Annie feels abandoned and alone. "[T]he last person left on earth couldn't feel more alone than I," as she remarks (93).

Living in the Shadow of the Contemptuous Mother:
Annie's Troubled Adolescence

Kincaid, describing her mother's cruelty, remarks on Annie Drew's "astonishing and harsh" way of humiliating her (Goldfarb 96). While Kincaid omits scenes of maternal abuse in the narrative, she does present scenes of maternal shaming as she describes Annie's relation with her mother. "The shamer is a person who may act inadvertently, but usually acts aggressively, to put down another," writes Joseph Berke. "He is like a parent who disciplines a child maliciously. The issue becomes more than moral convenience or control, but the systematic demoralization of one human being by another who gains considerable sadistic pleasure by so doing" (326). A prisoner of her childhood who remains trapped during adolescence in a shaming and abusive maternal environment, not only does Annie become angry and depressed, but she also suffers dissociative symptoms and experiences a frightening episode of self-disintegration.

When Annie turns fifteen, she is "more unhappy" than she "ever imagined anyone could be." Her unhappiness, which is "deep inside" her, takes the "shape of a small black ball, all wrapped up in cobwebs" (85). "[F]eeling like the oldest person who had ever lived and who had not learned a single thing," Annie is unable to explain how she became that way. "It must have come on me like mist," she remarks. "Everything I used to care about had turned sour" (86). Over time, Annie and Mrs. John develop two faces: a "good" public face and a "bad" private one. Around Mr. John, they are polite and kind and loving, and around Mrs. John's friends, Annie is obedient and well-mannered. But when the two are alone, everything darkens. "Something I could not name just came over us, and suddenly I had never loved anyone so or hated anyone so" (88). In a recurring dream that points, once again, to the shadow drama that haunts the narrative—that of the physically abusive mother—Annie envisions herself walking down a road. At first, her steps are light and quick and her voice happy as she chants the words, "My mother would kill me if she got the chance. I would kill my mother if I had the courage"—for her quickness seems to indicate that she will never give her mother the chance to kill her. But as she continues on the road, she says the words more and more slowly and in a sad way, and her feet and body become heavy as she seemingly recognizes that since she lacks courage, the chance will pass to her mother. Taught by her mother to see her dreams as real, Annie, after having the dream over and over, comes to measure various small incidents against it "to see if this was her chance or that was my courage" (89).

Isolated and vulnerable, Annie becomes subject to painful feelings of self-contempt and shame-depression. As she looks at her reflection in shop windows one day while walking alone on Market Street, she suddenly sees herself as "strange" in a moment of heightened self-consciousness and racial self-awareness. "My whole head was so big, and my eyes, which were big, too, sat in my big head wide open, as if I had just had a sudden fright. My skin was black in a way I had not noticed before, as if someone had thrown a lot of soot out of a window just when I was passing by and it had all fallen on me. . . . Altogether, I looked old and miserable" (94). Annie recalls a picture she had seen of a painting entitled *The Young Lucifer*. Seeing in Lucifer a reflection of her own "bad" identity,[22] Annie describes the misery behind her own defiant badness. In the painting, Lucifer, who has been cast out of heaven because of his bad deeds, is smiling, but it is "one of those smiles that you could see through, one of those smiles that make you know the person is just putting up a good front. At heart, you could see, he was really lonely and miserable at the way things had turned out" (94–95).

Annie's misery only deepens when she is insulted by four boys who undercut her secret identification with and idealization of Victorian heroines like that in her favorite novel, Brontë's *Jane Eyre*.[23] In a pointed mimicry of the Victorian—and English colonist—gentleman, the boys affectedly bow to Annie and intone bookish Victorian speech. "'Hallo, Madame. How are you this afternoon? . . . Ah, the sun, it shines and shines only on you,'" they say to Annie and then laugh. Even as Annie is being ridiculed by the boys, she is aware that their behavior is "malicious" and that she has done "nothing to deserve it other than standing there all alone" (95). Recognizing one of the boys as her former playmate, Mineu, Annie recalls the games they played as children in which Mineu, in a mimicry of the colonizer-colonized roles and also a rehearsal of the gender roles of adult life, assigned himself the master or leadership roles and Annie the lesser or servant roles. When Mineu, in turn, recognizes Annie and shakes her hand, smiling all the while in a knowing way at his friends, Annie is aware that Mineu and his friends are making fun of her, and she feels ashamed, actively humiliated in the presence of observing witnesses.

Attempting to rid herself of her shame, Annie, in a moment of shame-rage, wishes she could punish Mineu and his friends by turning them into cinder blocks. Annie's imagined punishment not only reveals her own feeling that she is being treated as a socially despised nonperson but also conveys the annihilating force of the other's contempt, which can make the shamed individual feel as if she is "'a nothing,' 'empty,' 'frozen'—'like a stone'" (Wurmser, *Mask* 83). During her walk home after this incident, Annie feels alternately so big that she takes up the whole street (as if her shame is visible to everyone) and so small that nobody can see her (that is, utterly disregarded and insignificant).[24] In describing Annie's emotional turmoil, Kincaid conveys the disorganizing and searing qualities of intense shame. "I wasn't aware of anything on the outside. Inside, however, the thimble that weighed worlds spun around and around; as it spun, it bumped up against my heart, my chest, my stomach, and whatever it touched felt as if I had been scorched there" (101).

Adding to Annie's misery, she subsequently learns that her mother was a witness to her encounter with the boys. When her enraged mother looks at her, Annie sees a "frightening black thing" leave her mother to meet and embrace her own "frightening black thing." In an open expression of contempt, Mrs. John speaks to Annie as if she were "not only a stranger but a stranger that she did not wish to know" (101). Denouncing Annie for making a public and shameful spectacle of herself with the boys, Mrs. John accuses Annie of behaving like a slut. "The word 'slut' (in patois) was repeated over and over, until suddenly I felt as if I were drowning in a well but instead of the well being filled with water it was filled with the word 'slut,' and it was pouring in through my eyes, my ears, my nostrils, my mouth." Attempting to temporarily rid herself of her shame by relocating it onto her mother, Annie talks back to her mother, returning her mother's contempt with her own countercontempt. "As if to save myself, I turned to her and said, 'Well . . . like mother like daughter'" (102), Annie's contemptuous words pointing indirectly to Kincaid's illegitimacy, which she would later admit was a profound source of shame for her when she was growing up.

By talking back, Annie temporarily overthrows her painful feelings of helpless shame through anger, a "powerful, surging" emotion that defends against shame (Goldberg 69). Annie enjoys a moment of triumph as she shames her mother: "I looked at my mother. She seemed tired and old and broken" (102). But then when her mother angrily rejects Annie—"Until this moment, in my whole life I knew without a doubt that, without any exception, I loved you best"—Mrs. John seems young and vigorous, and Annie is again the "tired and old and broken" one. Feeling as if the ground has opened up between her and her mother, "making a deep and wide split," Annie wonders what will become of her (103). At once Annie misses her mother and wants to live somewhere with her alone, and she hates her mother and wants to see her mother's withered corpse in a coffin at her feet. When Annie subsequently asks her carpenter father to make her a trunk, she begins her preparation for departure from home. Yet she remains aware of the power her mother has over her: "I could not be sure whether for the rest of my life I would be able to tell when it was really my mother and when it was really her shadow standing between me and the rest of the world" (107).

Debilitating Shame: Annie's Breakdown and Recovery

"Debilitating shame is an alienating feeling," remarks Carl Goldberg. "It conveys an anxiety that all is not right with one's life, that one's existence is not safe and harmonious. It carries the opprobrium that the sufferer is unlovable and should be cast out of human company" (8). Kincaid, in describing the autobiographical sources of Annie's mysterious illness, recalls that, like Annie, she had an illness, although she was seven when she was sick, and like Annie, she washed and powdered some family photographs during her illness (Bonetti 27). But while Kincaid suffered from whooping cough and delirium (Vorda 95), Annie's illness is presented as both a physical collapse and a psychic malady. Kincaid also incorporates an especially humiliating memory into her account of Annie's illness. "I want to try to live with my humiliations," she insists. "It's just life. I wet my bed until I was thirteen, and before I stopped wetting my bed, I was having my period and wetting my bed, and in the morning my sheets used to be just filled with my bloody pee. That was very embarrassing. But there it is. It did happen" (Goldfarb 98). If Kincaid is bent on exposing the "truth" of her humiliating past in *Annie John*, she also in part protectively conceals the fact of her bedwetting in the narrative by embedding it in a description of Annie's mysterious, but also symbolic and literary, illness, an illness, as Kincaid herself has suggested, that can be read as marking a "rite of passage" in Annie's life (Bonetti 27).

"I looked inside my head," Annie remarks, describing her illness. "A black thing was lying down there, and it shut out all my memory of the things that had happened to me. I knew that in my fifteen years a lot of things had happened, but now I couldn't put my finger on a single thing. As I fell asleep, I had no feeling in any part of my body except the back of my skull, which felt as if it would split open and spew out huge red flames. I dreamed then that I was walking through warm air filled with soot" (111–12). Annie, who before had experienced a heightened and painful sense of self-consciousness, comes to experience a loss of self as she succumbs to her illness and retreats into herself. Her symptoms recall at once the classic defense against shame—withdrawal—and the dissociative experiences associated with both extreme shame paralysis and trauma. During the time of her mysterious collapse, which lasts for three and one-half months, it rains every day. "The sound the rain made as it landed on the roof pressed me down in my bed, bolted me down, and I couldn't even so much as lift my head if my life depended on it." When Annie's parents speak to each other, the words travel toward Annie but then "fall to the floor, suddenly dead" as they reach her ears (109). Experiencing at times the dissociative state of "depersonalization" in which individuals report feeling a sense of unreality about the self or that the real self is distanced or that they are observing the self from the outside (Steinberg 62), Annie envisions herself as a small toy Brownie or imagines that she is sitting on one of the beams in the ceiling of her bedroom looking down on herself and her mother.

When the doctor offers a diagnosis of the fifteen-year-old Annie's condition by saying that she might be "a little run-down" (110), he inadvertently describes one of the root causes of her collapse, for Annie has been constantly "run-down," that is, shamed, by her contemptuous mother. In her illness, Annie becomes the image of the shamed individual. "In shame, there is . . . an implosion of the self. The head is bowed, eyes closed, the body curved in on itself, making the person as small as possible" (Helen Lewis, "Introduction" 18). Annie's symptoms also repeat, but in a prolonged way, the experiences of the shamed individual during an acute shaming event in which the individual may feel "small, helpless, and childish," her behavior and thought may seem "disorganized or disoriented," and she may feel at a "loss for words and also at a loss for thoughts" (Helen Lewis, "Introduction" 19, Scheff, "Shame-Rage Spiral" 111). In a childlike state of regression, Annie wets her bed when she is ill, and on a day when her parents leave her alone, going back to their usual routines, she washes the family photographs that document moments in her family's life, trying to wash them clean. In her destruction of the family photos, which include photographs recording painful, shameful memories like that about Annie's fight with her mother about her confirmation shoes, Annie acts out her desire to erase her past and thus escape her unendurable sense of shame.

Ultimately, Annie is helped not by her parents but by Ma Chess, her maternal grandmother who is a practitioner of obeah. When Ma Chess mysteriously arrives, she instinctively and wordlessly understands the source of Annie's illness and helps restore Annie by mothering her: "Sometimes at night, when I would feel that I was all locked up in the warm falling soot and could not find my way out, Ma Chess would come into my bed with me and stay until I was myself—whatever that had come to be by then—again. I would lie on my side, curled up like a little comma, and Ma Chess would lie next to me, curled up like a bigger comma, into which I fit" (125–26). Just as the rain mysteriously starts and then stops, so Annie's illness mysteriously comes and then goes.

Afterward, Annie, instead of feeling sad, is angry toward her mother. "I was feeling . . . how much I never wanted to feel her long, bony fingers against my cheek again, how much I never wanted to hear her voice in my ear again, how much I longed to be in a place where nobody knew a thing about me and liked me for just that reason, how much the whole world into which I was born had become an unbearable burden and I wished I could reduce it to some small thing that I could hold underwater until it died" (127–28). When Annie, who has grown taller during her illness, returns to school, she assumes, significantly enough, a classic shame posture, with her head held down, her back stooped, and her walk timid. At the same time, Annie has acquired a strange—presumably affected—accent, and she has perfected her mother's look of disdain. "If someone behaved toward me in a way that didn't meet with my approval, without saying a word I would look at them directly with one eyebrow raised. I always got an apology" (129). Just as Annie's mother turned her back on her daughter to express her contempt, so Annie leaves the company of her peers when she disapproves of the things they say or do. At one and the same time, Annie, with her stooped back and timid walk, exposes her abiding sense of shame while she also uses classic defenses against shame—contempt and affected arrogance—to bolster her sagging self.

The Dreadful Confusion of Dysphoria: Annie's Leave-taking

For many readers of *Annie John*, as Lizabeth Paravisini-Gebert has observed, one of the most troubling aspects of the mother character in the novel is the "absence of convincing evidence of the mother's iniquities," making it difficult to understand Annie's "burning anger" toward her mother (111). Indeed, some critics even view matrilinear bonding in the novel as ultimately empowering.[25] Contrary to these claims, what Kincaid is describing in *Annie John* is the potentially lethal impact of the mother's abuse and scorn. While part of Annie retains feelings of intense love for her mother, she also recognizes, ultimately, that she must leave Antigua—that is, leave the abusive and shaming maternal environment—in order to rescue herself. The "absence of convincing evidence of the mother's iniquities" in the novel reveals that Kincaid, even as she exposes her painful childhood in the novel, is engaged in a kind of cover-up. Yet in writing and publishing the novel, Kincaid is also effectively talking back to her mother, Annie Drew, as she bears witness to the suffering she experienced at her mother's hands and, in the process, wins the admiring approval of her reading public.

In the final chapter, the seventeen-year-old Annie is preparing to leave home to go to England where she will study to become a nurse. As Annie takes stock of the things in her room on the morning of her last day at home, she prepares to relinquish her life with her family in Antigua. "Everywhere I looked stood something that had meant a lot to me, that had given me pleasure at some point, or could remind me of a time that was a happy time. But as I was lying there my heart could have burst open with joy at the thought of never having to see any of it again" (131–32). Pronouncing her mother a "hypocrite" for claiming that she loved Annie while arranging for repeated separations from her daughter, Annie insists that she, like her mother, now has "hypocrisy" and "sharp eyes" to aid her (133). During her farewell breakfast, Annie wears a smile on her face as she watches her parents eat, disgusted at the clop-clop sound of her father's false teeth and at the sight of her mother's donkey-like chewing. Yet if Annie uses anger and scorn to protect herself, she remains extremely shame-sensitive. "Lying in my bed for the last time, I thought, This is what I add up to. At that, I felt as if someone had placed me in a hole and was forcing me first down and then up against the pressure of gravity" (133).

Deeply distressed, Annie feels as if she is "in a dream"—that is, she dissociates—as she walks with her parents to the jetty and reviews the places and formative events of her past: "I didn't feel my feet touch ground, I didn't even feel my own body—I just saw these places as if they were hanging in the air, not having top or bottom, and as if I had gone in and out of them all in the same moment" (143). As she confronts the reality of her leave-taking, she experiences the dreadful confusion of dysphoria. "I felt a familiar hollow space inside. I felt I was being held down against my will. I felt I was burning up from head to toe. I felt that someone was tearing me up into little pieces and soon I would be able to see all the little pieces as they floated out into nothing in the deep blue sea" (144). Behind Annie's feelings of hollow dread, vulnerability, and burning but impotent shame-rage is a fear of self-disintegration: that the contemptuous and oppressive (m)other will destroy Annie's vulnerable selfhood. Kincaid, who has commented that the closure of *Annie John* is "very disturbing," says that at the end Annie's apparent "hardness" is a "very fragile 'hard'" (Perry, "Interview" 495, Cudjoe 228). And indeed, as Annie is leaving home, she is almost overwhelmed by a flood of contradictory feelings: "[S]uddenly a wave of strong feeling came over me, and my heart swelled with a great gladness as the words 'I shall never see this again' spilled out inside me. But then, just as quickly, my heart shriveled up and the words 'I shall never see this again' stabbed at me. I don't know what stopped me from falling in a heap at my parents' feet" (145).

During her farewells to her parents in her small cabin, Annie and her mother smile at each other, "but I know the opposite of that was in my heart." Given Annie's need to escape her mother, Mrs. John's seemingly comforting words of farewell are, in fact, chilling: "It doesn't matter what you do or where you go, I'll always be your mother and this will always be your home" (147). After waving goodbye to her mother, Annie goes back to her cabin where she hears the sound of the waves lapping around the ship. "They made an unexpected sound, as if a vessel filled with liquid had been placed on its side and now was slowly emptying out" (148). A classic open ending, the closure describes Annie's departure from Antigua and thus from her mother. If the final image of the novel—that of a vessel emptying out—suggests a sense of loss and desolation, it also leaves open the possibility of renewal for Annie, who, in leaving behind her old life, is moving into an unknown future away from her homeland and mother.

Kincaid recalls that when she was sent to America to be a nanny, she thought she "would die" but also felt she would "rather die than stay" and would "rather be dead than to live a certain way." As she explains, "I felt very old and dark, sort of dead. . . . I think it's called depression" (Muirhead 41). Although brokenhearted when she left Antigua, she also felt that "this place, this situation had tried to squeeze the life out of me, and . . . I was going to live" (Birbalsingh 146). To Kincaid, coming to America "was like taking an enormous purgative. And I am just still on the toilet" (Ferguson, "Interview" 175). Explaining that the "immediate oppression" she wanted to free herself from was the mother-daughter relation, Kincaid also asserts that it was "good luck" that she came to America and not England, which is the destination of Annie John, for in America Kincaid was allowed to perform an "act of self-invention" (Bonetti 32, 33).

"[W]hen I crossed the ocean," Kincaid states, "I aspired to be with something grand and really great and better than me" (Garner). In her desire to leave the oppressive situation that was squeezing the life out of her and in her identification with something "better," Kincaid was trying to rescue her beleaguered self. And in writing *Annie John*, she was attempting to make sense of and also to free herself from her crippling memories of and obsessive ruminations about her mother-dominated and trauma- and shame-ridden Antiguan past. But in writing her next novel, *Lucy*, as we shall see in our continuing investigation of Kincaid's ongoing self-narration and her literary construction of an autobiographical, storied self and writer's identity, Kincaid still finds it necessary to talk and write back to the contemptuous and abusive woman she thought about each and every day for some twenty years after leaving Antigua and moving to the United States—the mother who wrote her life.

❧ 4 ❧

"As I Looked at This Sentence a Great Wave of Shame Came over Me and I Wept and Wept"

The Art of Memory, Anger, and Despair in *Lucy*

"My mother . . . was a betrayer of her sex," Kincaid remarks as she draws a connection between the mother character in her 1990 novel *Lucy* and her own mother, Annie Drew (Listfield). In *Lucy*, a novel Kincaid says is filled with "thick female stuff," she wants to be "very frank," "unlikable," and "even unpopular" (Listfield, Perry, "Interview" 506). *Lucy*, she insists, is not about "race and class" but instead is about "a person figuring out how to be an artist, an artist of herself and of things" (Kennedy). In her ongoing fictional recreation of her early life in *Lucy*, Kincaid describes her experiences after leaving Antigua and coming to the United States to work as a nanny. Because of the similarities in the experiences and memories of Annie John and Lucy Josephine Potter, who shares Kincaid's birthday and the surname of her biological father, Roderick Potter, and because of the close connection between Kincaid's life and that of her characters, informed readers are likely to read *Lucy* as a sequel to *Annie John*. In her remarks on the autobiographical sources of the novel, Kincaid comments that her characters are connected but are not identical, for Annie and Lucy are not "meant to be the same person," and *Lucy* is not a "continuation" of *Annie John*, and yet *Lucy*, like *Annie John*, is "a continuation . . . in the sense that it's about my life and it's the same life I'm writing about" (Vorda 99). *Lucy* is connected to but represents an important departure from *Annie John* not only in the physical sense as it records Kincaid's experiences after her leave-taking from Antigua but

also in the emotional sense as it describes Kincaid's attempt to forge a new invented writer's identity and become the self-possessed "Jamaica Kincaid" rather than the mother-dominated "Elaine Potter Richardson."

"I was only sixteen years old," Kincaid recalls as she describes leaving home in 1965 shortly after her sixteenth birthday. "I was a very depressed person, I wanted to leave, I wanted to go to America and . . . make sense of myself to myself." Even when she became homesick, she did not give up. "I was looking for control of my own life. . . . I was looking to close my door when I want[ed] to, open it when I want[ed], come when I want[ed]. I was looking to have some idea of myself" (Dilger 21). Kincaid recalls with great anger how her high school education was interrupted by her mother, who said that she needed her daughter at home to help care for her three young sons. "Some time before I was sixteen years of age, I might have taken a series of exams that, had I passed them, would have set me on a path that would have led me to be educated at a university, but just before all of that my mother removed me from school" (*My Brother* 74). Kincaid had hoped to stay in school and then go on to the university in Jamaica. Instead, her education was cut short, and she eventually got her high school diploma and completed some college in the United States.

When the sixteen-year-old Kincaid was sent to the United States to be a live-in babysitter for a family in Scarsdale, New York, she was supposed to help her family by sending money home. "It dawned on me that my mother had made a terrible mistake in her life, that she had had children she could not afford, and I was supposed to help. . . . I remember taking it very badly, that feeling. That was the beginning of feeling outrage and injustice in me, that I should bear that burden" (Jacobs). After working for the Scarsdale family for several months, Kincaid took a job on the Upper East Side of New York taking care of the four girls of the *New Yorker* writer Michael Arlen,[1] who would later become her colleague at the magazine—a job she kept for three years and that serves as the basis of Lucy's experiences in Kincaid's novel. "That is how I really left my mother," Kincaid explains. "Because I never told her where I was going, and I ended up not seeing her for nineteen years" (Garis). When Kincaid worked for Michael Arlen and his first wife, she was not "the nanny" or the "au pair," but instead, because of her "complexion and class," she was "the girl" (Donahue). Yet even though her situation with the Arlen family was that of a servant, she did not have "the mentality of a servant," she recalls. "When you see those young women from the Caribbean pushing those fair-skinned children around, no one thinks, 'Oh, there goes a future Ph.D.' or 'There goes a future writer' or a future anything important. I didn't know what my future held. But I knew it wouldn't be the life of a servant because that seemed bound to my family and to my past, and I wanted nothing to do with my past" (Mendelsohn).

Rather than supporting her family with the money she earned first as a nanny and, after she left the Arlens, doing filing and secretarial work, Kincaid spent the money on herself, buying clothes and taking courses at night. After winning a full scholarship to Franconia College in New Hampshire and spending over a year there, Kincaid returned to New York and worked as a receptionist in an advertising agency. Around this time she began to write for *Ingenue* and *The Village Voice*, publishing her first piece—an interview with Gloria Steinem—in *Ingenue* in 1973. When Kincaid, finding herself "living in a cold apartment in New York, hungry and penniless," wrote to her mother seeking some encouragement, she was stung by her mother's harsh reply: "'It serves you right, you are always trying to do things you know you can't do'" (*My Brother* 17).

During this period of her life, Kincaid lived selfishly, and although she did not really understand her behavior at the time, she came to see it as an act of self-rescue. Like her character Lucy, she felt that she had to "ruthlessly carve out some space" for herself, and years later she did not regret that, in her twenties, she was a "self-serving, self-absorbed, self-obsessed, ruthless person"—ruthless on her "own behalf" (Wachtel 63). If when she started writing, Kincaid wanted to send a message to her mother—"'Aren't you sorry that no greater effort was made over my education? Or over my life?'" (Bonetti 37)—her mother remained unimpressed with her daughter's success as a writer, something that Kincaid continues to find painful.

A novel full of bitterness and anger, *Lucy*, according to Kincaid, is written in her mother's "voice" (Bonetti 37), a contemptuous voice we often hear in Lucy's scornful thoughts and remarks about her mother and the white world of Lewis and Mariah. Told by her mother that she was named for Lucifer, Lucy employs a classic defense against shame—that of shamelessness—as she turns this maternal insult into a badge of honor. To Annie John, who also identifies with the figure of Lucifer, Lucifer, despite his smile, is a lonely and miserable figure, but to Lucy he is a defiant character. In *Lucy*, as in *Annie John*, Kincaid is both revealing and concealing as she describes what the mother has done to cause Lucy's intense animosity and rage and her open flaunting of her defiant Lucy/Lucifer identity. Even though Lucy/Lucifer represents an oppositional, shameless and "bad" identity—an identity forged in defiance of the repressive societal rules and regulations enforced by the shaming mother—Kincaid's character, despite her physical separation from her mother, still exists, as she comes to see, in the shadow of her powerful, and powerfully injuring, mother. Lucy talks and writes back to her mother, and yet to the extent that she has internalized her mother's angry voice, she, in effect, is her mother. And even as she attempts to free herself from her crippling past and ruthlessly carve out some space for herself, she becomes an artist not only of memory but also of anger and despair.

Lucy as the "Poor Visitor"

If, as Kincaid has remarked, when she came to the United States she wanted to have "nothing to do" with her Antiguan past (Mendelsohn), her memory-haunted character Lucy reveals just how difficult it is to escape the past. The linear, but fragmented, sections of the novel describing the nineteen-year-old Lucy's first year in the United States are so constantly interrupted by Lucy's intrusive memories of her past on a small unnamed island in the Caribbean that she seems to live as much in the past as in the present in an unnamed city, unspecified places that readers knowledgeable about Kincaid's life readily identify as Antigua and New York City.

During the ride from the airport to the New York apartment of Lewis and Mariah, Lucy recalls the daydreams she used to have about the famous landmarks in the city. "[A]ll these places were points of happiness to me; all these places were lifeboats to my small drowning soul, for I would imagine myself entering and leaving them, and just that— entering and leaving over and over again—would see me through a bad feeling I did not have a name for. I only knew it felt a little like sadness but heavier than that" (3–4). Like Annie John, Lucy suffers from not only shame-depression but also shame-rage, and she, too, is conflicted in her feelings about her family. Recalling books she used to read that included descriptions of homesickness, she remembers her impatience with characters who felt that they were in a "not very nice situation" and went to a place "a lot better" only to "long to go back where it was not very nice." Growing up in a "not very nice situation" herself, she "wanted to go somewhere else." Yet having arrived in New York City, she, too, longs to return to her Antiguan home and be with people "whose smallest, most natural gesture" provoked her to such a rage that she wanted to see all of them dead at her feet (6).

Plagued by the same depressive feelings that overwhelmed Annie John—"If I had had to draw a picture of my future then, it would have been a large gray patch surrounded by black, blacker, blackest"—Lucy imagined she could leave home and, with this "one swift act," escape her sad thoughts and feelings (6). Yet as she settles into her New York home, she recognizes the grip the past has on her: "I wondered if ever in my whole life a day would go by when these people I had left behind, my own family, would not appear before me in one way or another" (8). Hearing a song on the radio that seems to sum up her feelings—"'Put yourself in my place, if only for a day; see if you can stand the awful emptiness inside'" (8)—Lucy, like Annie John, is aware of the dreadful void within. And recalling Annie John's split into good/bad identities, Lucy reveals her own psychic split in a dream she has about one of her childhood flannel nightgowns. Although the flannel material shows scenes of (good) children playing with Christmas tree decorations, the nightgown bears the label "Made in Australia," a place, as Lucy recalls upon awakening, that was settled as "a prison for bad people" (9).

From the outset of her stay with Lewis and Mariah, Lucy is aware of her implicit subservient—and thereby shaming—role in the household. Finding herself sleeping in the maid's room, a small room like a box used to ship cargo, Lucy thinks, "But I was not cargo. I was only an unhappy young woman living in a maid's room" (7). To the black maid, Lucy is an object of contempt. Claiming that Lucy speaks and walks like a nun, the maid says that Lucy is "so pious" that it makes her "sick to her stomach and sick with pity" to look at Lucy (11). Recalling Kincaid's remark that when she came to the United States blacks were not kind to her while white people were the "most kind and loving" (Snell), Kincaid depicts the black maid as an openly hostile woman who deliberately shames Lucy while the white family, in contrast, is welcoming. When they invite Lucy to regard them as family and to make herself at home, she believes them to be sincere, knowing that such a remark would not be made to a member of their actual family. "After all, aren't family the people who become the millstone around your life's neck?" (8).

Teasingly called the "poor Visitor" because she seems distant from the American family, as if she is not "part of things" and is "just passing through" (14, 13), Lucy responds by telling Lewis and Mariah about a dream she has had about them. In the dream, Lewis chases a naked Lucy around the house while Mariah urges him to catch her, and eventually Lucy falls down a hole that contains silver and blue snakes. To Lewis and Mariah, the dream has obvious Freudian content, but to Lucy, who does not know who Freud is, the dream simply means that she has "taken . . . in" Lewis and Mariah, since the people who appear in her dreams are those who are "very important" to her (15). Because Kincaid, in effect, exposes the hubris of the American (Western) culture represented in Mariah and Lewis, who assume their interpretive and cultural superiority in explaining and thereby colonizing Lucy's dream, critics have claimed that Kincaid is intent on betraying the "ethnocentrism" of the white family or the "limitations of Western theoretical models" (Ferguson, *Jamaica Kincaid* 110, Donnell, "Dreaming" 48). But purely political readings of this scene do not fully explain what Kincaid is doing.

Unlike Kincaid, who not only has knowledge of but is reported to "love" Freud (Mendelsohn), her character, as Kincaid remarks, does not "understand" her dream but only "reports what happened" in it. "Of course, I understand it, but Lucy doesn't and isn't quite clear about it" (Vorda 100). Thus even as Kincaid uses this scene to urge white Western readers[2] to question their interpretive authority, their desire to take possession of the text and force it to yield up its hidden meanings, she also, in her self-conscious embrace of Freud both in *Lucy* and later in *The Autobiography of My Mother*, openly invites readers to see oedipal content in the dream, an interpretation in part verified by Lucy's remark that her dream means that she has "taken . . . in" the white couple, that is, internalized Lewis and Mariah as important figures, indeed as a kind of substitute family, in her psychic world.

If Kincaid deliberately offers a Freudian dream in depicting Lucy's developing (oedipal) attachment to Lewis and Mariah as a surrogate family, the dream also has cultural and historical resonances, as critics have pointed out, suggesting, as it does, the sexual oppression under slavery of black women by white men with the complicity of white women. And because Lucy, above all else, wishes to become self-possessed, her dream also communicates not only her fear of being pursued—and possibly taken over—by the white family but also her shame vulnerability as it dramatizes a common shame scenario: the fear that one is naked (exposed) accompanied by the feeling that one could "crawl through a hole" or "sink through the floor" in shame.

Because Lucy's relationship with the white family is typically read not so much as a psychological drama but instead as a political drama, critic after critic has insisted on the "mimicry of colonial control" or the "cultural imperialism" represented in the various actions of the family (Paravisni-Gebert 126, Ferguson, *Jamaica Kincaid* 124).[3] Yet from the outset Lucy is attracted, in part, to the white family for their cheerful optimism, which is so unlike Lucy's characteristically disillusioned response to life. The family photographs of Lewis and Mariah and their four daughters—which show "six yellow-haired heads . . . bunched as if they were a bouquet of flowers tied together by an unseen string"—capture their happiness, for they smile "out at the world" as if they find "everything in it unbearably wonderful" (12). Unlike Lucy, who as a girl was forbidden to use bad words, Mariah and Lewis's girls are unruly at the dinner table, but they are accepted by their parents even when they spill their food or refuse to eat it or make up rhymes about it ending in the words "'smelt bad.'" "I wondered what sort of parents I must have had, for even to think of such words in their presence I would have been scolded severely, and I vowed that if I ever had children I would make sure that the first words out of their mouths were bad ones" (13). Unlike Annie John or Lucy, the girls are accepted by their parents despite their assertive and ungirl-like behavior, the same kind of behavior that got Annie John pronounced as "bad." Lewis and Mariah's smiling acceptance of their daughters' "bad" behavior provides an alternative, and to Lucy, a healthier version of family life.

Mariah

Mariah and Sylvie

Ambivalent in her response to Mariah, Lucy is in part drawn to and even idealizes Mariah, who, Mary-like as her name suggests, is the idealized "good" mother. A woman who says she wanted and loves all four of her daughters, Mariah tells Lucy that she loves her. "I believed her, for if anyone could love a young woman who had come from halfway around the world to help her take care of her children, it was Mariah." When Lucy observes Mariah standing in the yellow light of the sun in her pale-yellow kitchen, she perceives her as the prototypically "good" woman: "Mariah, with her pale-yellow skin and yellow hair, stood still in this almost celestial light, and she looked blessed" (27).

Partly under Mariah's spell, Lucy, who appreciates the beauty of the winter snow, finds it hard to bear that the world can seem "soft, lovely, and nourishing," for she does not want "to love one more thing" or want one more thing in her life that can make her heart "break into a million little pieces" (23). Yet after living through her first winter—the first "past" that is her own and over which she has "the final word"— something "heavy and hard" settles inside her (23–24). "So this must be living, this must be the beginning of the time people later refer to as 'years ago, when I was young'"(24), Lucy thinks, repeating to herself the words the Antiguan woman Sylvie once used as she, in her hard voice, spoke of her past.

Thus even as Lucy finds herself succumbing to Mariah's spell, she reactively asserts her own defiant badness in her identification with Sylvie, who got into a fight with another woman over a man and was jailed for public misconduct. "Apparently Sylvie said something that was unforgivable," as Lucy recalls, "and the other woman flew into an even deeper rage and grabbed Sylvie in an embrace, only it was not an embrace of love but an embrace of hatred" (24).[4] Bitten by her attacker, Sylvie bears a disfiguring scar on her right cheek. Calling to mind Annie John's identification with the Red Girl, Lucy comes to see Sylvie, with her marked cheek, as a self-representation: an embodiment of Lucy's enraged "bad" self and her marked—that is, stigmatized or shamed—identity. Commenting that while the effects of stigmatization have long been known there has not been much discussion of the relationship between stigma and shame, Michael Lewis describes the shame of the stigmatized individual, who is publicly marked for her failure to meet social standards. Viewed by others as being "deviant, flawed, limited . . . or generally undesirable," the stigmatized individual suffers from a "spoiled identity" (194, 207). Even though Sylvie is marked by Antiguan society as a socially undesirable and tainted woman—as someone suffering from a spoiled identity—Lucy identifies with Sylvie's anger and bitterness, expressed in her "heavy and hard" voice. "That is how I came to think that heavy and hard was the beginning of living, real living; and though I might not end up with a mark on my cheek, I had no doubt that I would end up with a mark somewhere" (25).

To Lucy, as Kincaid has commented, Sylvie seems "more self-possessed" than Mariah. "Even in her embryonic consciousness-raising, she knows that it's better from a feeling of self-possession to be Sylvie rather than Mariah, spiritually speaking" (Vorda 101). Lucy observes that unlike Sylvie, Mariah has "no blemish or mark of any kind on her cheek or anywhere else, as if she had never quarreled with anyone over a man or over anything, would never have to quarrel at all, had never done anything wrong and had never been to jail." But to Lucy the unmarked, idealized Mariah is lacking. "The smell of Mariah was pleasant. Just that—pleasant. And I thought, But that's the trouble with Mariah—she smells pleasant. By then I already knew that I wanted to have a powerful odor and would not care if it gave offense" (27). By identifying with Sylvie, Lucy expresses her deeply rooted shame-rage and desire for retribution. In her insistence that she wants to be a dissmelling—and by extension—dirty individual, she exposes her feelings of self-contempt. The self-contempt script, which can both reactivate and reproduce the individual's original scenes of shame, as Gershen Kaufman remarks, "rejects the self." A "blend of dissmell and anger," contempt communicates rejection. "The object of contempt, be it self or other, is found offensive, something to be repudiated" (*Psychology* 108). What lies behind Lucy's oppositional defiance and desire to offend others is an abiding and painful sense of self-contempt and woundedness.

"How Does a Person Get to Be That Way?"

"How does a person get to be that way?" Lucy asks repeatedly as she observes Mariah, Lucy's refrain-like question becoming more pointed and scornful over time. Lucy, who is subject to feelings of self-contempt, uses the defending script of contempt in her relationship with Mariah. The source of judgmental or fault-finding or condescending attitudes toward others, contempt elevates the self above others, thus helping insulate the self against shame (Kaufman, *Psychology* 100). Even as Lucy finds herself drawn to Mariah, she repeatedly expresses scorn for Mariah's joyful embrace of life, which becomes symptomatic to Lucy of Mariah's political naïveté and unthinkingly privileged way of life.

Aware that Lucy has never experienced spring, Mariah tries to communicate to Lucy how she feels when she sees the first spring daffodils. Reacting with contempt, Lucy thinks, "So Mariah is made to feel alive by some flowers bending in the breeze. How does a person get to be that way?" (17). Lucy, who was forced as a girl to memorize Wordsworth's poem about daffodils,[5] recalls the enthusiastic applause she received when she recited the poem before an audience of parents, teachers, and her fellow students. At the height of her "two-facedness"—seeming one way on the outside and another on the inside—Lucy appeared appreciative, while vowing to erase every line and word of the poem from her mind (18). Her subsequent dream that she was being chased and then buried by daffodils, never to be seen again, exposed her feeling that she was being somehow smothered—obliterated—not only by her colonial education but also, recalling Annie John, by the young-lady behavior she was obliged to perform in public. In another related episode designed to demonstrate Lucy's nascent political consciousness, she recalls how, when she was around fourteen, she refused to sing "Rule, Britannia!" Taking particular offense at the line "Britons never, never shall be slaves," she told her choir mistress that she was not British and until not that long ago would have been a slave (135).[6]

When Lucy tells Mariah about her Antiguan experience reciting Wordsworth's poem, Lucy's anger surprises both women and also breaks their intimacy. "We were standing quite close to each other, but as soon as I had finished speaking, without a second of deliberation we both stepped back" (19). Later, when Mariah takes Lucy to see the spring daffodils, Lucy, before being aware of what kind of flowers they are, sees them as "simple" and "beautiful," yet, mysteriously, she wants to "kill them," to take a huge scythe and cut them down (29). Mistakenly thinking that Lucy is overjoyed at the sight of the daffodils, Mariah attempts to hug Lucy only to be rebuffed, reminded that when Lucy was ten she had to memorize a poem about some flowers she would not see in real life until she was nineteen. As Lucy casts Mariah's "beloved daffodils in a scene she had never considered, a scene of conquered and conquests; a scene of brutes masquerading as angels and angels portrayed as brutes," Mariah appears not only defeated but also shamed, for she averts her gaze and withdraws inside herself, her eyes sinking "back in her head as if they were protecting themselves." "It wasn't her fault. It wasn't my fault. But nothing could change the fact that where she saw beautiful flowers I saw sorrow and bitterness" (30).

In scenes that are at once political and psychological, Lucy finds fault with the wealthy, privileged Mariah, who is seemingly unaware of the hardships of others. Viewing Mariah as a woman "beyond doubt or confidence" because the right thing has always happened to her, Lucy thinks, "How does a person get to be that way?" (26). During the train trip to Mariah's summer home on the shore of one of the Great Lakes—a place Kincaid later specified as being on Lake Michigan near Chicago (see *My Brother* 152)—Lucy notices that the white diners in the train's dining car all resemble Mariah, and the black waiters resemble Lucy's relatives, although unlike Antiguans, American blacks are deferential and do not give "backchat." Oblivious to this racial—and class—divide, Mariah acts in her usual self-assured way, which conveys the message that "the world was round and we all agreed on that." Lucy, in contrast, feels vulnerable: "I knew that the world was flat and if I went to the edge I would fall off" (32). Lucy's feelings of vulnerability and fear of self-fragmentation are exposed in yet another dream of pursuit she has during the train journey in which she envisions herself being chased by thousands of people on horseback carrying cutlasses, all of them intent on chopping her into small pieces. Aware of the cultural, class, and racial differences between herself and Mariah, Lucy uses what Gershen Kaufman calls the "comparison-making script" in relating to Mariah. Evolving from an "awareness of difference between self and other," the comparison-making script "inevitably translates into an invidious comparison," and thus the individual feels "lesser, deficient" (*Shame* 218). Lucy's awareness of the class and racial divide in American society reactivates her deeply ingrained pattern of invidious comparison-making, a behavior that has its origins in her colonial past.

Lucy responds to her awareness of her difference—and implicit humiliation—with anger and contempt. When Mariah during the train ride tries to share with Lucy her pleasure at the sight of freshly plowed fields, Lucy remarks in a "cruel" tone of voice, "'Well, thank God I didn't have to do that'" (33). And Lucy is offended when Mariah reveals that she has American Indian blood, something Mariah had once looked forward to telling Lucy but comes to feel Lucy might take the wrong way. "Mariah says, 'I have Indian blood in me,' and underneath everything I could swear she says it as if she were announcing her possession of a trophy. How do you get to be the sort of victor who can claim to be the vanquished also?" (40–41).

Unmoved by Mariah's pleading, defeated look—her face is "miserable, tormented, ill-looking"—Lucy, her eyes and face "hard," shames Mariah, telling her, "'All along I have been wondering how you got to be the way you are.'" When Mariah reaches out to hug Lucy, Lucy rebuffs her, stepping out of her path and repeating, "'How do you get to be that way?'" Despite the anguished look on Mariah's face, which almost breaks Lucy's heart, Lucy refuses to yield. "It was hollow, my triumph, I could feel that, but I held on to it just the same" (41). Voicing her contempt for Mariah's character, Lucy pronounces Mariah unworthy. Because in expressing contempt the individual "feels elevated" by looking down on others, deeming them "inferior, beneath one's dignity" (Kaufman, *Psychology* 41), Lucy, in shaming Mariah, has a moment of triumph, a temporary escape from her own abiding feelings of self-contempt.

Mariah as a Mother Figure

In her Lake Michigan summer house—the same house where she spent her summers as a girl—Mariah wants Lucy and her children to share her enjoyment. Mariah's children are happy to "see things her way," but Lucy resists. Comparing Mariah to her mother, Lucy remarks, "I had come to feel that my mother's love for me was designed solely to make me into an echo of her; and I didn't know why, but I felt that I would rather be dead than become just an echo of someone" (36). As Lucy comes to recognize, "The times that I loved Mariah it was because she reminded me of my mother. The times that I did not love Mariah it was because she reminded me of my mother" (58).

Observing Mariah standing at the kitchen sink in the semidark looking at some herbs she has grown, Lucy thinks that to Mariah's five-year-old daughter, Miriam, Mariah might appear as the "beautiful golden mother pouring love over growing things." But to Lucy, who is responding to Mariah's anxiety about being forty years old, Mariah is "a hollow old woman, all the blood drained out of her face, her bony nose bonier than ever, her mouth collapsed as if all the muscles had been removed, as if it would never break out in a smile again" (46). Recalling Annie John's split perceptions of her mother, Lucy views Mariah as both the idealized and defeated maternal object.

On another occasion when Lucy sees Mariah, whom she grows to love, arranging peonies in a crystal vase at the kitchen table, she is so struck by Mariah's beauty that she cannot tear herself away. If Mariah reminds Lucy of the parts of her mother she loves, unlike her mother, Mariah is accepting of Lucy's unlady-like thoughts and behavior. When Lucy tells Mariah that the smell of the peonies makes her want to lie down naked and cover her body with peony petals, Mariah is delighted with Lucy's remark, making Lucy wish she could have had such a forbidden exchange with her mother. And even though Mariah sees Lucy's friend, Peggy, as a bad influence, she comes to accept Lucy's fondness for Peggy. "This was a way in which Mariah was superior to my mother, for my mother would never come to see that perhaps my needs were more important than her wishes" (63–64).

When Mariah becomes involved in the environmental movement, Lucy is aware of the refusal of people like Mariah to see the connection between their comforts and the degradation of the environment. Recognizing that Mariah's "kindness was the result of her comfortable circumstances" but also that many people in Mariah's position were "not as kind and considerate as she was" (72–73), Lucy forgoes demonstrating the contradictions of Mariah's position. "I couldn't bring myself to point out to her that if all the things she wanted to save in the world were saved, she might find herself in reduced circumstances; I couldn't bring myself to ask her to examine Lewis's daily conversations with his stockbroker, to see if they bore any relation to the things she saw passing away forever before her eyes. Ordinarily that was just the sort of thing I enjoyed doing, but I had grown to love Mariah so much" (73).

In her relationship with Mariah, Lucy relives but also, in effect, revises the past, undergoing a kind of corrective emotional experience that allows her to eventually confront her feelings about her mother. In a similar way, Lucy becomes attached to and relives the past through Miriam, one of Mariah's daughters who reminds Lucy of her "good" childhood self, the self loved and cared for by the mother. When Miriam cries in the night, Lucy treats her the way she was treated at the same age by her mother: she comforts her and allows her to sleep in bed with her. The times when Lucy is away from the family, she misses and continually thinks of Miriam. "I couldn't explain it. I loved this little girl" (53).[7]

In protecting Miriam in moments of vulnerability, Lucy revives and revises her own past by acting the role of the "good" mother, and she also engages in a symbolic act of self-mothering and self-rescue, dramatizing in her relationship with Miriam her own abiding need to protect her vulnerable selfhood. In a description that draws on Kincaid's own childhood fear of obeah, Lucy protectively carries Miriam when she takes her through the woods, imagining that there is "someone or something where there [is] nothing." Lucy recalls how in the Caribbean, where there is "no such thing as a 'real' thing," her mother was attacked by a *jablesse*, a demonic creature that appeared as a monkey and threw back the stone that her mother had thrown at it, almost killing her (54).[8] Undergoing yet another corrective experience, Lucy, despite her fear, begins over time to find "something beautiful" about the woods, giving her "one more thing to add" to her "expanding world" (55).

Mariah's Marriage to Lewis

"The whole thing had an air of untruth about it," Lucy remarks when Lewis, performing the role of the loving husband, embraces Mariah. "It was a show—not for anyone else's benefit, but a show for each other. And how did I know this? I just could tell—that it was a show and not something to be trusted" (47). Although Lucy comes to like Lewis, who at times treats her as if she were one of his daughters, her sympathies are with Mariah. "It was my mother who had told me that I should never take a man's side over a woman's; by that she meant I should never have feelings of possession for another woman's husband" (48).

From the outset, Lucy dislikes Mariah's friend, Dinah. When Dinah says to Lucy, "'So you are from the islands?'" Lucy senses contempt in her remark. Made to "feel like a piece of nothing," an enraged Lucy wants, in turn, to humiliate her humiliator by causing Dinah to feel like a disregarded nothing (56). If Dinah sees Lucy as "the girl," Lucy sees Dinah as "a cliché, a something not to be, a something to rise above, a something I was very familiar with: a woman in love with another woman's life, not in a way that inspires imitation but in a way that inspires envy" (58).

Happening upon Lewis and Dinah in a moment of physical intimacy, Lucy realizes that what she has seen is "not a show" but is "something real" (79). Lucy also is aware that Mariah "could imagine the demise of the fowl of the air, fish in the sea, mankind itself, but not that the only man she had ever loved would no longer love her" (81). While the family still appears to be a happy family, Lucy realizes that this is an illusion. Members of the family seem "healthy, robust" and "solid, authentic," but Lucy knows that she is "looking at ruins" (88).

The day Lucy discovers Lewis and Mariah together, Mariah's eyes red from crying, she realizes that the "ruin" is in front of her. "For a reason that will never be known to me, I said, 'Say "cheese"' and took a picture," Lucy recalls (118). Lucy, despite her affection for Mariah, expresses her contempt by taking a photograph of the shamed and defeated Mariah. And Lucy feels contempt for Lewis, a man she had liked and who had been kind to her. Viewing him as "a swine," she sees him as a cultivated but manipulative man, someone accustomed to getting his own way. "He was too clever, that man. . . . He would leave her, but he would make her think that it was she who was leaving him," as Lucy correctly predicts (119).

Replacing the original idealized and self-confident family portraits showing Lewis and Mariah as a happy couple, Lucy's photograph captures the humiliating image of the unhappy and defeated Mariah at the moment of her separation from Lewis. "There's something sad about Mariah and, ultimately, defeated," as Kincaid has remarked of her character. Unlike Sylvie, who is "the victor among the defeated," Mariah is "the victim among the conquerors." Never thinking that the world will "turn on her," Mariah is undone by her trust in human nature, according to Kincaid, something that is "not possible for Lucy, who trusts and mistrusts at once" (Vorda 101).

Lucy's Cold and Angry Heart: Lucy and Her Mother

When Mariah, her voice "filled with alarm and pity," remarks on Lucy's anger—"'You are a very angry person, aren't you?'"—Lucy, rather than denying her feelings, replies, "'Of course I am. What do you expect?'" (96). Lucy identifies, in part, with the despair and yearning of Gauguin[9] who, in Lucy's understanding of his life, left home because he found it an "unbearable prison" and rebelled against "an established order he had found corrupt." A banker who left his comfortable life in France and painted people living halfway across the world only to die an early death, Gauguin "had the perfume of the hero about him." Lucy identifies with Gauguin's heroic artist's life but also recognizes the limitations placed on her by her gender and her cultural background. She is not a man and not a European but, instead, is "a young woman from the fringes of the world" who had the shameful "mantle of a servant" wrapped around her when she left her Caribbean home (95). After living in the United States six months, Lucy knows that she never wants to live in her Caribbean homeland again, and if she were compelled to return there to live, as she remarks, "I would never accept the harsh judgments made against me by people whose only power to do so was that they had known me from the moment I was born" (51).[10]

From the beginning Lucy chafes at her memory of her family, longing, as she says, to see them all dead at her feet. Yet Kincaid not only defers explaining the cause of Lucy's rage, she also never provides a

detailed account of Lucy's troubled relationship with her family, especially her mother. As Lucy recalls the past, aspects of her personal history repeat and elaborate on Annie John's—and Kincaid's—girlhood.
Like Annie John, Lucy grew up in fear of women her father had had
children with, who tried to kill Lucy and her mother, and Lucy's mother,
like Annie's, consulted regularly with an obeah woman to prevent this
from happening (80); like Annie John, Lucy both idealized her mother—
she saw her mother's face as "godlike" (94)—and felt murderous hatred
for her; and like Annie John, she suffered defeat when she attempted to
"assert" her will against her mother (93). Yet while Lucy, like Annie
John, both loved and hated her mother while growing up, most of Lucy's
memories focus on her intense hatred of her mother. If Kincaid, in effect,
invites her readers to supplement the text by reading Annie John's past
into Lucy's history, she also repeats in *Lucy* the omissions and ambivalences of *Annie John*, halfway concealing, as she did in *Annie John*, the
specifically shameful and traumatic aspects of her character's—and her
own—personal history. Instead, readers are made aware of Lucy's
intense rage and shameless defiance, which result from, and also serve
to protect against, her feelings of injury and shame. Despite Kincaid's
frankness in discussing Lucy's, and by extension her own, anger, there
remains a curious emotional reticence about Kincaid's novel, a reluctance on Kincaid's part to describe in specific detail the mother's cruelty
toward her daughter.

"'Be a good girl. Write, write. . . . And remember not to bring
shame on your family,'" the mother suggestively says to the daughter in
"Antigua Crossings" (50), a story that, in describing the daughter's journey to Dominica to visit her grandmother also recalls the situation of
Annie John and Lucy who, in leaving home, carry with them the burden
of maternal shame. The fact that Lucy, who at first keeps her letters
from home inside her brassiere, feels that the letters are "scorching" her
breasts, points to the searing shame she associates with them. Rather
than openly acknowledging her shame, she insists that she carries the letters with her not out of "love and longing" but from "a feeling of
hatred." "There was nothing so strange about this, for isn't it so that
love and hate exist side by side?" (20).

Deciding after a while not to open her mother's letters, Lucy eventually has nineteen unopened letters, one for each year of her life. "I
could not trust myself to go too near them. I knew that if I read only
one, I would die from longing for her" (91). Lucy, who once believed
that she could change if she left Antigua, discovers, instead, a "sameness
in everything" as the present takes "the shape" of her past. "My past
was my mother," Lucy realizes (90). "Oh, it was a laugh, for I had spent

so much time saying I did not want to be like my mother that I missed the whole story: I was not like my mother—I was my mother. And I could see now why, to the few feeble attempts I made to draw a line between us, her reply always was 'You can run away, but you cannot escape the fact that I am your mother, my blood runs in you, I carried you for nine months inside me.' How else was I to take such a statement but as a sentence for life in a prison whose bars were stronger than any iron imaginable?" (90–91).

When Lucy's mother's goddaughter, the hated Maude Quick, unexpectedly visits Lucy in New York to hand deliver a letter from Lucy's mother, Lucy takes one look at Maude and sees that she is still a bully. Recalling *Annie John*'s veiled representation of maternal abuse, Maude can be read as an embodiment of the punishing and oppressive "bad" mother figure. If Lucy's mother viewed Maude as a good example to her adolescent daughter, Lucy, who, as a girl, had been placed under Maude's care, saw the hated Maude as a persecutory maternal figure. "I used to think of her as my own personal jailer," Lucy remarks, describing how Maude had rewarded her by insisting that she sleep in a cramped clothes basket and had threatened to place her in a barrel with the lid shut tight to punish her (111–12). Like the abused and shamed Annie John, who suffers from debilitating shame-depression, Lucy suddenly feels a revival of her girlhood feelings of insignificance and vulnerability when she comes face to face with her old nemesis and oppressor. "She said my name, and I felt as if all the earth's gravity had been gathered and made to center only on me; I was reduced to a tiny speck that weighed a world" (121–22).

Unlike Maude Quick who takes obvious pleasure in delivering the painful news that Lucy's father died a month earlier, Mariah, sensing Lucy's distress, physically comforts her by holding her close. "She must have known that I was about to break apart, and what she was doing was holding me together in one piece" (122). When Maude laughs at the sight of the speechless, paralyzed Lucy and then comments that Lucy resembles her mother, Lucy, who is "dying" of shame, is "saved" by Maude's anger-provoking remark. "She could not have known that in one careless sentence she said the only thing that could keep me alive. I said, 'I am not like my mother. She and I are not alike. She should not have married my father. She should not have had children. She should not have thrown away her intelligence. She should not have paid so little attention to mine. She should have ignored someone like you. I am not like her at all'" (123).

From her mother's letter, Lucy learns that her father's death has left her mother impoverished.[11] In part, Lucy acts the role of the dutiful daughter by sending her mother all the money that she has saved. But she also writes her mother a cold and condemning letter, asking how her mother could have married someone who would leave her in debt and accusing her mother of self-betrayal and of betraying her daughter. Continuing the story of Annie John by recalling a governing scene of shame in which Annie's mother denounced her daughter for behaving like a slut, Lucy first reminds her mother of the measures taken to prevent her from becoming a slut and then declares that she is finding her current life as a slut very enjoyable. Returning maternal contempt with counter-contempt, Lucy angrily defies her mother's rules, using the defense of shamelessness to counteract her deep-rooted sense of shame. A classic response to shame, shamelessness serves to defend against the feelings of powerlessness and vulnerability that accompany shame. But "if it is shame that is fought against by shamelessness," as Léon Wurmser has observed, "it is shame that returns in spectral form" in shameless behavior (*Mask* 262).

"I was not an only child, but it was almost as if I were ashamed of this, because I had never told anyone, not even Mariah," Lucy realizes, as she begins to explain to Mariah why she hates her mother (130). An only child until she was nine and her mother, in the space of five years, had three sons, Lucy ends up feeling betrayed by her mother who envisions her sons, but not her daughter, growing up to be people of importance and influence.[12] "[W]henever I saw her eyes fill up with tears at the thought of how proud she would be at some deed her sons had accomplished, I felt a sword go through my heart, for there was no accompanying scenario in which she saw me, her only identical offspring, in a remotely similar situation. To myself I then began to call her Mrs. Judas, and I began to plan a separation from her that even then I suspected would never be complete" (130–31). The fact that Lucy has avoided telling Mariah that she is not an only child reveals her protective need to prevent exposure of her deep-seated feelings of rejection and unlovability. Lucy's difficulty in telling her story—"I suddenly had to stop speaking; my mouth was empty, my tongue had collapsed into my throat. I thought I would turn to stone just then" (131)—is symptomatic of extreme shame anxiety in which the individual feels herself "freezing into complete paralysis and stupor" (Wurmser, *Mask* 84).

Mariah, in a misguided attempt to rescue Lucy, explains the universality of Lucy's experience of gender shaming and gives her a copy of Simone de Beauvior's *The Second Sex* to read.[13] Not only does Lucy feel that Mariah has misunderstood her situation, but she also experiences the shame that results from being objectified by another person, that is, "having one's status as a subject ignored, disregarded, denied, or negated" (Broucek 8). "I couldn't speak, so I couldn't tell her that my mother was my mother and that society and history and culture and other women in general were something else altogether" (131–32). To Lucy, her life situation as the daughter of a powerful and rejecting woman is "more simple and more complicated" than de Beauvior's analysis of women as the "second sex" under patriarchy. Eschewing the universalizing assumptions and cultural determinism of de Beauvior's feminist theory, Lucy focuses on her own subjective experiences as a daughter. Like Annie John, Lucy has been deeply injured by maternal rejection and the loss of her mother's love. She remarks, "[F]or ten of my twenty years, half of my life, I had been mourning the end of a love affair, perhaps the only true love in my whole life I would ever know" (132).

Lucy's Sexual Defiance and Shamelessness

Embracing her shame and anger, Lucy comes to defiantly flaunt her mother-defined "badness," which she associates with her name, Lucy/Lucifer.[14] Lucy recalls how, years before when she told her mother she wanted to change her name to "Enid," the name of an author she liked as a girl, Enid Blyton,[15] her mother flew into a rage because, as Lucy later learned, "Enid" was the name of a woman who had had a child with Lucy's father and who, consequently, had tried to kill Lucy and her mother through obeah. In her anger, Lucy's mother was "a ball of fury, large, like a god," making Lucy wonder, "for the millionth time, how it came to be that of all the mothers in the world mine was not an ordinary human being but something from an ancient book" (150). Much later, Lucy returned to the question of her name, asking her mother why she had named her "Lucy." "'I named you after Satan himself. Lucy, short for Lucifer,'" her mother replied under her breath. "'What a botheration from the moment you were conceived.'" Defiantly embracing her mother's insulting name for her, Lucy "went from feeling burdened and old and tired to feeling light, new, clean" the moment she learned the meaning of her name and thus "knew" who she was (152). "Lucy, a girl's name for Lucifer. That my mother would have found me devil-like did not surprise me, for I often thought of her as god-like, and are not the children of gods devils?" (153). Associating her "devil-like" badness with power, Lucy insists that her knowledge that she was named for Lucifer marked her transformation "from failure to triumph" (152). Years later in her letter to her mother, Lucy returns her mother's contempt for her with her own daughterly countercontempt as she defiantly and shamelessly flaunts her designated and denigrated "bad" girl identity.

Recalling Annie John's attraction to the Red Girl, Lucy befriends Peggy. When Peggy openly voices her disdain for her family, Lucy envies the anger and contempt in her friend's voice. Peggy, who hates children and has "nothing but hatred and scorn to heap on her own childhood," refers to her parents as "extremely stupid" people because they hate anyone who is not Irish, and she calls her family "a bunch of absolutely nothing" (61, 91). Deciding not to live with her parents anymore, Peggy, who eventually shares an apartment with Lucy, tells Lucy that she is "sick" of her parents, "as if her parents were a style of dressing she had outgrown." Unlike Lucy, who views her own parents as larger than life, Peggy sees her parents as "trivial, trinketlike, mere pests" (146).

An embodiment of Lucy's defiant selfhood, Peggy gives verbal expression to Lucy's contempt for her family. And Peggy, who smokes Lucky Strike cigarettes, uses slang, wears tight jeans and fake-snakeskin boots and always appears in sunglasses, is also a representative "bad" girl who breaks the rules governing proper femininity. In a female appropriation of the objectifying male gaze, Peggy and Lucy look over men on their Sunday afternoon walks in the park, carefully examining their bottoms, legs, shoulders, and faces, in particular, their mouths, deciding the men with whom they might want to have sex. Yet Peggy, despite the bad girl image she projects, always finds fault with the selected men, insisting that their hands are too small and that small hands mean a small penis, and thus Lucy and her friend never actually approach any of the men in the park.

Taught by her mother to be "clean, virginal, [and] beyond reproach" (97), Lucy self-consciously uses her sexuality to defy and thus separate herself from her mother, and yet her experiences also show, as Kincaid has remarked, that a woman's sexuality can be an "incredible source of shame" (Garner). Attracted to Dinah's brother, Hugh, Lucy feels that she is "made up only of good things" when she and Hugh lie naked together in the grass only to be "filled with confusion and dread" when she realizes that she forgot to use protection during intercourse (67). Like Annie John, Lucy recalls her adolescent distress over her sexually maturing body, "a sign that certain parts of my life could no longer be kept secret from my mother, or people in general" (68). Remembering how her mother once instructed her on which herbs to use "to strengthen the womb" to bring on a missed period—her mother's circumlocution for ending a pregnancy—Lucy realizes how difficult it would be to write to her mother and ask for the abortion herbs. "I had always thought I would rather die than let her see me in such a vulnerable position—unmarried and with child," Lucy remarks, revealing how the fear of pregnancy revives her deep-seated feelings of sexual shame (70).

Despite—or perhaps because of—Peggy's warning that Paul is a "pervert," Lucy finds herself attracted to him. When she first meets him and asks, "'How are you?'" in her "small, proper" good girl voice, she feels the opposite of good when he kisses her on the cheek, wanting to be "naked in a bed with him" (97). Yet Lucy's childhood memory when she sees Paul's death-like hands in a fish tank—his hands look "strange," the flesh resembling "bone" (102)—reveals her unacknowledged anxieties about being touched by him. Lucy recalls a girl from her childhood, Myrna, who was the daughter of a cruel mother and who, as if in response to maternal rejection, never attained "a normal size" (102). Yet Lucy was jealous when she discovered that Myrna had been chosen by Mr. Thomas, a fisherman, to secretly meet him in an alley near a latrine so he could treat her like a slut by paying her money for allowing him to put his middle finger up inside her. When Lucy asked Myrna if Mr. Thomas had hurt her, "The look she gave—I was the one who felt like dirt" (108). To Mr. Thomas, Lucy, unlike the sluttish Myrna, appeared to be "a teenage girl so beyond reproach in every way that if you asked her a question she would reply in her mother's forty-year-old voice—hardly a prospect for a secret rendezvous" (107). Even though Lucy claims to be upset that "such an extraordinary thing" happened to Myrna and not to her (105), she nevertheless associates Myrna's secret meetings with the unattractive Mr. Thomas near a latrine with feeling "like dirt," that is, with sexual contamination and shame. And the fact that Lucy connects Paul's hands with Mr. Thomas's hands is suggestive, pointing as it does to the feelings of sexual excitement but also shame that subtend Lucy's conscious embrace of the life of a slut. Despite Lucy's claim that she is "thrilled by the violence" of having sex with Paul (113), her initial focus on his death-like hands suggests that she finds his lover's touch, even as it sexually excites her, dangerous, even potentially lethal.[16]

Inventing a New Identity

After being in the United States for one year, Lucy feels that the person she was a year before has "gone out of existence" and the person she has become is someone she does not "know very well" (133). Aware that she is reinventing herself and doing this "more in the way of a painter than in the way of a scientist," Lucy takes stock of her personal assets. "I could not count on precision or calculation; I could only count on intuition. I did not have anything exactly in mind, but when the picture was complete I would know. I did not have position, I did not have money at my disposal. I had memory, I had anger, I had despair" (134).

To Lucy, who was living "silently in a personal hell" one day and then was "not living like that at all," the past is like a line: "[Y]ou can draw it yourself, or sometimes it gets drawn for you; either way, there it is, your past, a collection of people you used to be and things you used to do. Your past is the person you no longer are, the situations you are no longer in" (136–37). After determining to break off contact with her mother and sending her mother a final letter, Lucy begins the process of leaving Mariah. "I could not wait to put this period of my life behind me, and each moment felt like a ball of lead; at the same time, I wanted to understand everything that was happening to me, and each day felt like a minute." Lucy, like Annie John, suffers episodes of shame-depression as she prepares to embark on her new life: "I noticed how hard and cold and shut up tight the ground was. I noticed this because I used to wish it would just open up and take me in, I felt so bad" (140).

Lucy begins her new life when she moves into an apartment with Peggy. Initially, Lucy sees in Peggy a mirror reflection of her own "restlessness" and "skin-doesn't-fit-ness," but she also recognizes the differences that threaten to separate them and engender feelings of "life-long loathing" between them (145). Suspecting over time that Peggy and Paul are seeing each other, Lucy is relieved, not upset. For when Paul begins to act as if he possesses Lucy, she grows tired of him. "He kissed me now in that possessive way, lingering over my mouth, pressing my whole body into his; and though I was not unmoved, it was not as special as he believed" (156). It is revealing that Lucy, first in her relationship with Hugh and then with Paul, remains emotionally distanced. Although Lucy, in Kincaid's description, "enjoys" sex, she "has just escaped a certain possession from her mother, and she doesn't want to be possessed again" (Vorda 103).

"I was twenty years old—not a long time to be alive—and yet there was not an ounce of innocence on my face," Lucy remarks as she looks at herself in the mirror. "If I did not know everything yet, I would not be afraid to know *everything* as it came up. That life might be cold and hard would not surprise me" (153). Even though Lucy is living the life she always wanted—"I was living apart from my family in a place where no one knew much about me; almost no one knew even my name, and I was free more or less to come and go as pleased me" (158)—she is not happy or fulfilled. "I was alone in the world. It was not a small accomplishment. I thought I would die doing it. I was not happy, but that seemed too much to ask for" (161).

As Lucy attempts to invent—and indeed write—a new identity at the novel's end, she remains a prisoner of her unhappy past. In her final act in the novel, Lucy begins to write in the red leather notebook given to her by Mariah in commemoration of Lucy's remark, when she left Mariah, that her life "stretched out ahead" of her "like a book of blank pages" (163). For Lucy, the act of writing, as the novel's closure makes clear, will be a painful process of recovering the past and confronting her own abiding feelings of vulnerability and shame. "At the top of the page I wrote my full name: Lucy Josephine Potter. At the sight of it, many thoughts rushed through me, but I could write down only this: 'I wish I could love someone so much that I would die from it.' And then as I looked at this sentence a great wave of shame came over me and I wept and wept so much that the tears fell on the page and caused all the words to become one great big blur" (163–64).

Refusing to provide a happy ending to *Lucy*, Kincaid, in her on-going fictional-autobiographical reconstruction of her life, points to the deep shame attached to her beginnings as a writer. "If you're ashamed of something," Kincaid remarks, "it holds you in its sway," and "you must say it, because if you don't, it gives people power over you" (Wachtel 64). Growing up in a household where the tradition of "not speaking" led Kincaid to conduct "enormous conversations" in her head with the person she was not speaking to—conversations she now carries on in her books (Goldfarb 96)—Kincaid writes out of memory, anger, and despair as she talks back to her mother in *Lucy*. "I don't know if many people in my position retain memory, but I do have memory. And anger. I think that people are ashamed of anger," Kincaid comments. "[A]nd I've written a great deal out of despair. That's another thing perhaps one's ashamed of, to be despairing or to be in a state of despair or to be unhappy somehow. . . . I don't have despair every day, but I think I have memory every day, and I certainly have anger if I think about things long enough" (Wachtel 68). Writing out of memory and especially anger in *A Small Place* and "On Seeing England for the First Time," Kincaid, as we shall see in the next chapter, uses to great effect the contemptuous voice that pervades *Lucy*—the contemptuous voice of the mother—as she, in her very personal politics, angrily talks behind the backs of, and writes back to, the authorities.

PART II

A Very Personal Politics

5

"Imagine the Bitterness and the Shame in Me as I Tell You This"

The Political Is Personal in *A Small Place* and "On Seeing England for the First Time"

"*Apparently, I'm a very angry person*. . . . I hope I never lose it," Kincaid remarks. "If I ever find myself not getting angry, . . . I'll go to a psychiatrist to regain my anger" (Mendelsohn). In writings that openly engage political issues, Kincaid famously vents her anger not only at the British colonialism of the Antigua she grew up in and the social and political corruption of postindependence, self-ruling Antigua in *A Small Place* but also at the England she visited for the first time in 1985 in "On Seeing England for the First Time." Claiming that had she immigrated to England and not the United States she might not have become a writer or even "one-half of the person" she became, in part, because she would not have been able to express her anger in England, and finding herself unable to live in Antigua, Kincaid comes to regard America as "a wonderful place to be in exile" (Birbalsingh 139, Ferguson, "Interview" 186). The United States is "a place that has allowed me to denounce it," she remarks. "To America's credit, I've become— at least verbally—a politically conscious person" (Vorda 105). Yet while Kincaid openly expresses her political anger in *A Small Place*, her 1988 book is also autobiographical.[1] "[M]y growing up is very much in *A Small Place*. Practically everything I've written is autobiographical, and if it isn't I make it so" (Muirhead 45). In a similar way, she acknowledges that whenever she travels to England she confronts her "past" (Vorda 101), something that becomes evident in her 1991 essay on England.

If as Kincaid becomes more politically aware, she comes to voice the commonplace critical view that her descriptions of the "mother" are also about the "Mother Country" (see, e.g., Ferguson, "Interview" 176–77), her work nevertheless stays focused on the familial, and her politics remains highly personal. In 1991, Kincaid remarked that she felt herself "intellectually going towards" viewing the mother-daughter relation as a "prototype" for the relation of the powerful and powerless and claimed that she wanted "to look at power without the dressing of" her relationship with her mother (Birbalsingh 144). And yet, as we shall see, Kincaid remains a mother-haunted woman in works such as *The Auto-biography of My Mother* and *My Brother*, both written in the 1990s and both continuing to express her intense anger toward her mother, Annie Drew. Thus even as Kincaid attempts to gain a kind of rational insight into and mastery over her feelings about her mother, her anger toward her mother persists as a potent and driving force in her writings. Ridiculing the contemporary critical fascination with identity politics, Kincaid says that she finds the word "identity" to be "repellent" because it is "so limiting." "There are so many things that make up a person and one of them is not 'an identity.' It sounds like something on your passport" (Cryer). Even as Kincaid moves toward a political interpretation of her Antiguan past, she continues to emphasize the importance of the autobiographical and personal in her writing. "I personalize everything," she states. "I reduce everything to a domestic connection" (Perry, "Interview" 504).

Despite the common politicized readings of Kincaid that focus on the cultural determinants of her writings and view the mother-daughter relation as metaphoric of the colonizer/colonized relationship, Kincaid's writings, including her openly political works, remain highly personal. That meaning is "both cultural and personal at the same time," as Nancy Chodorow argues (*Power* 4), is evident in Kincaid's political writings. "[P]articular cultural symbols appeal to particular individuals," Chodorow observes, "because they can personally infuse these symbols with their own psychobiographically particularized unconscious fantasies and emotions" (*Power* 195). If Kincaid's obsession with the cultural story of the victor and the vanquished grows out of her own personal-familial history as well as her upbringing in British Antigua, the voice she adopts as she denounces the British and American tourists in Antigua and the English people she sees in England is a familiar one—the contemptuous voice of the mother. And the feelings that overcome Kincaid when she returns to Antigua—feelings of loss, betrayal, resentment, profound shame, and anger—repeat the constellation of feelings she attaches to the mother-daughter relationship in her work. In a similar way, Kincaid's love/hate relationships with England and Antigua recall her repeated representations of the daughter's love/hate relationship with the mother in her work. "Every time I go to England I almost have a nervous breakdown. I have such conflicting feelings of England. I love it, and I hate it," Kincaid remarks (Vorda 101). And while Kincaid says of Antigua that she had to "face the little" she came from when she began to write and claim it as her own—"I would be nothing if I hated it"—her writing in fact expresses her intense love/hate relationship with Antigua, which she characterizes as "a narrow place with narrow people" (Birbalsingh 140, Goldfarb 96). That "[s]pecific cultural patterns are always given an individual cast" (Chodorow, *Power* 225) becomes evident in Kincaid's political writings, writings that resonate with and are given narrative force by Kincaid's ambivalence and her deep—and deeply personal—anger.

A Small Place

A Small Place, Kincaid recalls, was written for the readers of *The New Yorker*, whom she "had come to think of as friends in some peculiar way," and William Shawn, the editor, loved it and bought it. But then Shawn was replaced with a new editor, Bob Gottlieb, who said that *A Small Place* "was very angry. Not badly written. Angry." When Gottlieb refused to publish it, Kincaid, encouraged by Shawn, ended up publishing it as a book (Perry, "Interview" 497–98). Writing *A Small Place*, in Kincaid's account, helped her clarify her politics. "I didn't know that I thought those things. I didn't go around saying them to myself. But then, somehow, once I had the opportunity to think them, I just did. . . . I wrote with a kind of recklessness in that book. I didn't know what I would say ahead of time. Once I wrote it I felt very radicalized by it." When reviewers repeatedly remarked on the book's anger, Kincaid came to "love anger" even more, insisting that "the first step to claiming yourself is anger. You get mad. And you can't do anything before you get angry. And I recommend getting very angry to everyone, anyone." In writing *A Small Place*, she realized that she "had all this feeling and that it was anger" and she wanted the book to be "crude and impolite—and all the other things that civilized people are not supposed to be" (Perry, "Interview" 498). Despite the openly political content of *A Small Place*, writing it for Kincaid was like "going to a psychiatrist"—it was "getting something" out of her head that if she had not would have driven her "absolutely insane" (Perry, "Interview" 498, Ferguson, "Interview" 174).

Written for *New Yorker* readers—"white people in the suburbs,"
as Kincaid once described them (Cudjoe 221)—*A Small Place* was
attacked in a "vicious" way by a black American man, and nonblacks
were "the most sympathetic." In Antigua, people who read the book
said to Kincaid's mother, Annie Drew, "'It's true, but did she have to say
it?'" To Kincaid, the Antiguan response was "very revealing" of their
mentality: "They think you shouldn't mention the unpleasant truth, and
maybe it will go away" (Dilger 24). Kincaid not only was unofficially
banned for five years from Antigua "[i]n retaliation" for *A Small Place*
(Hayden)—from 1988 to 1993—but she even voiced concern at one
point that she could get killed if she returned to Antigua. "God knows
if they would shoot me, but it's a criminal place. I wouldn't be surprised
if they had henchmen who would do it, because politics in the West
Indies is very tribal" (Vorda 98–99). But while the Antiguan government
"was a little afraid" that the book would cost them politically, so "they
sort of banned it," they were nevertheless "reelected by an overwhelming majority," Kincaid recalls (Perry, "Interview" 499). And Kincaid
ended up being treated with deference by her fellow Antiguans, who
were "very respectful" of her as "Jamaica Kincaid," whereas they might
have felt free to slight or confront her as "Elaine Potter Richardson,"
something she did not give them the opportunity to do. "You know, I
silenced them," she tellingly remarks (Muirhead 45).

If in silencing them, Kincaid—that is, "Jamaica Kincaid," the
highly respected author—assumes a position of power over Antiguans,
she nevertheless identifies with the powerless native, not the powerful
tourist, even though she "occupies both worlds" and is "often in the
position of" the tourist and has the tourist's "economic clout." But her
consciousness, she insists, is that of the "powerless group," the native.
While she is a "resident of a very powerful and rich country" and is "not
at the bottom of its social class," her consciousness remains "formed by
the situation of the natives" (Muirhead 40). Moreover, because she is
"drawn" to individuals who dissent, she "could never have the consciousness of a tourist" (Muirhead 44). It is from this position that Kincaid attacks not only the powerful white European and American
tourists but also the powerful—and to Kincaid powerfully corrupt—
black ruling elite in Antigua. Yet while Kincaid identifies herself with the
powerless native, she clearly speaks from a position of authorial power,
and she writes for the white *New Yorker* reader—a reader that presumably shares her disdain for the ugly white tourist who, in traveling to
Antigua, is bent not on gaining cultural enrichment or a deepened
knowledge of the Antiguan people but on feeling culturally superior and
having what Kincaid calls "a rubbish-like experience" (Vorda 96).[2]

As Kincaid attacks the white tourist's feelings of cultural superiority, she borrows from and makes effective use of the shaming discourse of white racism as she returns the open contempt of the white tourist with the hidden countercontempt of the black Antiguan. Combining the affect of anger with dissmell, contempt, as shame theorists have observed, underlies various expressions of prejudice, including white prejudice against blacks. "By combining anger with dissmell, contempt functions as a signal and motive to others . . . of either negative evaluation or feelings of rejection," explains shame theorist Gershen Kaufman. "The face pulls away in dissmell from the offending, 'bad-smelling' other" (*Psychology* 40). The contemptuous individual feels elevated and looks down on others, who are "found lacking or seen as lesser or inferior beings" (*Psychology* 100). Moreover, "it is the affect of contempt which partitions the inferior from the superior in any culture or nation. As such, contempt is the principal dynamic fueling prejudice and discrimination" (Kaufman, *Shame* 241). If in the "actions and reactions" between various groups—such as white Europeans and black Antiguans—each group "enacts its own scripted part" (*Shame* 241), in *A Small Place* Kincaid deliberately sets out to challenge the white tourist's feelings of superiority and to rescript the traditional roles of white superiority and black inferiority. Kincaid, in viewing the white tourist as an object of contempt, acts out not only a contempt script but also rage and power scripts—all defending scripts against shame. For just as rage protects against the feelings of vulnerability and exposure that accompany shame, so gaining power over others defends against feelings of helplessness. "When power scripts combine with rage and/or contempt scripts, the seeking of revenge is a likely outcome," Kaufman explains. A recasting defense, the aim is to "reverse roles with the perceived humiliator" so that "the humiliated one, at long last, will humiliate the other" (*Psychology* 101).

Adopting a misleadingly intimate tone in the first section of *A Small Place* as she mocks the glossy tourist-brochure descriptions of Antigua, Kincaid's speaker addresses the would-be European or American tourist as "you," which serves to make her eventual humiliation of the perceived white humiliator all the more personal. Upon first emerging into the "hot, clean air" of Antigua, the white tourist, who is "implicitly coded as male" (Poon, para. 22), feels "cleansed," "blessed (which is to say special)," and "free" (5). Thoughtlessly pleased at the hot, dry Antiguan climate, the tourist is concerned about having a rain-free holiday and not about the suffering of Antiguans, who live in perpetual drought even though they are surrounded by the sea. During the cab ride[3] to the hotel, the tourist is equally oblivious to the Antiguan school he passes, which looks like "some latrines"; the hospital, which is staffed with incompetent doctors that locals refer to, not as doctors, but as "the three men"; and the library, which was damaged in the 1974 earthquake and which, years later, still bears the sign "REPAIRS ARE PENDING" (7–9).

If, in describing the poor public services in Antigua, Kincaid is leveling an attack against the corrupt current government—an issue she will return to and develop at length later—she also uses this as an occasion to attack the white tourist for his willful ignorance of the past. According to the official Western version of economic history to which the white tourist subscribes, Europeans and Americans became rich not because they historically exploited people such as the Antiguans for their "free"—or "got-for-nothing"—and then "undervalued" labor, but because of Western ingenuity and inventiveness. Expressing outrage, Kincaid's speaker dialogically contests this official Western account of economic progress. "[I]sn't that the last straw; for not only did we have to suffer the unspeakableness of slavery, but the satisfaction to be had from 'We made you bastards rich' is taken away, too." Calling attention to the moral obtuseness of the white male tourist, she uses his self-justifying rhetoric to condemn him. "[Y]ou needn't let that slightly funny feeling you have from time to time about exploitation, oppression, domination develop into full-fledged unease, discomfort; you could ruin your holiday. They are not responsible for what you have; you owe them nothing; in fact, you did them a big favour, and you can provide one hundred examples" (10). Ironically enough, to the white tourist, the favors he has bestowed include the Antiguan Government House, the Prime Minister's Office, the Parliament Building, and the American Embassy—places that later are shown to be seats of governmental corruption, a corruption black Antiguan leaders have learned from years of British rule.

Aware of the holiday fantasies of the white tourist—that he sees himself walking on the beach, or meeting new people, or wading in the sea—the speaker sets out to undermine his idyllic tourist-brochure vision of the perfect Caribbean vacation. When the tourist looks out and sees a beautiful boy windsurfing in the sea, he also sees a couple walking on the beach, but unlike the boy they are not lithe and beautiful but are "incredibly unattractive, fat, [and] pastrylike-fleshed" (13). The beautiful water the tourist sees himself wading in is, in fact, contaminated with sewage so that the contents of his lavatory just might wash against his ankles when he wades in the sea, the same sea that once "swallowed up" countless black slaves as if they, too, were nothing more than human waste (14). In his vacation escape to Antigua, the white tourist has thoughtlessly returned to the scene of a great crime committed by his ancestors against the African Caribbean people of Antigua. Yet as he visits "heaps of death and ruin," he feels "alive and inspired at the sight of it" (16).

In a classic turning-the-tables shame drama and attack-other script, Kincaid's speaker views the white tourist, who initially feels "blessed" and "special" upon arriving in Antigua, as an object of contempt. In the shame-reversing attack-other script, as shame theorist Donald Nathanson explains, anger is used to repair, at least temporarily, shame. "Have we been made to feel small? The other will be made to feel even smaller. Have we been made the butt of a joke, laughed at by others? Then the rebuttal will reduce our tormentor even further" (*Shame* 362–63). Manifested in the "put-down, ridicule, contempt, and intentional public humiliation," the attack-other script seeks a remedy to social inferiority with its "Someone must be made lower than I" defense (*Shame* 313). In *A Small Place* one of Kincaid's goals is to undermine the complacent superiority of the white tourist through her shame-reversing attack. Indeed, at the emotional core of *A Small Place*'s attack on the white tourist are the same emotions historically directed at blacks by white racists: what affect theorists refer to as the "hostility triad" of disgust, contempt, and anger (see Rozin 589).[4]

Just as black Antiguans were long viewed as objects of contempt by the British colonizers, leading to feelings of learned cultural shame among Antiguans, so contemporary Antiguans see white tourists as contemptible. Aware that shame is derived from the shame sufferer's "vicarious experience of the other's scorn" (Helen Lewis, "Introduction" 15), Kincaid's speaker works to provoke, if not coerce, the white tourist to see himself through the contemptuous gaze of the Antiguan native. Through her shame-reversing attack-other script, she attempts to induce shame-anxiety—which is "evoked by the imminent danger of unexpected exposure, humiliation, and rejection" (Wurmser, *Mask* 49)—in the white tourist. If at home the tourist is "a nice person, an attractive person, a person capable of drawing . . . the affection of other people" (15), in Antigua he is an object of contempt. "An ugly thing, that is what you are when you become a tourist, an ugly, empty thing, a stupid thing, a piece of rubbish pausing here and there to gaze at this and taste that." Actively undercutting the pride of the white male tourist and his feeling of cultural superiority, the speaker asserts that Antiguans not only secretly mock and ridicule him but also view him with contempt-disgust. If the British once mocked Antiguans for their appearance, behavior, and speech, so contemporary Antiguans mock their white visitors:

> [I]t will never occur to you that the people who inhabit the place
> in which you have just paused cannot stand you, that behind their
> closed doors they laugh at your strangeness (you do not look the
> way they look); the physical sight of you does not please them; you
> have bad manners (it is their custom to eat their food with their
> hands; you try eating their way, you look silly; you try eating the
> way you always eat, you look silly); they do not like the way you
> speak (you have an accent); they collapse helpless from laughter,
> mimicking the way they imagine you must look as you carry out
> some everyday bodily function. They do not like you. (17)

Through her shame-reversing attack-other script, Kincaid attempts
to promote feelings of learned cultural shame in the white tourist who
spends his days and nights in Antigua with people who despise him and
people that he, in turn, would not want as his neighbors. Yet the
Antiguans, Kincaid insists, also envy the white tourist because he has
economic resources unavailable to them. Both tourist and native are
bound in the same lives of "overwhelming and crushing banality and
boredom and desperation and depression," Kincaid's speaker insists
(18). But unlike the tourist, the natives are "too poor to go anywhere"
or even "to live properly in the place where they live, which is the very
place you, the tourist, want to go—so when the natives see you, the
tourist, they envy you, they envy your ability to leave your own banality and boredom, they envy your ability to turn their own banality and
boredom into a source of pleasure for yourself " (19).

Continuing her attack-other script in the second section of the
essay, Kincaid's speaker targets the racist English colonizers of her
remembered past as she describes to the tourist the Antigua she grew up
in, an Antigua that does not exist any longer, in part because "the bad-
minded people who used to rule over it, the English, no longer do so."
No longer the culturally superior empire builders with "one quarter of
the earth's human population bowing and scraping before them," the
English, she insists, "have become such a pitiful lot these days, with
hardly any idea what to do with themselves" (23). Kincaid's speaker
points to the shame-pride dynamics of colonialism as she describes the
historical encounter between the English colonizers and the people they
colonized. Attempting to turn the places they colonized into England
and the native populations they encountered into English people, they
caused profound harm to people such as the Antiguans. "[N]o place
could ever really be England, and nobody who did not look exactly like
them would ever be English, so you can imagine the destruction of people and land that came from that. The English hate each other and they

hate England, and the reason they are so miserable now is that they have no place else to go and nobody else to feel better than" (24).

What the speaker was taught to respect, if not revere, in the past, she now denigrates as she describes, for example, how the street names in the St. John's where she was raised—Nelson, Rodney, Hood, Hawkins, and Drake—commemorated English "maritime criminals"; or how the English princess who visited the island when the speaker was a girl—Princess Margaret—was "putty-faced"; or how the founders of Barclays bank, the Barclay brothers, were slave traders, who turned to banking only after slavery was abolished (24, 25, 25–26). Especially galling to the speaker is the fact that people a bit older than she is "can recite the name of and the day the first black person was hired as a cashier at this very same Barclays Bank in Antigua." Speaking directly to her white tourist addressee, she expresses her deep sense of outrage at this example of English racist practices. "Do you ever wonder why some people blow things up? I can imagine that if my life had taken a certain turn, there would be the Barclays Bank, and there I would be, both of us in ashes. Do you ever try to understand why people like me cannot get over the past, cannot forgive and cannot forget?" (26).

Invoking and then reversing the discourse of white racism, with its polarizing binarisms of white/black, civilized/uncivilized, human/animal, and pure/polluted, Kincaid's speaker sets out to humiliate the humiliator in yet another turning-the-tables shame drama. Recalling the whites-only policy of the Mill Reef Club of the past,[5] she remarks that Antiguans viewed the white members as bad-mannered people "behaving in a bad way, like pigs" (27). For they lived as "strangers" in the "home" of the Antiguans and then refused to associate with, or "have anything human, anything intimate," to do with their Antiguan hosts, making them like "pigs living in that sty (the Mill Reef Club)" (27–28). As the speaker recalls how the Czechoslovakian "doctor" and the Irish headmistress treated blacks in the Antigua she grew up in, she comes to a new, political understanding of their bad-mannered behavior. An escapee from Hitler, the Czechoslovakian "doctor"—a dentist who claimed he was a doctor specializing in childhood illnesses—treated the black Antiguan children brought under his care as if they were potentially dissmelling, dirty objects:[6] that is, as objects of contempt. And the Irish headmistress of a girls' school openly insulted the black girls in her charge by repeatedly telling them "to stop behaving as if they were monkeys just out of trees" (29). Frantz Fanon, in his well-known account of the black feeling of inferiority that comes through the experience of being "dissected under white eyes," describes the shaming experience of being seen as an object of contempt—as a "Dirty nigger!"—in the eyes of whites (116, 109). Viewed through the shaming gaze of whites, "Negroes are savages, brutes, illiterates," writes Fanon as he, in recounting the racist myths that historically undergirded the cultural construction of black inferiority, reports on the process of the "internalization—or, better, the epidermalization"—of a sense of inferiority (117, 11).

Returning white contempt with black countercontempt and dissecting whites under black eyes, Kincaid's speaker inferiorizes the white colonizers. "We thought these people were so ill-mannered and we were so surprised by this, for they were far away from their home, and we believed that the farther away you were from your home the better you should behave. . . . We thought they were un-Christian-like; we thought they were small-minded; we thought they were like animals, a bit below human standards as we understood those standards to be. We felt superior to all these people" (29). Yet even as the speaker insists that the black Antiguans felt superior to the badly behaved and "ugly, piggish" whites, she also admits to her deep-seated sense of humiliation and rage and loss as she ponders the crime committed against her people, "millions of people . . . made orphans: no motherland, no fatherland, no gods . . . and worst and most painful of all, no tongue" (31). As she speaks of the crime committed against blacks, the only language available to her is "the language of the criminal who committed the crime," a language that is used to justify "the criminal's deed" and that is unable to "contain the horror of the deed, the injustice of the deed, the agony, the humiliation inflicted" on her (31–32). Consequently, she is unable to communicate with the English criminal, who understands the word "wrong" to mean that he did not "get his fair share of profits from the crime just committed" and who asks, "'But why?'" when she expresses her outrage. "[N]othing," she asserts, "can erase my rage—not an apology, not a large sum of money, not the death of the criminal—for this wrong can never be made right. . . . And so look at this prolonged visit to the bile duct that I am making, look at how bitter, how dyspeptic just to sit and think about these things makes me" (32).

If, during the speaker's youth, the Antiguan people lacked a political perspective on the ill-mannered and bad-minded whites in their midst—the English, the Irish headmistress, the Czechoslovakian "doctor," and the members of the Mill Reef Club—all of them, the narrator now sees, were, in fact, racists. Raised in an Antigua that "revolved almost completely around England" so that she "met the world through England" (33), she comes to discern the shaping influence of the English in the corruption of the contemporary, postcolonial Antiguan society and government. "Have you ever wondered to yourself why it is that all people like me seem to have learned from you is how to imprison and murder each other, how to govern badly, and how to take the wealth of our country and place it in Swiss bank accounts? Have you ever wondered why it is that all we seem to have learned from you is how to corrupt our societies and how to be tyrants? You will have to accept that this is mostly your fault" (34–35). Talking back to the racist whites from her youth, in particular the Irish headmistress, Kincaid's speaker asserts, "Even if I really came from people who were living like monkeys in trees, it was better to be that than what happened to me, what I became after I met you" (37).

In blaming the English for Antiguan corruption, *A Small Place* enacts a shaming script. Yet even as Kincaid's speaker actively shames the English by pronouncing them blameworthy, she realizes that they continue to feel superior to contemporary postcolonial Antiguans. Watching Antiguans do to themselves "the very things" the English once did to them, the English feel vindicated in their belief that blacks "cannot run things" or "understand the notion of rule by law" (36). If one of Kincaid's goals in *A Small Place* is to pronounce the English culpable, she also, in the next section, enacts yet another blaming and shaming script as she accuses the self-ruling black government in contemporary Antigua of betraying the Antiguan people through their mimicry of corrupt English practices.

"Imagine . . . the bitterness and the shame in me as I tell you this," laments the speaker at the beginning of the next section as she asks whether self-ruled Antigua is "a worse place than what it was when it was dominated by the bad-minded English" (41). Even as Kincaid blames the English, she also holds Antiguan authorities accountable, finding them, as she has stated, "worse in some ways, because although it hurts to be betrayed by a stranger, when you are betrayed by someone close to you, it's more painful" (Birbalsingh 141). In her view, "Antiguans are locked in shame over a situation in which their own people, who look like them, are now more cruel to them and have less pity on them than the former colonial government" (Nurse). For Kincaid, when black people behave just as the colonial powers did, it is like having people in your "own family doing these terrible things to you" (Vorda 85). Because for Kincaid the political is also very personal, it is not surprising that her various comments about her feelings about contemporary Antigua and the Antiguan government recall the daughter's feelings about the mother in her fiction. Not only does she remark, for example, on how painful and shameful it is to be betrayed by someone close or by people who are like family, she also describes the ruling elite in Antigua as "mean" (Dilger 25) and expresses her very personal feelings of bitterness and shame as she witnesses what has happened to her

102 ❦ *Jamaica Kincaid*

homeland under a self-ruling government. People in Antigua "don't think," as she has commented, and they lack a sense of the "public good," and so "public institutions that are the foundations of a good society do not exist there. Education and health do not exist there. And it used to, actually. I mean, say what you can about the British. The hospital was quite OK, and the schools were good. Look at me. I had a really good education from there" (Ferguson, "Interview" 174). Indeed, as a result of her education, as Kincaid states, she knows "a lot of things about language" that she can "use against" the English who educated her "very well" (Ferguson, "Interview" 175).

Perhaps in a sidelong glance at, and an expression of affinity for, the *New Yorker* readers for whom she originally wrote *A Small Place*, Kincaid focuses attention on a place she particularly loved as a girl growing up in Antigua—the public library—in her exposé of the deterioration of Antiguan public institutions under self-rule. In her account, Kincaid not only refers to her own girlhood passion for books but also to the fact that she stole books from the Antiguan public library when she was growing up.[7] Even as Kincaid's speaker mocks the colonial content of the English-authored books that were housed in the library of her youth—books that instilled in young Antiguans like her a fairy-tale-like belief in the greatness and beauty of the English and their right to dominate black Antiguans—she expresses nostalgia for the old public library. With its open windows and rows and rows of book-filled shelves and its reading tables, the public library was a place of quiet refuge and escape, where she would "sit and look at books and think about the misery" of being herself (45). Unable to part with a book once she had read it, she stole books from the library, sneaking them past the head librarian, an "imperious and stuck-up" woman who was "proud" of the work she did, but who now "looks the opposite of her old self" as she "stands over the shame of what is now the library" (44–45).

Kincaid's speaker, who is "undone" at the sight of "the dung heap that now passes for a library in Antigua" (42, 43), is also upset at the current state of postcolonial education in Antigua. If earlier the speaker described the English language as the "language of the criminal" who committed crimes against her people, here she objects to the near illiteracy of the current generation of young people in Antigua where young news media personalities "speak English as if it were their sixth language" (31, 43). Recalling a teenage pageant she attended in which young men and women recited poems they had written about slavery, she comments: "What surprised me most about them was not how familiar they were with the rubbish of North America—compared to the young people of my generation, who were familiar with the rubbish of

England—but, unlike my generation, how stupid they seemed, how unable they were to answer in a straightforward way, and in their native tongue of English, simple questions about themselves. In my generation, they would not have been allowed on the school stage, much less before an audience in a stadium" (44). To Kincaid's speaker, the fact that Antigua's Minister of Education also serves as the Minister of Culture and the Minister of Sport is exemplary of the cultural decline in Antigua where "cricket is sport and cricket is culture." When a country has a Minister of Culture, this means either that the people "have no culture or are afraid they may have no culture. . . . And what is culture, anyway? In some places, it's the way they play drums; in other places, it's the way you behave out in public; and in still other places, it's just the way a person cooks food. And so what is there to preserve about these things?" (49).

Not unlike the white woman who wants to restore the old library—a woman who enrages the speaker when she assumes a position of cultural superiority and takes obvious pleasure "in pointing out . . . the gutter into which a self-governing—black—Antigua had placed itself" (47)—Kincaid's speaker similarly seems to halfway enjoy her public disclosure of the deterioration of Antiguan culture, and she, too, assumes a position of cultural superiority over contemporary Antiguans. Living in "a small place," people in Antigua "cannot see themselves in a larger picture" or "give an exact account, a complete account of events (small though they may be)" (52, 53). In making the small place–small mind equation and describing Antiguans as politically naïve, indeed, as children, the speaker actively shames the people of Antigua even as she sets herself up as the informed—and culturally and intellectually superior—insider/outsider. If Kincaid, in describing the political situation in contemporary Antigua, has remarked on how painful it is to be "betrayed by someone close"—that is, by her fellow black Antiguans—she, in turn, has been condemned for her "perceived betrayal of her 'cultural home'" in *A Small Place* (Birbalsingh 141, Donnell, "She Ties Her Tongue" 110). There may, indeed, be something very personal behind Kincaid's ridicule of the Antiguan people: a wish to humiliate the humiliator and thus settle old scores. For as we have already observed, Kincaid not only was the target of maternal—and also public—ridicule when she was growing up, but when she began to write she hid her identity under the name *Jamaica Kincaid* because she was afraid that she would be laughed at for attempting to write. Insisting that she could not have become a writer had she stayed in Antigua, she states, "[F]or me as a writer I think the mental, the verbal, the spiritual scorn from my community would have been more painful, in a way, than being stoned to death. There is something so deeply cruel about the place I am from" (Goldfarb 96).

Just as Kincaid, in earlier sections of *A Small Place*, humiliates the white humiliators—both contemporary European and American tourists and the English colonizers of her youth—here she humiliates the black humiliators. Yet at the same time she aims to enlighten contemporary Antiguans, urging them to see their complicity in their own degradation. Behind Kincaid's political anger at the Antiguan embrace of the tourist industry there is something highly personal, for when Kincaid was sent to America at the age of sixteen to become an au pair, she felt that her parents viewed her as nothing more than a servant, an identity she found humiliating. Thus she is outraged that in postcolonial, self-ruling Antigua, the celebrated Hotel Training School "teaches Antiguans how to be good servants, how to be a good nobody, which is what a servant is" (55). Elaborating on her small place–small mind equation and on the Antiguan inability to see the larger picture, she insists that Antiguans cannot see that there is a connection between their obsession with slavery and emancipation and not only their acceptance of the servant role but also their election of corrupt men to govern them, men who have "given their country away to corrupt foreigners" (55). Unaware of the inner forces that act on them in their daily lives, Antiguans turn the event into the everyday and the everyday into an event. "And might not knowing why they are the way they are and why they do the things they do put in their proper place everyday and event, so that exceptional amounts of energy aren't expended on the trivial, while the substantial and the important are assembled (artfully) into a picture story ('He did this and then he did that')?" As the speaker reflects on her fellow Antiguans, she is unable to determine whether they are "children, eternal innocents, or artists who have not yet found eminence in a world too stupid to understand, or lunatics who have made their own lunatic asylum, or an exquisite combination of all three" (57).

In what she calls the "strange voice" of Antiguans—a voice suggesting at once "innocence, art, [and] lunacy" (68)—Kincaid makes public the kinds of governmental scandals that the people talk about among themselves. As Kincaid's speaker assumes the role of the insider-informant and talebearer, the reader becomes a kind of eavesdropper on island gossip about governmental corruption. Providing example after example—and page after page—of alleged and reported governmental misdeeds and crimes, Kincaid carries out a war of words with the officials who have betrayed the public trust of their fellow Antiguans. In Antigua, as islanders discuss among themselves, it is an open secret that government-owned vehicles are Japanese-made because Antiguan officials hold shares in the Japanese-car dealership owned by a Syrian national; that some government ministers are hidden owners of businesses that not only sell mainly to the government but are granted sole importing rights by the government; that associates of the Prime Minister run a house of prostitution; that a government minister uses off-shore banks to deposit the money he gets from drug trafficking; that government officials accept bribes to allow United States mobsters to control hotel gambling casinos; that eleven million dollars in aid money given to the Antiguan government by France has disappeared; that the government-owned airwaves are used to stifle political opposition; and that an official who was investigating the government for financial wrongdoing died under suspicious circumstances.

Audacious and unabashed in her account as she exposes shameful secrets about the government, Kincaid's speaker also expresses dismay at her fellow Antiguans as they gossip about official corruption, "pausing to take breath before this monument to rottenness, that monument to rottenness, as if they were tour guides; as if, having observed the event of tourism, they have absorbed it so completely that they have made the degradation and humiliation of their daily lives into their own tourist attraction" (68–69). If, in speaking about the "degradation and humiliation" of Antiguans, Kincaid attempts to prod the people of Antigua into a political awareness and shame them into acting to change things, she also risks being accused not only of betraying but also of humiliating them. Interestingly just as Kincaid's mother, who is "notorious for her political opinions" and making "a great hubbub," once silenced the Minister of Culture with her accusation that he was involved in a lucrative stamp-stealing scheme (50), so Kincaid makes an even greater "hubbub" as she attacks the government and attempts to silence her opponents. Indeed, in her fierce attack on postcolonial Antigua, she arrogates to herself the right, not unlike that of the mother or the hated colonizers depicted in her fictional works, to speak of and for others. It is revealing, then, that Kincaid's critique of Antigua "displays a disturbing reliance on the vocabulary and positional superiority of the very objects of her oppositional writing—Western colonizers and neocolonizers"—and that her anger "seems to be directed at all except herself" (Poon, paras. 27, 30). For what underlies the at-times theatrical, dissident politics of *A Small Place* is a very personal drama as Kincaid assumes a position of superiority over and chastises her fellow black Antiguans[8] for accepting a government that is run by the Prime Minister and two of his sons like a family business.

If in her no-holds-barred attack on the Antiguan government and people, Kincaid effectively vents her anger, she also enacts, in part, a reparative gesture in the brief concluding section of *A Small Place*. "Antigua is beautiful. Antigua is too beautiful. Sometimes the beauty of it seems unreal," the speaker remarks as she delineates the strange beauty of Antigua in a lyrical speech that recalls *At the Bottom of the River* and anticipates descriptive passages found in *Mr. Potter*. "Sometimes the beauty of it seems as if it were stage sets for a play, for no real sunset could look like that; no real seawater could strike that many shades of blue at once; . . . no real day could be that sort of sunny and bright, making everything seem transparent and shallow; and no real night could be that sort of black, making everything seem thick and deep and bottomless" (77). Even as she celebrates the natural yet unreal beauty of Antigua—the part of Antigua that attracts tourists—she also directs attention to the parts of Antigua avoided by tourists as she describes the poverty found in the village life of the drought-stricken island, discovering even there a kind of beauty in the "one-room houses painted in unreal shades of pink and yellow and green" or in the Saturday morning market "where the colours of the fruits and vegetables and the colours of the clothes people are wearing and the colour of the day itself, and the colour of the nearby sea, and the colour of the sky . . . all of this is so beautiful, all of this is not real like any other real thing that there is" (78–79).

That Kincaid's speaker ends up viewing Antigua's unreal beauty as a "prison" calls to mind Kincaid's own very personal response to the Antigua in which she was raised.[9] Existing in such "heightened, intense" and yet prison-like surroundings, Antiguans live in the present and thus lack a historical perspective, for they have "no big historical moment to compare the way they are now to the way they used to be. No Industrial Revolution, no revolution of any kind, no Age of Anything" (79). And the "unreal" beauty of the Antigua they now live in as free people is the same "unreal" beauty their ancestors lived in as slaves. A small island, nine miles wide by twelve miles long, Antigua "was settled by human rubbish from Europe, who used enslaved but noble and exalted human beings from Africa . . . to satisfy their desire for wealth and power, to feel better about their own miserable existence, so that they could be less lonely and empty—a European disease. Eventually, the masters left, in a kind of way; eventually, the slaves were freed, in a kind of way. The people in Antigua now, the people who really think of themselves as Antiguans . . . are the descendants of those noble and exalted people, the slaves" (80–81). By referring to the white masters as "human rubbish" and the African slaves as "noble and exalted," *A Small Place* continues with its original strategy of reversal as it rescripts the traditional roles of white superiority and black inferiority. Yet even as Kincaid uses a shame-reversing attack-other script to turn the tables once again on the white oppressors, she also critiques the postcolonial rhetoric she invokes. A new grand narrative, the postcolonial story of the exalted slave and debased master is not truly empowering, she suggests. Instead, it is a new kind of debilitating fairy tale. For in placing emphasis on the passive victimization of blacks, it serves to perpetuate a kind of political acquiescence among Antiguans under self-rule so that instead of openly protesting against the government, the people tolerate a continuation of exploitative and corrupt governmental practices.

If in *A Small Place* Kincaid famously settles scores and expresses her indignation at not only the white colonizers and tourists but also her fellow Antiguans, she also, in the closing passage, gestures toward healing. "Of course, the whole thing is, once you cease to be a master, once you throw off your master's yoke, you are no longer human rubbish, you are just a human being, and all the things that adds up to. So, too, with the slaves. Once they are no longer slaves, once they are free, they are no longer noble and exalted; they are just human beings" (81). In describing the white colonizers and tourists and the black Antiguans as "just human beings," Kincaid seeks a remedy to the historical and continuing hierarchical division of people into superior and inferior groups, and she also looks for a way out of the unending cycles of contempt and countercontempt that grow out of such divisions. Yet this hoped-for solution, proffered as it is in the context of *A Small Place*'s sustained use of attack-other scripts, does little to ameliorate or resolve the anger that drives Kincaid's narrative, an anger that resurfaces again full force in her 1991 essay, "On Seeing England for the First Time."

"On Seeing England for the First Time"

Growing up in an Antigua where "[e]verything seemed divine and good only if it was English" (Cudjoe 217) and where it was impossible for black Antiguans to live up to the English ideal, Kincaid ended up being deeply influenced by but also resentful of the English. "In my generation," she admits, "we are very English in some way, certainly through literature, and we see the world not in a European but an English way" (Wachtel 57–58). But Kincaid recalls that she also had "very anti-colonial feelings and very anti-British feelings" when she was growing up (Wachtel 59). When she visited England for the first time in 1985 and realized how familiar the places she visited were to her, she became angry (Mendelsohn). After a 1990 visit, she remarked that every time she visited England, a place she both loved and hated, she almost had "a nervous breakdown." "[W]hen I go to England," as she explained, "what happens is that I also confront my past" (Vorda 101).

In "On Seeing England for the First Time," which like *A Small Place* is at once a political and a highly personal essay, Kincaid again employs a shame-reversing attack-other script as she explains the shameful legacy of her "very English" Antiguan upbringing. Self-dramatizing and profoundly angry, Kincaid's speaker describes her rage when she first travels to England as "a grown-up woman" and "the wife of someone, a person who resides in a powerful country" (37). Coming to first see England as a child in Antigua through idealistic representations found in pictures, paintings, and especially books, Kincaid's speaker explains that when she finally visits the real England for the first time as an adult "the space between the idea of it and its reality had become filled with hatred, and so when at last I saw it I wanted to take it into my hands and tear it into little pieces and then crumble it up as if it were clay, child's clay" (37). That there is something childlike in her angry fantasy—her wish to tear England into pieces and crumble it as if it were child's clay—points to the childhood sources of the speaker's adult rage.

As she reviews her personal history, she recalls the first time she saw England—that is, the map of England—as a schoolgirl in Antigua. "[T]hough it looked like a leg of mutton, it could not really look like anything so familiar as a leg of mutton because it was England. . . . England was a special jewel all right, and only special people got to wear it. The people who got to wear England were English people." When the teacher said, "'This is England,'" the "authority, seriousness, and adoration" in her voice let the students know that "England was to be our source of myth and the source from which we got our sense of reality, our sense of what was meaningful, our sense of what was meaningless— and much about our own lives and much about the very idea of us headed that last list" (32). But as a girl she was unaware that the teacher's repeated command during every test to "'Draw a map of England'" was "worse than a declaration of war." Having "long ago been conquered," she did not realize that this command was part of an insidious process that would ultimately lead to her "erasure" and that it was meant to make her feel "in awe and small" when she heard the word "England": in awe of England's existence and small because she was not from England (34). But what really made her "feel like nothing" was the England she came to know through English literature. Bookish expressions—"'When morning touched the sky'" or "'Evening approaches'"— made lasting impressions on her, for in Antigua mornings "came on abruptly, with a shock of heat and loud noises," and evenings "did not approach" (34–35). In English books "there were gentle mountains and low blue skies and moors over which people took walks for nothing but pleasure, when where I lived a walk was an act of labor, a burden." And in English literature she learned that there were "people whose eyes were blue and who had fair skins and who smelled only of lavender, or sometimes sweet pea or primrose" and that there were parents who "loved their children" and sent their children "to their own rooms as a punishment, rooms larger than my entire house." Ultimately, what she learned from English literature was that the English "were special; everything about them said so. . . . The world was theirs, not mine; everything told me so" (35).

If viewing English life through literature made her feel like an outsider with her nose pressed against a glass window as she looked in at the plentitude of English life, it also provided her with a temporary escape from the shameful reality of her life as a black Antiguan—the "hole filled with nothing" from which she had been rescued. "[A]nd that was the word for everything about me, nothing. The reality of my life was conquests, subjugation, humiliation, enforced amnesia" (36).[10] Because her ideal version of self was based on an unattainable English identity, she could not help but feel ashamed: that is, that her whole self was a failure and inferior in comparison with the English ideal (see Morrison, *Shame* 12). Measuring her life against the yardstick of an idealized representation of English life reflected in literature,[11] she felt as if she were being punished for her badness: that she "must have done something to deserve" her fate (36).

Deeply shamed as a child, the speaker, as an adult, is consumed by feelings of rage toward the English. No longer the inferiorized Antiguan but an empowered woman living in a powerful country when she visits England as an adult, she feels hatred for the English and actively humiliates her childhood humiliators. To her, the English people, with their pale skin, are not powerful and beautiful as depicted in books; instead, they appear to be "fragile," "weak," and "ugly." In a classic turning-the-tables revenge fantasy, she imagines the English as slaves, banished from their homeland and sent to a place such as Antigua where the sun's constant presence would "rid them of their pale complexion," making them look more like her. "[W]hat if all this was in my power? Could I resist it? No one ever has." Rather than being a polite and gracious people, the English are "rude to each other" and dislike each other in the same way they dislike people like her, making her realize that their dislike for people like her is "one of the few things" upon which they agree (38).

During her tour of England with an English "friend," she comes to question her years of friendship with the woman after an incident in a store where she shops for a shirt and tie for her husband. The "slavish, reverential, awed" tone of the salesclerk when he shows her a shirt and tie set bearing the crest of the Prince of Wales angers her so much that she wants to hit him. When she retorts that she and her husband "hate princes" and that her husband would refuse to "wear anything that had a prince's anything on it," both the salesclerk and her friend stiffen. Subsequently told by her friend that the prince is "a symbol of her Englishness," she sees her friend in a new light (38). "She was an English person, the sort of English person I used to know at home, the sort who was nobody in England but somebody when they came to live among the people like me." Aware that her friend resembles the English people who first introduced her to England when she was a child, she questions whether, during her years of friendship with the woman, she "had had a friend or had been in the thrall of a racial memory" (39). Struck by how familiar everything is when she visits Bath and drives through the English countryside—the narrow winding roads, the hedges, and the English villages all seem familiar even though she has never visited England before—she reflects on what the English did to her when she was growing up in Antigua: they made her feel that she was "incomplete, or without substance, and did not measure up" because she was Antiguan and not English (40).

Actively undercutting the cultural—and racial—superiority of the English, Kincaid's speaker mocks them by using their own racist rhetoric against them in a shame-reversing attack-other script. Had she said to her English friend what she was thinking—"the English are a very ugly people, the food in England is like a jail sentence, the hair of English people is so straight, so dead looking, the English have an unbearable smell so different from the smell of people I know"—she would have been accused of being prejudiced. Aware that because her "prejudices have no weight to them" and "no force behind them," they remain her "personal opinion," she is overcome by "a great feeling of rage and disappointment" as she looks at England (40). In a scene that recalls Lucy's rage at the sight of daffodils, the speaker, when she sees the white cliffs of Dover, feels deep anger and contempt. Often described as a "'cold' affect," a form of aggression that wants to "eliminate the other being," contempt says, in effect, "'Get out of my sight: Disappear!'" (Wurmser *Mask*, 81, 80, "Shame" 67). Expressing her deep contempt, the speaker remarks that when she sees the white cliffs of Dover she wishes that "every sentence" and "everything" she knows that begins with "England" would end with this phrase: "'and then it all died; we don't know how, it just all died'" (40). When asked about this passage, Kincaid explained that the "it just all died" wish was meant as "a sort of childish indulgence," not unlike a child saying "'I wish you were dead'" (Ferguson, "Interview" 182). Rather than providing a reparative gesture in the closure, Kincaid abruptly ends her essay on an angry note. "The white cliffs of Dover, when finally I saw them, were cliffs, but they were not white; . . . they were dirty and they were steep; they were so steep, the correct height from which all my views of England, starting with the map before me in my classroom and ending with the trip I had just taken, should jump and die and disappear forever" (40).

"[I]t became clear to me when I was writing the essay that became 'On Seeing England for the First Time,'" Kincaid has remarked, "that I was writing about the mother—that the mother I was writing about was really Mother Country" (Ferguson, "Interview" 176–77). Yet even as Kincaid voices her political grievances against the mother country in her essay, she also acts out a very personal mother-daughter drama. For not only does her expression of rage at and contempt for the once idealized but now hated England repeat the daughter's rage at and contempt for the once loved but then hated mother in Kincaid's fiction, but her desire to verbally retaliate against and humiliate the English who humiliated her as a child recalls the daughter's desire to talk back to the humiliating mother, returning the mother's contempt with the daughter's countercontempt.

Remarking that people say that she is "awful and angry," Kincaid insists, "[T]he combativeness that people complain about is that I don't like to take crap from horrible people" (Conover). Asserting that anger is important to her and that she might not have been able to express her anger had she ended up in England instead of the United States, she feels that because she lived in America when she began to write she was able to write in her "own" voice (Birbalsingh 139, 142). Yet even as Kincaid writes in her own voice, she also incorporates into her own combative, denunciatory speech the contemptuous voice of the mother. No longer the humiliated daughter and powerless Antiguan, she is the highly renowned and powerful author, Jamaica Kincaid, an individual Antiguans treat in a "very respectful" way (Muirhead 45). Clearly energized by her anger, Kincaid takes obvious pleasure in settling old scores and making "a great hubbub" in her political-personal essays as she gains public attention and recognition by both talking behind the backs of and writing back to the authorities.

PART III

Family Portraits

6

"I Would Bear Children, but I Would Never Be a Mother to Them"

Writing Back to the Contemptuous Mother in *The Autobiography of My Mother*

An unremittingly bleak and bitter novel permeated with feelings of despair, contempt, and rage, Kincaid's 1996 novel *The Autobiography of My Mother* is at once a continuation of and a departure from her autobiographical-fictional project, her attempt to use fiction to write herself a life and make sense of her troubled relationship with her mother. A book that, like *Annie John* and *Lucy*, Kincaid says she "couldn't help but write," *The Autobiography of My Mother* "took a long time to finish," and "[t]here was a lot of it" she did not understand (Garner). When Kincaid completed the novel after working on it for some five years, she did not think people would like it. "But if I'd thought that nobody would like it as I was writing it, I would have written it even more," she insists (Jacobs). In part, Kincaid had a conscious political agenda in telling the story of her seventy-year-old narrator, Xuela, whose mother died the moment she was born. Explaining that Xuela's life can be read as a metaphor for the African diaspora, Kincaid remarks, "At the moment African people came into this world, Africa died for them. . . . The birth of one is the death of the other" (Lee). But for Kincaid *The Autobiography of My Mother* also has a very personal meaning, and, indeed, she said that after writing the novel she felt that she had made "sense" of her own childhood (Jacobs). "You know, I didn't just fall out of the sky," she remarks. "I come with all these human attachments so they come into it. But I am really always writing about myself. Especially when I write something as explicitly not about myself as *The Autobiography of My Mother*, which was not really about my mother but about a woman who could be my mother and so therefore could be me" (Brady).

Continuing to investigate the formative influence of her childhood relationship with her powerful and destructive mother in *The Autobiography of My Mother*, Kincaid incorporates family stories into her narrative. Like Kincaid's mother, Annie Drew, Kincaid's narrator, Xuela Claudette Richardson, is from Dominica and is part Carib Indian, African, and Scots, and she bears Kincaid's mother's family name, Richardson.[1] Kincaid also incorporates into the life of her character obeah stories told to her by her mother: Annie Drew's story about the *jablesse* that took the form of a monkey and attacked her by throwing a stone at her; about the death of her brother from an obeah spell that caused a worm to come out of his leg just as he died; and about the drowning of a boy lured into a flooded river by a *jablesse*, which appeared as a beautiful beckoning woman bathing in a deep part of the river.[2] If Kincaid is intent on examining her matrilineal roots as she includes family stories and looks back to her mother's Carib Indian origins in *The Autobiography of My Mother*, she also is driven by the daughterly imperative to assert herself and assume power by talking back—or, more accurately, writing back—to her powerful and powerfully destructive mother. Indeed, what lies at the center of the book, as Kincaid has remarked, is the narrator's decision not to be a mother, which, in turn, is drawn from Kincaid's and her brothers' view of their mother. For even though all of Annie Drew's children are "quite happy to have been born," they are also "quite sure" that she should not have been a mother. "I feel comfortable saying that publicly, I think. I try not to corner my mother anymore. Because I have at my disposal a way of articulating things about her that she can't respond to. But I feel comfortable saying that the core of the book—and the book is not autobiographical except in this one way—derives from the observation that my own mother should not have had children" (Garner).

If in *The Autobiography of My Mother* Kincaid expresses her anger against her mother in telling the story of her destructive mother character, she also, in her account of the childhood of her character, presents Xuela as a daughter-victim, emphasizing Xuela's obsession with her idealized but dead mother and her abuse at the hands of a series of bad mother substitutes. Like Kincaid's earlier fictional personas and daughter-victims, Annie John and Lucy, Xuela uses anger to defend against deeply entrenched feelings of shame-vulnerability and shame-depression. That Xuela, like Annie John and Lucy, is an embittered and cold-hearted individual suggests that Kincaid, in describing her own angry feelings and "badness" through her destructive "bad" mother character, also locates her own mother as the source of these feelings and actively reprojects these feelings back onto her mother. By articulating things Annie Drew was unable to "respond to" in *The Autobiography of My Mother*, Kincaid turns the tables on her mother and thus returns maternal contempt with her own daughterly countercontempt.

There is something highly personal about this novel, which can be read at least in part as the daughter's written vendetta against the "bad" mother. But Kincaid also seems intent on deflecting attention away from the personal drama enacted in the narrative by creating tantalizing literary puzzles in the text. Indeed, the novel's title—*The Autobiography of My Mother*—as one critic has astutely observed, immediately raises questions in the reader's mind: How can one narrate someone else's story of the self? Is this the story of the writer's self in which Xuela writes the story of her unknown mother, who died in childbirth, in order to tell the story of the self? Is this Kincaid's mother's auto/biography, and if so is Kincaid present as the "ghost" writer/biographer? (Donnell, "When Writing" 127). The resulting "confusion over who speaks, for whom and about whom" in the narrative and the "slippage between mothers and daughters, mothers and mothers" (Donnell, "When Writing" 127) are deliberate on Kincaid's part. When asked about the novel's title, Kincaid explained that her purpose was to write "the life of a certain kind of woman from the British-ruled West Indies," and although it was not her life or her generation, she wanted to say things "in a voice that seemed autobiographical" in the novel. "The tradition of autobiography of course is that it's your own life you're talking about, but I believe that I can trace my line legitimately through the maternal, and that all the female lives that came before mine are part of me, so I can think of it as my own life, my own biography, though strictly speaking it's not that at all" (Wachtel 68–69). In *The Autobiography of My Mother* Kincaid, the daughter/ghostwriter, tells a fabricated story of her mother that includes family stories passed down by her mother as well as the story of Kincaid's own girlhood and adult relation with her angry and contemptuous mother, who becomes an internalized part of Kincaid heard in her angry and contemptuous authorial voice. Just as Xuela, in response to the contemptuous hostility of others, enacts power, rage, and contempt scripts as she learns to humiliate the humiliator,[3] so Kincaid as a retrospective storyteller assumes a similar power over her mother.

The Autobiography of My Mother, then, grows out of Kincaid's troubled relationship with her mother, and it also considers, in a more self-conscious and extended way than her earlier novels, the damaging impact of cultural forces and internalized colonialism on her character's developing personality. Interestingly, while the mother figure in Kincaid's earlier novels is represented as an upholder of repressive English colonial codes of "lady-like" conduct, in *The Autobiography of My Mother* the mother-Xuela refuses the restricted life of the socially respectable and "lady-like" woman. If Annie John is accused by the mother of behaving like a slut, and if Lucy shamelessly declares herself a slut to defy her mother, Kincaid, in effect, turns the tables on the contemptuous mother of her earlier works by describing the mother-Xuela's shameless expressions of her "sluttish" life. Adding to the complexity of Kincaid's blurring of her characters, Xuela's sexual empowerment also recalls the experiences of the earlier daughter character, Lucy. For as she is growing up, Xuela, like Lucy, uses her sexuality to defy maternal control, and for Xuela, as for Lucy, sexuality is an area in which she can gain power over the men in her life, including for Xuela the white Englishman whom she eventually marries and dominates as she plays out in her marriage, just as she does in all her significant relationships, a victor/vanquished power and shame script.

Xuela and Her Dead Mother

The primacy of the lost mother-daughter relationship in the narrative's psychic structure is apparent in the novel's opening statement, which introduces Xuela's recurring refrain-like statement about her mother's death: "My mother died at the moment I was born, and so for my whole life there was nothing standing between myself and eternity; at my back was always a bleak, black wind" (3). The death of the mother, Kincaid remarks, carries a symbolic political meaning—the loss of the mother country of Africa. "For Africans, Africa died the minute they were born into the new world," and for Kincaid "[t]hat loss is not recoverable" (Jaggi, Jackson). Yet even as Kincaid consciously attaches a political meaning to the mother's death, she also replays in *The Autobiography of My Mother* a very personal story that animates the accounts of her earlier fictional personas and daughter-victims, Annie John and Lucy.

Like *Annie John*, *The Autobiography of My Mother* associates maternal loss with the black despair and shame of the unloved child. "The helplessness of the searching eye and of the cry for love is the helplessness of feeling doomed to unlovability," Léon Wurmser writes in his description of "basic shame" as the wound of feeling unloved and unlovable. "To be unlovable means not to see a responsive eye and not to hear a responding voice, no matter how much they are sought" (*Mask* 97). Xuela, whose mother died the moment she was born, is doomed to feelings of helplessness and unlovability. "[A]t my beginning was this woman whose face I had never seen, but at my end was nothing, no one between me and the black room of the world" (3). Like Annie John and Lucy, Xuela lacks a sense of self-stability and security because of the profound maternal loss she has suffered. "I came to feel that for my whole life I had been standing on a precipice, that my loss had made me vulnerable, hard, and helpless; on knowing this I became overwhelmed with sadness and shame and pity for myself" (3–4). Left a "small child vulnerable to all the world" (4), Xuela, even in her dreams of her mother, remains the abandoned child of the faceless and remote, but idealized, mother. Appearing in Xuela's dreams in the white dress associated in the colonized mind with moral and sexual—indeed angelic—purity, Xuela's mother comes down a ladder over and over again, but only her heels and the hem of her white gown are visible to the dreaming Xuela. Even as Xuela's dream captures the sense of abandonment and loss she feels, it also recalls Annie John's description of how her mother, in a moment of contempt and disgust, turned her back on her disobedient daughter.

In *The Autobiography of My Mother*, the loss of the idealized, good, and protective mother is experienced as a crippling, festering wound that never can be healed, and this loss puts the child at the mercy of a series of persecutory bad mother figures, who not only fail to nurture or confirm but also seek to dominate the child. Making use of a psychoanalytic paradigm by rooting Xuela's intrapsychic life and interpersonal relations in this originary moment of maternal loss, *The Autobiography of My Mother* also points to the broader connection between the lack of maternal recognition of the developing self and a mode of relating based not on mutuality but on domination. In her psychoanalytic study of intersubjectivity, Jessica Benjamin discusses the necessity of mutual recognition in the mother-child relationship—that is, "the necessity of recognizing as well as being recognized by the other" (23). "In order to exist for oneself, one has to exist for an other," as Benjamin remarks (53). Xuela not only never recognizes or is recognized by the idealized good mother, but she also is treated like an object of contempt by her mother-surrogate figures, who refuse Xuela's assertions of self and attempt to dominate and control her. The underlying fantasy structuring relations in the novel is described by Benjamin in what she calls "the dialectic of control": "If I completely control the other, then the other ceases to exist, and if the other completely controls me, then I cease to exist. A condition of our own independent existence is recognizing the other. True independence means sustaining the essential tension of these contradictory impulses; that is, both asserting the self and recognizing the other. Domination is the consequence of refusing this condition" (53). Existing not in a relational world of mutual recognition but in a maternal—and colonial—world of dominator and dominated, Xuela determines to survive the best she can: by becoming one of the dominators.

Ma Eunice

In describing how her father[4] leaves her under the care of Eunice Paul, the same woman who washes his clothes, Xuela suggests that her father is unable to recognize or confirm her developing selfhood. A vain man who cares about his appearance, it is possible, Xuela remarks, that in giving Ma Eunice the two bundles—his daughter and his soiled clothes—her father "would have expected better care for one than the other, but which one I do not know" (4). During her father's fortnightly visits to Ma Eunice's to pick up his clean clothes, he asks Xuela how she is, "but it was a formality; he would never touch me or look into my eyes" (6). Xuela is emotionally neglected by her father and mistreated by Ma Eunice. "Ma Eunice was not unkind: she treated me just the way she treated her own children—but this is not to say she was kind to her own children. In a place like this, brutality is the only real inheritance and cruelty is sometimes the only thing freely given. I did not like her, and I missed the face I had never seen" (5). At once the lost, lonely child and the enraged bad child, Xuela exhausts herself in tears as she looks out at the "unpitying" landscape of sea and mountains at Ma Eunice's house, but she also, when her teeth grow in, bites Ma Eunice's hand[5] as she is being fed, her "first act of ingratitude" (5, 6).

Like *Annie John* and *Lucy*, *The Autobiography of My Mother* splits the mother figure into good and bad parts as it links the daughter's loss of the love and protection of the "good" mother to her abuse at the hands of a series of "bad" mother figures. In describing Ma Eunice's cruel behavior toward her children, *The Autobiography of My Mother* points to the colonial sources of this oppressive behavior by insisting that "brutality is the only real inheritance" in Dominican culture. But it also focuses attention on the parental transmission of this lethal cultural heritage and the impact of colonialism on the family and, in particular, on the psyche of the developing child. Like the victor/vanquished relationship fostered under colonialism, the power-imbalanced abusive parent-child relationship can resemble a cruel power game in which the parent, in the name of molding or socializing or breaking the will of the disobedient child, attempts to dominate, humiliate, and punish her. As Alice Miller has observed, such an adult assertion of power over the child is "a use of power that can go undetected and unpunished like no other," pointing to the insidious effects of what Miller calls "poisonous pedagogy," an abusive form of child-rearing that can lead, as it ultimately does in Xuela, to an attempt on the part of the victimized individual to become "senselessly hard" and to suppress "all signs of weakness" in herself (*For Your Own Good* 17, 80).

When Xuela breaks a treasured object owned by Ma Eunice—a bone china plate depicting an idealized English countryside scene with the gold-lettered word *heaven* written underneath—she is unsympathetic to Ma Eunice's sadness over the loss of the plate. To Ma Eunice, the plate's illustration of a wide-open, grassy field with flowers on a sunny day is "a picture of heaven" that offers "a secret promise of a life without worry or care or want" (9). Although Xuela, at the time, does not know of the existence of the English countryside, her obsessive curiosity about and destruction of the plate suggests her fascination with but also resistance to English colonial values. In her punishment of Xuela, the angry Ma Eunice reveals that she has internalized the power-imbalanced colonizer/colonized relationship as she, the autocratic mother-oppressor, exerts complete power over the willful, disobedient child-victim. "She made me kneel down on her stone heap, which as it should be was situated in a spot that got direct sun all day long, with my hands raised high above my head and with a large stone in each hand" (9–10).

Xuela, who refuses to say that she is sorry, is forced to remain in this position until Ma Eunice exhausts herself cursing not only Xuela but also Xuela's dead mother and her father. Placing emphasis on this punishment and explaining its broader cultural and historical significance, the narrative draws a connection between maternal abuse of the child and colonial abuse of the colonized subject. Making a lasting impression on Xuela, Ma Eunice's punishment is "redolent . . . in every way of the relationship between captor and captive, master and slave, with its motif of the big and the small, the powerful and the powerless, the strong and the weak, and against a background of earth, sea, and sky, and Eunice standing over me, metamorphosing into a succession of things furious and not human with each syllable that passed her lips" (10). Recalling representations of the angry, powerful mother figure in Kincaid's earlier works, Ma Eunice transforms, in her anger, into a persecutory figure— the mother-monster—and yet at the same time she is the inferiorized and dirty, that is, shamed, colonized subject, for Xuela also observes in minute detail Ma Eunice's unwashed, uncombed hair and her dirty dress. Ma Eunice's children, rather than being sympathetic to Xuela's plight, further victimize and humiliate Xuela by throwing bread pellets at her and laughing at her as she kneels in the hot sun. If Xuela claims to remember everything that happened to her during this episode, her description of the sound of the overripe breadfruit falling off a tree—she likens the sound to that of "a fist meeting the soft, fleshy part of a body" (11)—suggests that Xuela was physically beaten by Ma Eunice and that she has protectively distanced herself from this physical trauma through dissociative denial. Like *Annie John*, *The Autobiography of My Mother* omits scenes of physical beatings even as it makes a veiled reference to the physical abuse Kincaid suffered as a child at the hands of her mother.

Xuela's wish for a safe holding environment during her ordeal is expressed in her comforting fantasy of the three land turtles she watches while she is kneeling in the sun: "I fell in love with them, I wanted to have them near me, I wanted to speak only to them each day for the rest of my life" (11). After her ordeal is over, Xuela takes on the role of the mother-caretaker figure as she watches over and feeds the turtles only to transform over time into the abandoning, and tyrannical, mother-destroyer. Making the turtles totally dependent on her for their survival, she places them in an enclosed space, and when they withdraw into their shells and refuse to come out when she calls them, she decides to teach them a lesson. She covers up the holes their heads and necks emerge from with mud, which dries, and places stones over the enclosed area where she keeps them and then forgets about them. Days later, when she returns to the enclosure, the turtles are dead.

The designated child victim who is treated as an object of manipulation and control by the domineering Ma Eunice, Xuela not only internalizes the victim/victimizer roles, which become entrenched parts of her personal identity, but she also identifies with the aggressor. Setting up a potentially hostile relationship with the reader-listener, Xuela, the daughter-victim, takes the position of the mother-violator. Assuming active mastery over passive suffering, Xuela repeats a pattern commonly found in violent families: the child victim's identification with the aggressor-parent and her incorporation and enactment of the patterns of aggressive and punitive behavior inflicted on her by the abusive parent (see Waites 75). Vengeful and punitive, Xuela internalizes and repeats the violence done against her in a drama that is at once personal and psychological and, in repeating the colonial victor/vanquished relationship, historical and political.

Internalized Colonialism and the Educational Process

In *The Autobiography of My Mother*, as in *Annie John*, *Lucy*, and also *A Small Place*, Kincaid points to the insidious and shaming effects of internalized colonialism on the developing child. When the four-year-old Xuela says her first words—"Where is my father?"—she speaks, not in French or English patois, languages associated with social inferiority and shame, but in standard English, a language she has never heard spoken. "That the first words I said were in the language of a people I would never like or love is not now a mystery to me; everything in my life, good or bad, to which I am inextricably bound is a source of pain" (7). Similarly, the first words she learns to read in school—THE BRITISH EMPIRE—are English words that are prominently displayed on the top of a map in her classroom (14).[6] Xuela is aware that her African Caribbean teacher views her own African heritage as "a source of humiliation and self-loathing, and she wore despair like an article of clothing, like a mantle, or a staff on which she leaned constantly, a birthright which she would pass on to us" (15). Because Xuela is both African and Carib Indian, she is viewed as an object of contempt by her schoolmates, for while the African people in Dominica "had been defeated but had survived," the Carib people "had been defeated and then exterminated, thrown away like the weeds in a garden." When others look at Xuela, they see "only the Carib people" in her (16).

A lonely girl whose basic need for the affirming recognition of the other remains unfulfilled, Xuela wishes "to see people in whose faces" she can "recognize something" of herself (16). To assuage her loneliness, she talks to herself, enjoying the sweet sound of her voice, and when she learns, at the age of seven, how to write a letter in a "decorative penmanship . . . born of beatings and harsh words," she writes a series of letters that are addressed to her father but are really written to her dead mother. Writing the same thing over and over, she describes her mistreatment at the hands of Ma Eunice: "'I am beaten with words, I am beaten with sticks, I am beaten with stones . . . only you can save me'" (19).

When one of her classmates, a pitiless, malicious boy who lacks any impulse to defend the weak, sees Xuela putting the letters in her secret hiding place—under a large stone outside the school gate—he removes them and gives them to the teacher. Assuming that the letters are about her, the teacher accuses Xuela of lying and publicly berates her, saying she is ashamed of her. Aware that the other students enjoy seeing her "humiliated" and "brought so low," Xuela, rather than feeling humiliated, views her contemptuous teacher as an object of contempt: "I could see her teeth were crooked and yellow, and I wondered how they had got that way. Large half-moons of perspiration stained the underarms of her dress, and I wondered if when I became a woman I, too, would perspire so profusely and how it would smell" (21). Xuela's desire to crush with her bare hand the spider she sees on the wall behind the teacher reveals the intense rage she feels toward her teacher, rage that masks her feelings of humiliation.

When the teacher sends the letters to Xuela's father, Xuela learns of the power of verbal expression. Having been subjected to the teacher's scolding words, which felt like "a series of harsh blows," Xuela discovers that she can use words to change her situation and rescue herself. "To speak of my own situation, to myself or to others, is something I would always do thereafter. It is in this way that I came to be so extremely conscious of myself, so interested in my own needs, so interested in fulfilling them, aware of my grievances, aware of my pleasures. From this unfocused, childish expression of pain, my life was changed and I took note of it" (22).[7] As Xuela rides off with her father toward her new home, she is able, for the first time, to leave behind the past. "This most simple of movements, the turning of your back, is among the most difficult to make, but once it has been made you cannot imagine it was at all hard to accomplish. . . . If I were ever to find myself sitting in that schoolroom again, or sitting in Eunice's yard again, sleeping in her bed, eating with her children, none of it would have the same power it once had over me—the power to make me feel helpless and ashamed at my own helplessness" (25).

Xuela and Her Stepmother and Father

Because the seven-year-old Xuela is a visible reminder of her dead mother, her stepmother, from the outset, views her as a threat. Overwhelmed when she first arrives at her father's house—"I did not know who I was or why I was standing there in that room"—Xuela faints, and the first thing she sees when she comes to is the face of her stepmother, "the face of evil," looking down at her (28). Like *Annie John* and *Lucy*, *The Autobiography of My Mother*, as it focuses on the issue of domination, also deals with the annihilating power of maternal contempt. "Contempt says: 'You should disappear as such a being as you have shown yourself to be—failing, weak, flawed, and dirty. Get out of my sight: Disappear!'" (Wurmser, "Shame" 67). An embodiment of the abusive, bad mother who wants to dominate and annihilate the daughter-victim, Xuela's stepmother, Xuela insists, never stops wishing her stepdaughter dead. After the stepmother gives Xuela moldy food to eat in an apparent attempt to make her stepdaughter sick, Xuela prepares her own food. When the stepmother gives Xuela a necklace to wear, trying to use obeah to kill her, Xuela places the necklace around the neck of her stepmother's dog, and within twenty-four hours the dog goes mad and dies.

Aware that her stepmother does not like or love her, Xuela insists that while love would always "defeat" her, she can "live well" in an "atmosphere of no love" (29). Yet Xuela also feels alone and in danger as she becomes aware of her stepmother's annihilating contempt for her. When her stepmother privately speaks to her in French patois, not in the English she uses in front of Xuela's father, Xuela recognizes that her stepmother wants to "make an illegitimate" of her by associating her "with the made-up language of people regarded as not real—the shadow people, the forever humiliated, the forever low" (30–31). A verbally abusive woman, the stepmother heaps scorn on Xuela, viewing her as a dirty and dissmelling person. Using shamelessness as a defense against her stepmother's contempt, Xuela loves what she is told to hate about herself. "I loved the smell of the thin dirt behind my ears, the smell of my unwashed mouth, the smell that came from between my legs, the smell in the pit of my arm, the smell of my unwashed feet. Whatever about me caused offense, whatever was native to me, whatever I could not help and was not a moral failing—those things about me I loved with the fervor of the devoted" (32–33).

The stepmother treats Xuela with contempt, and when she has two children, a boy and a girl, she, predictably, favors her son over her daughter.[8] The stepmother's contempt for her daughter, as Xuela explains, is the expected behavior among women who learn to despise what is most like themselves: their daughters. To Xuela, her half sister's "tragedy was greater than mine; her mother did not love her, but her mother was alive, and every day she saw her mother and every day her mother let her know she was not loved. My mother was dead" (53). Yet while Xuela feels sympathetic toward her half sister, Elizabeth views Xuela as an enemy, for she has been told by her mother that Xuela is "like a thief in the house," waiting to rob her father's family of their inheritance (52).

Finding herself in a family situation "full of danger and treachery," Xuela learns how to protect herself in her stepmother's home. "I was not indifferent to the danger my father's wife posed to me, and I was not indifferent to the danger she thought my presence posed to her. So in my father's house, which was her home, I tried to cloak myself in an atmosphere of apology" (41). Xuela wears the mantle of proper femininity as a disguise, performing the role of the pious, quiet, and sexually modest "good" girl. Forced in her daily life to negotiate "many treacherous acts of deception," Xuela remains clear in her mind about who she "really" is (42). Recalling the mingling of physical pain and sexual pleasure in Kincaid's other works and the daughter-characters' use of their sexuality to resist maternal control, the narrative describes how Xuela gets in touch with her real identity at night in her bed. As she hears the spirits of the dead slaves and her Carib ancestors, she masturbates:

[i]f I listened again I could hear the sound of those who crawled on their bellies, the ones who carried poisonous lances, and those who carried a deadly poison in their saliva; I could hear the ones who were hunting, the ones who were hunted, the pitiful cry of the small ones who were about to be devoured, followed by the temporary satisfaction of the ones doing the devouring. . . . And it ended only after my hands had traveled up and down all over my own body in a loving caress, finally coming to the soft, moist spot between my legs, and a gasp of pleasure had escaped my lips which I would allow no one to hear. (43)

Determined to survive in a hostile maternal environment, Xuela, over time, learns how to interpret her stepmother's silences. "Sometimes in these silences there was nothing at all; sometimes they were filled with pure evil; sometimes she meant to see me dead, sometimes my being alive was of no interest to her" (55).[9] Aware that her need for maternal recognition is unmet, Xuela realizes that without the "invisible current" between child and parent—the "observed and observer, beheld and beholder"—the individual life is not "complete" or "whole." "No one observed and beheld me, I observed and beheld myself; the invisible current went out and it came back to me. I came to love myself in defiance, out of despair, because there was nothing else" (56–57). When Xuela, at the onset of puberty, undergoes bodily changes, she is not frightened at the sight of her "changing self" in the mirror, and she never doubts that she will like whatever comes to stare back at her in the mirror (58).

Xuela learns to read the behavior of her stepmother, but her father remains a kind of enigma to her: "Who was he? I ask myself this all the time, to this day. Who was he?" A tall, mixed-race man with red hair and gray eyes, Xuela's father is a policeman who subtly abuses his power, making him "part of a whole way of life on the island which perpetuated pain" (39). Mimicking the behavior of the colonizers, he treats people disrespectfully by making appointments with them and then forcing them to wait or never showing up. A smiling man who appears trustworthy, he wears the mask of benign colonial power that covers his pleasure in robbing and humiliating others to bolster his own sense of importance and social standing. "The more he robbed, the more money he had, the more he went to church; it is not an unheard-of linking. And the richer he became, the more fixed the mask of his face grew" (40–41).[10] Describing her father's invention of himself, Xuela likens her father's personality to a suit of clothes he has made for himself and worn so long that "it became impossible to remove, it covered completely who he really was; who he really might have been became unknown, even to himself." Her father believes that he is "a man of freedom, honest and brave," but he is, in fact, a thief, a liar, a coward, and a jailer—a man who takes advantage of those who are weak—and yet his true character remains "unknown to him" (54).

To Xuela's father, who has inherited the "ghostly paleness" (49) of his Scottish father, other African Caribbean children are objects of contempt. He tells Xuela what other parents tell their children: that she "cannot trust these people," and yet "'these people' were ourselves," people who resembled each other physically and "shared a common history of suffering and humiliation and enslavement" (47–48). Because Xuela's colonizer-identified father finds African Caribbean culture embarrassing, he tells her that she is mistaken when she reports that she has encountered a *jablesse*, an apparition of a beautiful naked woman in a deep part of the river who beckoned to Xuela and her schoolmates as they crossed the river and caused the disappearance of the boy who tried to swim out to the "something that took the shape of a woman" (37).[11]

Recognizing that her belief in the beckoning woman is "the belief of the illegitimate, the poor, the low" (38), Xuela nevertheless affirms the reality of what she has witnessed even though some of her schoolmates who saw the apparition later come to question its reality. "This is no longer without an explanation to me. Everything about us is held in doubt and we the defeated define all that is unreal, all that is not human, all that is without love, all that is without mercy. Our experience cannot be interpreted by us; we do not know the truth of it" (37). Kincaid's narrator, even as she makes a political point by insisting on the reality of the *jablesse*, also describes her own psychic reality—her experience of the good/bad mother—in her account of the beautiful, nurturing woman-apparition surrounded by mouth-watering, ripe mangoes who lures a child to his death.

Xuela and the LaBattes

Because Xuela's father wants to enhance his reputation by being able to say some day that his daughter is a schoolteacher, she is sent at age fifteen to continue her education in Roseau, where she boards at the home of the LaBattes. To Xuela, there is a "malicious intent" behind her education, for as she learns the history of peoples she will never meet—the Romans, Gauls, Saxons, Britons, and the British—she is made to feel "humiliated, humbled, small" (59). Her education at an all-girls school, where she is surrounded by "the eventually defeated, the eventually bitter," fills her with unanswered questions and with anger, and she does not like what it will lead to: "a humiliation so permanent that it would replace your own skin" (80, 79).

To the motherless Xuela, Madame LaBatte seems at first to be a good and kindly mother figure, for she tells Xuela to think of her as if she were her mother and to feel safe in her presence. Yet Xuela also becomes aware that Lise LaBatte wants something from her as the older woman tacitly consents to, and even encourages, the sexual arrangement between her husband and Xuela. At the home of the LaBattes, Xuela learns that "the respectable, the predictable" will not be her "destiny" (73) as she, assuming the oedipal role of the daughter-rival to Lise LaBatte, has an affair with Jacques LaBatte, who, like Xuela's father, is a money-obsessed, greedy man.

Aware of the power imbalance between husband and wife, Xuela views the relationship of the LaBattes as one of victor and vanquished: an energic exchange in which the husband's energy and power exist at the expense of the wife's. The embodiment of masculine vitality, Jacques LaBatte has a "strong body," "strong hands," and a "strong mouth" (64). Lise LaBatte, in contrast, is a frail, exhausted woman who is worn out by the "strength" of the "weapon" her husband carries "between his legs" (65). Childless, her womb "lay shriveled inside her; perhaps her face mirrored it: shriveled, dried, like a fruit that has lost all its juice" (76). If Xuela feels at once sympathy and revulsion for the defeat she sees in Lise, she also becomes aware of her own sexual vitality in the presence of the older woman. Not only does she feel young, strong, and new, but she enjoys the "sweet smelly stickiness" between her legs. "I was alive; I could tell that standing before me was a woman who was not. It was almost as if I sensed a danger and quickly made myself a defense; in seeing the thing I might be, I too early became its opposite" (66).

Aware that Lise wants to make a gift of her young boarder to her husband, Xuela spends her days with the older woman and her nights with Lise's husband. The first time Xuela has sex with Jacques LaBatte, she finds his unclothed body unattractive and yet is enthralled as she anticipates how his body will make her feel. "And the force of him inside me, inevitable as it was, again came as a shock, a long sharp line of pain that then washed over me with the broadness of a wave, a long sharp line of pleasure: and to each piercing that he made inside me, I made a cry that was the same cry, a cry of sadness, for without making of it something it really was not I was not the same person I had been before" (71). Recalling the link between physical pain and sexual enjoyment in the experience of the daughter-character Lucy, Xuela, afterward, associates her aching body with sexual pleasure. Xuela insists that she acts from instinct in her relation with Jacques LaBatte, as she, like Lucy, asserts her independence from the restricted life of the socially respectable woman by shamelessly embracing her sexuality.

Xuela's Refusal of Motherhood

Able to speak without words by exchanging thoughts with Lise LaBatte, Xuela realizes, over time, that the older woman wants the child that she might have. "I did not let her know that I heard that, and this vision she would have, of a child inside me, eventually in her arms, hung in the air like a ghost, something only the special could see" (77). When Xuela eventually becomes pregnant, she is terrified at the prospect of having a child and attempts to "expel" the foetus by the "sheer force" of her will, but to no avail (81).[12] Feeling that she no longer has a future, she begins "to want one," despite its uncertainty. "[W]hat such a thing could be for me I did not know, for I was standing in a black hole. The other alternative was another black hole, this other black hole was one I did not know; I chose the one I did not know" (82). After undergoing a painful abortion, Xuela is permanently changed. "I was a new person then, I knew things I had not known before, I knew things that you can know only if you have been through what I had just been through. I had carried my own life in my own hands" (83).

Xuela, who shamelessly embraces her sexuality, is nevertheless reduced to an object of shame and contempt when she undergoes an abortion. Lying down in a small hole on a dirt floor, she spends four days in a "volcano of pain" and another four days bleeding (82). When she awakens from a dream in which she claims her birthright as she walks through her inheritance—"an island of villages and rivers and mountains and people who began and ended with murder and theft and not very much love" (89)—she sees her father standing over her. As he looks down on her, his face "like a map of the world," she is reduced to a dirty, dissmelling object lying on a bed of rags on a bare-earth floor giving off the metallic odor of fresh blood and the "sweet rotten stink" of old blood (91).

Aware when she returns to the LaBattes that the defeated Lise is in mourning, Xuela is "not unmoved" at the sight, but she also senses that Lise wants "to consume" her (94). Openly voicing her defiance, the motherless Xuela angrily declares her rejection of the maternal role, linking the fact she never had a mother to her refusal to become a mother. "I would never become a mother, but that would not be the same as never bearing children. I would bear children, but I would never be a mother to them. I would bear them in abundance; they would emerge from my head, from my armpits, from between my legs; I would bear children, they would hang from me like fruit from a vine, but I would destroy them with the carelessness of a god." In a scene deliberately staged by Kincaid to voice her anger at her own rejecting, contemptuous mother, Xuela casts herself as the all-powerful and consuming and abusive mother-destroyer. "I would bear children in the morning, I would bathe them at noon in a water that came from myself, and I would eat them at night, swallowing them whole, all at once. They would live and then they would not live" (97).

At one and the same time Kincaid expresses her daughterly rage against her mother and identifies with the powerful mother as she, in the role of the contemptuous, rejecting daughter-destroyer, acts out a power script as she tells the story of her mother. Adding to the complexity of Kincaid's relationship to her mother-character, Xuela is also a self-representation of the daughter-victim. Like Kincaid's other self-representational daughter figures, Xuela is not only deeply injured by maternal abandonment and abuse, but she also is subject to intense feelings of shame-depression. Isolated from others and speaking to no one, not even herself, after the abortion, Xuela mourns the loss of her motherhood: "Inside me there was nothing; inside me there was a vault made of a substance so heavy I could find nothing to compare it to; and inside the vault was an ache of such intensity that each night as I lay alone in my house all my exhalations were long, low wails" (99). Defending against her feelings of empty despair, Xuela insists that love is beyond her and that she has become hardened by her experience. But the motherless Xuela also attempts to repair her abiding sense of unlovability and rejection by worshiping and loving herself. "My own face was a comfort to me, my own body was a comfort to me, and no matter how swept away I would become by anyone or anything, in the end I allowed nothing to replace my own being in my own mind" (100).

The Defeat of Xuela's Stepfamily

Recognized by her father, who, in a letter, asks her to return home, Xuela suddenly finds herself weary of the life she has been leading, so she returns to her father's house even though she feels like an outsider. "I felt I did not want to belong to anyone, that since the one person I would have consented to own me had never lived to do so, I did not want to belong to anyone; I did not want anyone to belong to me"

(104). Even as Xuela insists that the defeated-looking woman with a swollen belly that she encounters on her journey back to her father's house is not symbolic of anything, the fact that she refers to the woman as martyr-like suggests that she sees in the woman an image of her own cast-off pregnant and defeated—and also shameful—identity. In the family drama that unfolds when Xuela returns to her father's house, the once-defeated and shamed Xuela witnesses the defeat and shaming of her family members in an enactment of a classic attack-other revenge script in which the humiliator is at long last humiliated.

Xuela's half brother, Alfred—who, like his father, bears the name of the English conqueror and king, Alfred the Great[13]—dies a gruesome, shameful death. Said to be suffering from yaws or to be possessed by an evil spirit, his sore-covered body becomes a "river of pus," and, recalling an incident from Kincaid's mother's family history, as he dies a large worm crawls out of his left leg (111).[14] After the loss of his son, Xuela's proud and powerful father feels "small again, insignificant, helpless against life" (111) while her stepmother feels as if she has died. "I felt sorry for her then," Xuela remarks, "but not enough to forgive and forget that she had once tried to make me dead also, and most certainly always wished me dead and would make me dead if she could ever bring herself alive enough to accomplish this" (112).

After the death of Alfred, Elizabeth, Xuela's half sister, is rejected by her father, who "had never really looked at her," and by her mother, who "could not look at her, for what a waste she was, she was the wrong one to be alive" (114). Aware that Elizabeth is devalued by her parents because of her sex, Xuela in part sympathizes with her, and when her half sister becomes pregnant, Xuela helps her end the pregnancy. Yet afterward, Elizabeth, rather than expressing gratitude toward Xuela, demonstrates her continuing contempt and disgust by spitting on the ground in front of Xuela and insulting her.

Elizabeth is a woman in love with herself, and yet "hers was not a self worth loving" (119). After having a bicycle accident while returning home from a secret meeting with her lover, she becomes a semi-invalid. When Elizabeth, some seven years later, marries her lover—a vain man Xuela has had sex with and found incapable of providing sexual pleasure—she remains "completely disfigured by the accident: her eyes were unable to focus properly, one leg was longer than the other, and she walked with a limp" (127). Becoming "more arrogant, she acquired a coarseness to her voice, her gaze became a hard stare, her figure grew wide and slow" (128). A deeply contemptuous woman, Elizabeth is, in turn, presented as an object of contempt by Xuela, who, as storyteller, assumes the power to humiliate the humiliator.

Philip and Roland

In her affairs with Philip and Roland, both married men, Xuela enacts power, not romance, scripts, as she seeks the satisfaction of her sexual needs, and as she assumes sexual dominion over Philip, the white man she eventually marries. Xuela also enacts power and contempt scripts with the wives of these men as she, in yet another version of the oedipal scenario, triumphs over not the kindly wife-mother figure embodied in Lise LaBatte but the hostile wife-mother. Presented as sexual, familial, and also political dramas of the colonizer/colonized and the powerful/powerless, Xuela's sexual relations repeat the victor/vanquished scenarios she has long enacted in her personal relationships.

In her "short, bitter sermonette" on the relationship between the white male colonizer and the African Caribbean colonized, Xuela inveighs against the man "proud of the pale hue of his skin" who, through no effort of his own, has been chosen for "special privilege in the hierarchy of everything" (138, 131). In contrast, African Caribbeans are a defeated people who have been "reduced to shadows" and, in internalizing the religious beliefs of the colonizer, are "walking in a trance, no longer in their right minds" (133). Contrary to the Christian hymn that refers to Jesus as both master and friend, Xuela insists that "a master cannot be a friend," for "a master is one thing and a friend is something else altogether, something completely different" (134). "I did not mind my defeat, I only minded that it had to last so long," Xuela remarks as she, in her relationship with Philip, the married doctor[15] and master/friend she works for, assumes sexual power over him (139).

If during their initial sexual encounter Xuela assumes the pose of the sexual slave—naked, she binds his belt around her wrists, raises her hands in the air, and stands with her chest against the wall—she also stage-manages their encounter. "I made him stand behind me, I made him lie on top of me, my face beneath his; I made him lie on top of me, my back beneath his chest" (154). A man who, like most men, is obsessed with sex even though he is not very good at it, Philip follows Xuela's directions, complying when she orders him to kneel before her and to eat until she is totally satisfied. "I did not mean peace to him (as he did not mean peace to me); I could not mean peace to him, it would have been dangerous for him if that had been so, the temptation to see him die I would have found overwhelming, I would not have been able to resist it" (155).

Not only does Xuela assume sexual power over Philip, but when she has sex with him she thinks of her black lover, Roland, who is the opposite of Philip. An unheroic man who does not have either a country or a history, Roland is "a small event in somebody else's history," but he also is "a man" (167). Though an "unpolished" man, Roland, who is a stevedore, carries himself as if he were "precious," and Xuela associates him with the landscape, finding herself attracted to Roland's mouth, which expands across his face "like an island"—a "dangerous" mouth that can "swallow things whole that were much larger than itself" (167, 177–78). But if Xuela wonders when she first gazes at Roland who will be the captive and who the captor in their relationship, she, inevitably, comes to see him as the defeated one. And in yet another replay of an oedipal scenario, Xuela also defeats Roland's wife.

Initially, Roland's wife appears "like a sentry—stern, dignified, guarding the noble idea, if not noble ideal, that was her husband" (170). An angry, contemptuous woman, Roland's wife is yet another replay of the contemptuous mother that haunts Kincaid's fiction, the mother who accuses her daughter of sluttish behavior. After verbally assaulting Xuela—calling her "a whore, a slut, a pig, a snake, a viper, a rat, a lowlife, a parasite, and an evil woman"—she slaps Xuela (171). When Xuela dismisses her adversary—"I consider it beneath me to fight over a man," Xuela says to her (172)—Roland's wife becomes so enraged that she grabs Xuela, renting her dress from neck to waist. Yet even as Roland's wife is attacking Xuela, Xuela notices that her adversary is barefoot: that is, she is one of the defeated. Unlike Roland's wife, who is intent on possessing her husband, Xuela chooses to possess herself. In describing the defeat of Roland's wife, Xuela emphasizes her own beauty and strength. "I looked delicate, but any man I held in my arms knew that I was strong. . . . My face was beautiful, I found it so" (174).

Xuela defies and defeats Roland's wife, and she also ends up seeing Roland as one of the defeated, for when she hears the long list of names Roland's wife has committed to memory—names of Roland's former lovers—she comes to view his life as one that has been "reduced to women." In describing her own strength, Xuela rehearses Roland's defeat. "[M]y legs were long and hard, as if they had been made to take me a long distance; my arms were long and strong, as if prepared for carrying heavy loads. I was in love with Roland. He was a man. But who was he really?" Even though he has not crossed oceans or had mountains or valleys named for him, he still wants something "beyond ordinary satisfaction—beyond one wife, one love . . . for it would all end only in death" (176). Although denying the "small uprisings within him," Roland at times is overcome with a "cold stillness," that is, a premonition of death. Unable to find words for what he is experiencing, he is "momentarily blinded with shame" (177).

Xuela's Defeat of Moira and Marriage to Philip

In yet another enactment of an oedipal scenario, Xuela, in her relationship with Philip, becomes the hidden rival of Philip's wife, Moira, who
is ultimately defeated. A proud and contemptuous woman, Moira is
"pleased to be of the English people, and that made sense, because it is
among the first tools you need to transgress against another human
being—to be very pleased with who you are" (156). Aware of the black
feeling of inferiority that comes through the shaming experience of being
"dissected under white eyes" (Fanon 116), Xuela, in turn, dissects
whites under black eyes. Transgressing against the transgressor, Xuela
views Moira, who likes her white skin and sees herself as a kind and
decent and graceful woman, as an object of contempt. To Xuela, Moira's
white skin is "waxy, ghostish, without life" (156). A thin and bony
woman who is given a "malicious quality" by the all-black, all-gray, or
all-white clothes she wears, Moira looks "like a vector, a vector of
malaise," and when Moira speaks in long sentences without saying anything, Xuela must resist the impulse to stop the annoying sound of
Moira's voice "with a swift blow" (157).

Returning white contempt with black countercontempt and dissecting whites under black eyes, Xuela describes how, to the African
Caribbeans, the English are viewed as "something other" and as "not
human." Xuela is aware of the "otherness" of Moira when she looks at
Moira's blue eyes set in her "bone-dry face"—features that confirm the
"ungenerous nature" of the English woman (158). "[S]he was a lady, I
was a woman, and this distinction for her was important; it allowed her
to believe that I would not associate the ordinary, the everyday—a
bowel movement, a cry of ecstasy—with her, and a small act of cruelty
was elevated to a rite of civilization" (158–59). To Xuela, "a lady is a
combination of elaborate fabrications, a collection of externals, facial
arrangements, and body parts, distortions, lies, and empty effort."
Xuela, in contrast, defines herself as a "woman," for she has two
breasts, a vagina, and a womb, and to her such a description "has at its
core the act of self-possession" (159).

Staging the defeat and death of the repressive mother-colonizer figure, Xuela remarks that Moira's life—and also the life of all who look
like Moira and Philip—is the "result of a great triumph, a life that no
one seems able to resist, dominion over others." But it also is "a life of
death . . . a living death, for each deed, good or bad, holds inside its self
its own reward, good or bad" (159–60). Finding an appropriate textual
punishment for Moira, the narrative describes her slow self-poisoning as
she drinks a tea that induces a sense of well-being and pleasurable hal-

lucinations, a state not unlike that induced by the pleasurable life of the colonizer. Before she dies a painful death, the white humiliator is humiliated, for Moira's skin turns black, the color of the people she despises. As an English woman, Moira believed that "with the arrival of her and her kind, life had reached such perfection that everything else, everything that was different from her, should just lie down and die" (208). Receiving her comeuppance, Moira, instead, lies down and dies in a classic turning-the-tables revenge drama.

"She died. I married her husband, but this is not to say that I took her place," Xuela remarks of her marriage to Philip, a man she does not love (160). "He loved me and then after that he longed for me and then after that he died" (206). In marrying a member of the conquering class, Xuela is placed in the superior position in the eyes of her half sister, Elizabeth. "That Philip was empty of real life and energy, used up, too tired even to give himself pleasure, that I did not love him, never occurred to her; it never occurred to her that my marriage represented a kind of tragedy, a kind of defeat" (211–12). If Xuela is one of the "vanquished" and "defeated," in her defeat lies the origins of her "great victory" and "great revenge" as she, in her marriage to one of the victors, acts for the defeated people of which she is part (215–16).

Xuela defeats Philip by using his love for her against him. Because Philip comes to love the sound of her footsteps and voice, she walks soundlessly and remains silent for days on end. "He worshipped me, he loved me; that I did not require these things only increased the feelings he had for me" (221). Even though Philip, a representative white colonizer, finds his colonizer's inheritance burdensome and has a sense of justice and even condemns himself, Xuela never forgets the past or forgives him for what he represents. When Philip attempts to create his own natural, and to Philip, beautiful, world through gardening, Xuela pointedly describes his gardening as an "act of conquest," and when he spends time rearranging his collection of books—white Western books on history, science, philosophy, and geography—she says that he is busying himself with "the dead" (143, 224).

Xuela is aware of Philip's suffering when she sees him standing alone at the edge of a cliff facing east toward England, the direction in which he asks to be buried. But she remains unmoved, refusing to "consider his entire being in such a way that would make his suffering real," and as his life grows "darker," and she sees him standing at the cliff's edge, she wants to "push him over, into the abyss, and not with deliberate anger but with a tap-tap, as if of recognition, as if of a friend, as if to say to him, You were not the great love of my life and so I understand you completely" (219, 227). A restless man who is unable to find peace,

Philip ends up feeling lost and dying alone. "I blocked his entrance to the world in which he lived; eventually I blocked his entrance into all the worlds he had come to know," Xuela comments, describing her defeat of the white conqueror. "He became all the children I did not allow to be born" (224).

The Death of the Father

Not long after Xuela marries Philip, her father dies. When her proud and wealthy father undergoes a prolonged and painful death, the suffering he endures "almost" makes Xuela "believe in justice, but only almost, for there are many wrongs that nothing can ever make right, the past in the world as I know it is irreversible" (209). Contesting her dying father's view of his life as "splendid," Xuela reiterates her charge against him: that he, acting the part of the conqueror, robbed others to amass his wealth. "He died a rich man and did not believe that this would prevent him from entering the gates of the place he called heaven," she pointedly remarks (210).

Death, to Xuela, is the ultimate—and commonly shared—humiliation and defeat. When her proud father dies, Xuela, as she looks down on his body, sees him as someone who can be looked down upon. "[S]eeing him dead, I felt superior, I felt superior in the fact that I was alive and he was dead, and even though I knew and believed that death was my fate also, I felt superior to him, as if such a humiliation, death, would never happen to me" (213). Xuela's description of the humiliation of her father in death points to the connection between shame and death. There is a "close affinity of shame and death," as Carl Schneider explains, not only because of the sense of exposure death brings, including the dying person's exposure to the curious and intrusive gaze of others, but also because of the "twin traits of which shame and death remind us—our limits and our vulnerability" (88, 84). "More fundamental . . . than the offense and stigma of particularly shameful deaths, or the degeneration . . . of the body, is the offense and shame of *death* itself" (83). Just as dying "becomes a kind of ontological shame," death can be experienced as "a humiliating defeat" (84, 87).

Yet another drama of victor and vanquished, the narrative stages the humiliating defeat and death of Xuela's father, a man of mixed-race origins who identifies with and mimics the white colonizer. As Xuela provides a scathing indictment of her father, Alfred, she retells and also extends her account of her father's personal history, seeking the familial and intergenerational roots of his identification with the victors. The colonizer-victor and exslave-vanquished meet in Alfred, who was fathered by John Richardson, a Scots *man*, and mothered by Mary, a woman of the African *people*. The distinction between *man* and *people* remains important to Alfred, who is aware that the African people "came off the boat as part of a horde, already demonized, mind blank to everything but human suffering," while the white man "came off the boat of his own volition, seeking to fulfill a destiny, a vision of himself he carried in his mind's eye" (181). Like the other sons of John Richardson, Alfred is proud to have his father's red hair, seemingly unaware of the misery his drunken father has left behind by having many children with a number of different women. If, according to the official family history, John Richardson was lost at sea, Xuela, as a retrospective storyteller, speculates that he might, in fact, have deliberately abandoned his Caribbean family and returned to Scotland.

In the mixed-race Alfred, the Scots *man* and African *people* meet. But Alfred, who looks more like the victors with his copper-colored skin, rejects the "complications of the vanquished," choosing instead "the ease of the victor" (186). He becomes a vain man in love with his appearance and an ambitious man who loves, not people, but money. And he comes "to despise all who behaved like the African people: not all who looked like them, only all who behaved like them, all who were defeated, doomed, conquered, poor, diseased, head bowed down, mind numbed from cruelty" (187). A man in whom there exists "at once victor and vanquished, perpetrator and victim," he proves himself "commonly human" in choosing the mantle of the victor, "for except for the saints who among us would not choose to be among the people with head held up, not head bowed down, and even the saints know that in the end of ends they will be among the ones with heads held up" (192).

Parental Loss as a Family Legacy

Xuela condemns her father as she describes his proud demeanor, yet she also imagines him as a boy who suffered from the loss of his father just as she suffered from the death of her mother. Admitting that she never truly knew him, she remarks that "this must be a point of shame for all children—it was for me—that this person who was one of the two sources of my own existence was unknown to me, not a mystery, just not known to me" (197).[16]

Extending her autobiographical awareness by looking back to her own origins, Xuela imagines her father's first sexual encounter with her unknown mother, one of the last survivors of an extinct people, the

Caribs, who lost not only "the right to be themselves" but also "themselves" (198). Repeating the refrain-like words of loss that haunt the narrative—"she died at the moment I was born"[17]—Xuela gives story to the unstoried life of her mother, finding the roots of her own unhappy life in her mother's life. Like Xuela, her mother suffered the trauma of maternal loss, for Xuela's mother was abandoned by her own mother and raised by French nuns. "The attachment, spiritual and physical, that a mother is said to have for her child, that confusion of who is who, flesh and flesh, that inseparableness which is said to exist between mother and child—all this was absent between my mother and her own mother. How to explain this abandonment, what child can understand it?" Xuela, who has been abandoned like her mother, connects her childhood loss of her mother to her adult refusal to have children. "[T]hat confusion of who is who, flesh and flesh, which was absent between my mother and her mother was also absent between my mother and myself, for she died at the moment I was born, and though I can sensibly say to myself such a thing cannot be helped—for who can help dying—again how can any child understand such a thing, so profound an abandonment? I have refused to bear any children" (199).

As Xuela imaginatively reconstructs the life of her mother, she, in effect, authors—and authorizes—her mother's story, which becomes part of Xuela's self-narration. Elaborating on the few facts she knows about her mother, she speculates on the joylessness of her mother's childhood spent with the nuns who raised her, and she imagines that the first time her father saw her mother, he was attracted to the beauty residing in her mother's "sadness, her weakness, her long-lost-ness, the crumbling of ancestral lines, her dejectedness, the false humility that was really defeat" (200). Xuela wonders what her mother thought when she first saw her father, thinking that perhaps he seemed like "yet another irresistible force" in her life or that possibly she loved him (201–02). As Xuela imagines the life of her mother, she feels "sad to know that such a life had to exist." After her mother died within a year of being married, her father is said to have suffered over this loss. "[P]eople say he was broken by this. . . . [B]ut people cannot say that because of his own suffering he identified with and had sympathy for the suffering of others; people cannot say that his loss made him generous, kindhearted, unwilling always to take advantage of others, that goodness in him grew and grew, completely overshadowing his faults, his defects; people cannot say these things, because they would not be true" (201).

As Xuela meditates on life's mysteries and reconstructs her own origins, situating her life in the lives of her parents, she does not gain a healing sense of continuity and connection, but, instead, a heightened awareness of the precariousness of life. "You are conceived; you are born: these things are true, how could they not be, but you don't know them. . . . You are a child and you find the world big and round and you have to find a place in it. How to do that is yet another mystery, and no one can tell you how exactly." Becoming a woman, "you put trust in the constancy of things" only to step into the yard one day and fall into a bottomless hole. "The mystery of the hole in the ground gives way to the mystery of your fall; just when you get used to falling and falling forever, you stop; and that stopping is yet another mystery, for why did you stop, there is not an answer to that any more than there is an answer to why you fell in the first place. Who you are is a mystery no one can answer, not even you. And why not, why not!" (202).

The Still Self of Death

As the seventy-year-old Xuela approaches the end of her narration, she focuses not only on the mystery of her own origins and that of her parents but also on the death of her parents and her own approaching death. She recalls her feeling of superiority when she stood over the body of her dead father but also her loneliness. "The two people from whom I had come were no more. I had allowed no one to come from me. A new feeling of loneliness overcame me then" (213). She comes to love her father "but only when he was dead, at that moment when he still looked like himself but a self that could no longer cause harm, only a still self, dead" (214). Once Xuela had feared the moment when she would be parentless and thus alone. But near the end of her life, she comes to accept her aloneness as an essential fact of life. "[A]t last a great peace came over me. . . . I was alone and I was not afraid, I accepted it the way I accepted all the things that were true of me: my two hands, my two eyes, my two feet, my two ears, all my senses, all that could be known about me, all that I did not know. That I was alone was now a true thing" (223).

"Who was I? My mother died at the moment I was born. . . . This fact of my mother dying at the moment I was born became a central motif of my life," Xuela remarks as she, near the end of her life, hears "the sound of much emptiness," a "soft rushing sound . . . waiting to envelop" her (225, 226). Having outlived her father, stepmother, half sister, half brother, and husband, Xuela, while being one of the vanquished and defeated, triumphs over others. Seemingly self-possessed and defiant to the end, she refuses to belong to a nation or a race or to have a child, a way to perpetuate the "crime" of racial and national identities (226). Yet she remains, in effect, a prisoner of her origins, still mourning at the end of her life her originary loss of her mother. Her autobiographical account, she insists, is as much about her mother's life as it is about her own life. "In me is the voice I never heard, the face I never saw, the being I came from. In me are the voices that should have come out of me, the faces I never allowed to form, the eyes I never allowed to see me. This account is an account of the person who was never allowed to be and an account of the person I did not allow myself to become" (227–28).

Stripping her life down to its bare essentials, the seventy-year-old Xuela focuses on her maternal origins and her inevitable end as she closes her account, looking beyond—or behind—the masks of cultural, racial, and national identities. "I long to meet the thing greater than I am, the thing to which I can submit," she remarks. "It is not in a book of history, it is not the work of anyone whose name can pass my own lips. Death is the only reality, for it is the only certainty, inevitable to all things" (228). If death is humiliation and defeat, it also is the only certainty in the ongoing struggle between victor and vanquished that has marked the troubled and tormented life of Kincaid's narrator: a motherless child and a woman who refuses to bear or mother any children of her own. Both an individual and also a representative voice—the voice of her lost mother and the voice of the defeated—Xuela breaks the long silence imposed on vanquished peoples. Yet behind her defiance and will to be heard echoes the primal sense of mourning and dread heard in the often-repeated refrain that begins her account: "My mother died at the moment I was born, and so for my whole life there was nothing standing between myself and eternity; at my back was always a bleak, black wind" (3). As Xuela voices her sense of loss and despair, she lays claim to the right to speak of her own bereavement and shame and sadness before her urgent and insistent voice is swallowed up by the bleak, black wind always blowing at her back.

A bitter and angry book that Kincaid says is "about a woman who could be my mother and so therefore could be me" (Brady), *The Autobiography of My Mother* exposes Kincaid's continuing anger toward her mother. Indeed, the maternal loss that haunts the novel—the death of Xuela's "good" mother—also points to Kincaid's relinquishing of the idealized "good" mother of *Annie John* and *Lucy* in her portrait of the bad and powerfully destructive mother who should never have had children. In an interesting and telling exchange, Kincaid, her mother, and her daughter were photographed in 1996 for a book of portraits—*Generations of Women: In Their Own Words*—which included a few words from each on their relationship. Describing her daughter-writer as her "support," the seventy-seven-year-old Annie Drew stated, "All of us get on nicely. Jamaica looks after us and we love her. Even if sometimes she may say one or two things that are fiction, I'm never vexed. As a writer, what she will write is just fiction." Speaking back to her mother, Kincaid provided a very different account of their relationship. "I have powerful feelings of despair, dislike, and even sometimes revulsion toward my mother," she remarked. "I don't know her really, and I don't know if she wanted any of us. She did some incredibly loving and intimate things, and then some things [that] were not acts of love at all" ("Portraits: Jamaica Kincaid" 20). Describing in an interview her mother's impact not only on her but also on her brothers, Kincaid commented, "I don't think anyone could destroy us as powerfully as she did" (Mehren).

Able through her writing to articulate things that her mother could not respond to, Kincaid, in *The Autobiography of My Mother*, talks and writes back to her mother, returning maternal contempt with daughterly countercontempt. An author whose writing "reconfigures the literary imperatives of intertextuality," Kincaid "rarely places her work in open dialogue with that of other authors, choosing instead to consistently mine and cross-reference her own texts," observes Louise Bernard. "It is in the taxonomic ordering of this self inventory and the connections that emerge between her fictional and nonfictional voices that Kincaid pushes against the boundaries of autobiography and memoir" (118). Just as Kincaid writes about herself in *The Autobiography of My Mother* even as she creates a fictional memoir of her mother, so in her next book, a memoir of her youngest brother Devon who died of AIDS in Antigua, Kincaid tells the story of the failed life she might have led if she had remained in Antigua under the influence of Annie Drew, a mother hated not only by her daughter but also, as we learn in *My Brother*, by her three sons.

❧ 7 ❧

"I Shall Never Forget Him Because His Life Is the One I Did Not Have"

Remembering Her Brother's Failed Life in *My Brother*

"This might have been me, dying young," Kincaid remarks of the death of her youngest brother, Devon Drew, who died of AIDS in Antigua at the age of thirty-three in January 1996. "I felt instinctively that of all the lives I might have had, this might have been me" (Mehren). Ostensibly a memoir describing the life and lingering death of Devon, *My Brother*, in describing Kincaid's identification with the failed life of her brother, continues to tell the story of Kincaid and her troubled relationship with her cruel and humiliating mother, Annie Drew. A book about personal and family memory, *My Brother*, published in 1997, not long after Devon's death, renders, in a frank and disturbing way, the story of Devon's death and Kincaid's recollections of her own early life in Antigua prompted by her return to visit her dying brother. Through its circling, repetitive, and digressive style, *My Brother* captures the obsessive, haunted quality of Kincaid's memory as she carries on her incessant inner dialogue with her mother. Yet even as Kincaid attempts to be brutally honest in her account, the digressive and circling style of *My Brother*—a style characteristic of the classic shame narrative—suggests some reluctance on her part to confront the humiliations of her Antiguan past.

In her remarks on *My Brother*, Kincaid insists on the importance of memory and the recollection of the "truth" about what happened in the past. Unlike her mother who "plays with memory" by remembering things the way they "did not happen" as a means of protecting herself from "all sorts of humiliations," Kincaid insists that "if something really happened, it *really happened*," and she also says that she wants "to try to live with" her "humiliations" (Goldfarb 98). When asked why she decided to go public with Devon's death from AIDS, Kincaid explained that to her "writing isn't a way of being public or private; it's just a way of being. The process is always full of pain, but I like that. It's a reality, and I just accept it as something not to be avoided. This is the life I have. This is the life I write about" (Snell). Kincaid, in her earlier fictional-autobiographical works, totally ignored or made only passing references to her three brothers, including Devon, the youngest, who was three when Kincaid left Antigua in 1965 at the age of sixteen, not to return for some twenty years. Yet when she became involved with Devon many years later, especially after his diagnosis with AIDS when he was thirty, she began to see his life in Antigua as the life she had escaped from many years before when she left Antigua—and her mother—and fashioned a life for herself in the United States. Her interest in him, as she came to see, derived in part from the fact that had circumstances been different, Devon's life "might have been" her life. "What distinguished my life from my brother's is that my mother didn't like me. When I became a woman, I seemed to repel her. I had to learn to fend for myself. I found a way to rescue myself" (Snell).

Kincaid's memoir of her brother's life and death, then, is also a self-narration, for in Devon's failed life she sees the life she might have lived had she remained in Antigua under the control of her tyrannical mother. As Kincaid records painful and humiliating memories of her personal past in *My Brother*, she also tells what she sees as the complex and brutal truth about her brother's reckless, wasted life and his painful and disfiguring illness. Indeed, she presents Devon's lingering death from AIDS as a shameful death by dwelling on his deteriorating body and his disgusting symptoms, including his offensive body odors, and by exposing his symptoms of physical degeneration to the curious, and intrusive, gaze of her reading public. Kincaid also condemns Devon for his thoughtless ingratitude. "You have to understand that helping my brother was the most thankless thing in the world," she states. "At the end of his life, he was a monster. If he could have brought us all with him, he would have" (Goldfarb 98).

Remarking that she has only ever written about members of her family, Kincaid comments that she has "never written about them so frankly" as she does in *My Brother* (Goldfarb 99), a book she felt compelled to write. Kincaid, who suffers from insomnia, recalls that she would start to write after 9:00 P.M. and write for hours, often "staggering up to bed" at 4:30 A.M., and that while she was writing the "words flowed out of her fingertips so quickly she sometimes couldn't type fast enough to keep up" (Mehren, Goldfarb 96). Asked whether Devon's lifetime silence about his homosexuality contributed to his tragedy and perhaps even cost him his life, Kincaid replied that to her the ability to speak and act freely and truthfully is almost like "a divine right," a "right to self-realization." Just as Devon would have been "scorned" as a homosexual in Antigua, causing him more "mental pain" than he could have endured, so Kincaid could not have been a writer had she stayed in Antigua. "[F]or me as a writer I think the mental, the verbal, the spiritual scorn from my community would have been more painful, in a way, than being stoned to death. There is something so deeply cruel about the place I am from" (Goldfarb 96).

A book that reads like an impassioned and painful self-conversation about her troubling memories and turbulent feelings about her family of origin, *My Brother* repeats, elaborates on, and continues the personal and emotional drama limned in Kincaid's novels as it tells the story of Kincaid's visits to Antigua during the final three years of Devon's life. Even though Kincaid was a successful and highly celebrated author when she visited her dying brother and was happy in the life she had built for herself in Vermont as a wife and mother, she remained plagued by humiliating memories of her Antiguan past and found herself frustrated and all but overwhelmed when she was in the presence of her still powerful, and powerfully contemptuous, mother. Unlike Devon, who had been taught by Annie Drew not to remember, Kincaid relentlessly remembers and records the past. "I always say, Do you remember?" (19), Kincaid remarks, describing how her family hates her memory, her ability to recall what others want to forget. "'What a memory you have!'" Annie Drew says of her daughter's unwelcome ability to recollect the past (6). For Kincaid's mother, "an old story is a bad story, a story with an ending she does not like" (25).

As Kincaid recalls her own Antiguan past, as well as unflattering fragments of Devon's past, in *My Brother*, she tells old bad stories as well as a new bad story: a noneulogistic story of her brother's life and death, and a story with an ending her mother would not like. "I can see clearly even now," Kincaid says of her mother, "the moment she turned on me with that razorlike ability to cut the ground out from beneath her children, and said I remembered too much ('You mine long, you know')" (75). Turning the quality her mother hates into a writerly asset—indeed into a source of writerly pride—Kincaid insists on remembering too much. In a classic turning-the-tables drama, Kincaid uses her own razorlike writer's ability against the mother who caused her such pain. The mother who attempted to consign Kincaid to a servant-like existence and who ridiculed her daughter's writerly aspirations is exposed yet again as a formidable and destructively cruel woman who, like Xuela in *The Autobiography of My Mother*, should have never had children.

Positioning the reader as a confidant—the recipient of family gossip and shameful family secrets—and also as a witness-listener, Kincaid asserts her own daughterly power in *My Brother* as she talks back to the mother in her brutally frank account of her relationship with her mother and also of Devon's wasted and wasteful life. Bound in classic emotional impasses—the shame-shame feeling trap (in which feelings of shame beget yet more shame in an endless cycle) and the shame-rage feeling trap (which involves an inevitable and self-perpetuating sequence of emotions from shame to humiliated fury back to shame)—Kincaid writes to settle old scores with her mother and also to make sense of her Antiguan past. In part trying to understand the mystery of Devon's life and death, Kincaid searches for meaning—the meaning of his life and her own—as she tells the story of his disease and death. "I shall never forget him because his life is the one I did not have, the life that, for reasons I hope shall never be too clear to me, I avoided or escaped" (176). Driven to write about Devon's dying in order to save herself, she states, "I became a writer out of desperation, so when I first heard my brother was dying I was familiar with the act of saving myself: I would write about him" (195–96). But she also confesses that she enjoys having the last word. "[T]hat is one of the reasons to outlive all the people who can have anything to say about you, not letting them have the last word," as she puts it (110–11). Once treated in a contemptuous way by her family, Kincaid in a sense has the "last word" in her ongoing quarrel with her mother as she creates not only an unsentimental but also in places an angry and contemptuous portrait of her Antiguan family.

"Falling into a Deep Hole": Kincaid's Troubled Return to Antigua

When Kincaid left Antigua shortly after she turned sixteen not to return for some twenty years, she attempted to put behind her the misery of her Antiguan childhood. Even though in her current American life in Vermont she is surrounded by a loving and supportive family, she still carries with her the acute pain attached to her humiliating memories of her troubled past. "[I]n a society like the one I am from, being a child is one of the definitions of vulnerability and powerlessness," she remarks, generalizing from her own childhood experiences (32). Antiguans, she insists, "are not an instinctively empathetic people; a circle of friends who love and support each other is not something I can recall from my childhood" (42). It is revealing that when she travels to Antigua to visit her dying brother, Kincaid fears that the plane will crash or "in some way not at all explainable" she will "never come back" to Vermont (92). For the adult Kincaid, returning to her Antiguan family means to risk falling once again into a deep hole, the deep hole of the shame-depression she experienced while growing up.

At Devon's bedside during her visits in his final three years, Kincaid misses her Vermont life. "I missed my children and my husband. I missed the life that I had come to know. When I was sitting with my brother, the life I had come to know was my past, a past that does not make me feel I am falling into a hole, a vapor of sadness swallowing me up" (23). Kincaid recalls that when she returned to Vermont after her first visit to Devon after his diagnosis, she continued to think and talk about him. "Whatever made me talk about him, whatever made me think of him, was not love, just something else, but not love; love being the thing I felt for my family, the one I have now, but not for him, or the people I am from, not love, but a powerful feeling all the same, only not love," she remarks. "My talk was full of pain, it was full of misery, it was full of anger, there was no peace to it, there was much sorrow, but there was no peace to it. How did I feel? I did not know how I felt. I was a combustion of feelings" (51).

In *My Brother*, as Kincaid ostensibly sets out to tell Devon's story and come to terms with her "combustion of feelings" about her Antiguan family, she continues and also elaborates on the personal story told in *Annie John* and *Lucy*, and, in part, in *The Autobiography of My Mother*. In incremental and repeated installments—a device that serves to entice reader interest by slowly divulging new information—she recalls her January 1986 visit to Antigua some twenty years after she left home and her mother's subsequent visit to her Vermont home in 1990, a visit that so traumatized Kincaid that she had to seek out psychiatric help after her mother left. As Kincaid reconstructs the early and intensely unhappy period of her Antiguan life after the birth of her brothers, she sets this against her adult relationship with Devon, who was three years old when she left Antigua, twenty-three when she saw him again in 1986, and thirty when he was diagnosed with AIDS. Yet even as Kincaid tells the story of her relationship with Devon, the story of her relationship with her mother inexorably seeps into her account, threatening to overtake her memoir of her brother as it has all but overtaken her life. Turning her razorlike writer's ability against her mother, Kincaid puts her mother's tyrannical character on display in *My Brother*, arraigning Annie Drew for mistreating and humiliating not only her daughter but also her three sons: Devon, the youngest, Dalma, the middle, and Joseph, the oldest son. In describing the relationship between the adult sons and their mother, Kincaid achieves a kind of delayed vindication, a brotherly acknowledgment of the rightness of her ongoing quarrel with her mother.

Kincaid, who is "so vulnerable" to her family's "needs and influence" that she removes herself from them at times, was in one of her periods of not speaking to her mother when one of her mother's friends called her in Vermont to tell her about Devon's illness. When she first learned that Devon was ill, Kincaid responded without her "usual deliberation" about having contact with her Antiguan family but at a great cost. "I felt I was falling into a deep hole, but I did not try to stop myself from falling. I felt myself being swallowed up in a large vapor of sadness, but I did not try to escape it" (20). As she does in *Annie John*, *Lucy*, and *The Autobiography of My Mother*, Kincaid associates her Antiguan family—and especially her mother—with deep-seated and abiding feelings of vulnerability, shame, and despair. And in *My Brother* Kincaid harks back to incidents already described in *Annie John* and *Lucy*, recalling, for example, how a six-year-old girl and Miss Charlotte died in her mother's arms (4–5); how, as a girl, she attended the funeral of a hunchback girl (182–83); how her once beautiful mother changed after the birth of Devon, becoming a bitter and quarrelsome woman (71); how she was sent to the United States to help out her family financially after her stepfather became ill, plunging the family into a disaster she did not create but was expected to help remedy (150); and how, when she wrote a despairing letter to her mother during her early days in New York City, her mother wrote back these words to her: "'It serves you right, you are always trying to do things you know you can't do'" (17).

Calling to mind the scene in *Annie John* in which Annie says "like mother like daughter" when her mother accuses her of behaving like a "slut," Kincaid remarks in *My Brother* on her illegitimacy. "[M]y mother and father were not married at the time I was conceived, my mother and father were never married at all," she states (140), admitting to a part of her family heritage that she experienced as shameful when she was growing up and that she would later elaborate on in her fictional memoir of her biological father, *Mr. Potter*. As the illegitimate daughter of a bitter and increasingly impoverished woman, Kincaid, by age fourteen, felt "already disappointed and already defeated, already hopeless, thinking and feeling that I was standing on a fragile edge and at any moment I might fall off into a narrow black hole that would amount to my entire earthly existence" (140–41). Recalling a scene in *Lucy*, Kincaid describes how, ten years after she had left Antigua, she learned of the death of her stepfather, David Drew, some three months after he had died and been buried. "My mother and I were in one of our periods of not speaking to each other, not on the telephone, not in letters. In the world I lived in then, my old family was dead to me," Kincaid remarks. "I did not speak of them, I spoke of my mother, but only to describe the terrible feelings I had toward her, the terrible feelings she had toward me, in tones of awe, as if they were exciting, all our feelings, as if ours had been a great love affair, something that was partly imaginary, something that was partly a fact; but the parts that were imaginary and the parts that were only facts were all true. She did not like me, I did not like her; I believe she wanted me dead, though not actually; I believe I wanted her dead, though not really" (118–19).

Unlike *Annie John* and, to a lesser extent *Lucy*, which elaborate on the daughter-characters' "great love affair" with the mother, *My Brother*, like *The Autobiography of My Mother*, dwells on Kincaid's intense hatred of and resentment toward her mother. In a relentless way, Kincaid puts her mother's arrogant, obstinate character on display as she describes her mother's contemptuous treatment of her sons and their response to her antagonistic personality. Annie Drew, Kincaid openly asserts, "hates her children" and is a "cruel" woman (154, 180). Kincaid also admits to her long hate-filled obsession with her mother. "I once did not see my mother for twenty years, even though I thought of her first thing in the morning and last thing at night, and almost all my thoughts of her were full of intense hatred" (154). "[Y]ou are a very bad mother to a child who is not dying or in jail," Kincaid thinks when she returns to Antigua to visit her dying brother, continuing to carry on her interminable inner dialogue with her mother (27). Kincaid does express admiration for the devoted way her mother cares for the sick Devon, remarking on how Annie Drew, during her hospital visits, bathes her son and feeds him the food she has prepared for him at home. "[T]his too is a true picture of my mother," Kincaid states (14). But she also asserts that her mother is capable of loving her children only when they are "weak and helpless and need her" and that she turns her love for her children "into a weapon for their destruction" (16–17, 53). To her mother, as Kincaid remarks, "her inferiors are her offspring," and were she to outlive her children—her inferiors—she would feel "regal, triumphant" (131).

As Kincaid tries to puzzle out the personal meaning of her childhood and adult relationship with her Antiguan family, she repeatedly refers to her dead stepfather as "the father of my brothers, who was a father to me, though at the same time not my father at all"; similarly, she refers, at times, to her mother as "our mother" or as "the mother of my brothers," explaining that when she is not talking to her mother,

Annie Drew "is someone else's mother, not mine" and that when Annie Drew is "our mother, she's another entity altogether" (149, 114, 89, 115). A hostile, contemptuous woman who subjects her adult sons to her "famous tongue-lashings," Annie Drew "protects and reserves her right to verbally humiliate her children" (53). Kincaid recalls that when she visited Antigua in 1986, she no longer got in her mother's way: "I had removed myself from getting in her way, I was in a position in my own life that did not allow for getting in my mother's way, she could not curse me, I no longer needed her" (115). But with her adult sons, Kincaid's mother continues to carry on her "small war of words" so that the middle son, Dalma, no longer speaks to his mother, and when forced to speak to her, "his voice is full of hatred and despair" (53, 54). Telling Kincaid that he is sorry he never understood before when she told him how "awful" Annie Drew had been to her, Dalma says that his mother is "evil," repeating this every time he talks to Kincaid "as if it is a new discovery to him" (54). Like Dalma, Devon, before he got sick, called his mother "Mrs. Drew," reverting to "Mother" and then his childhood nickname for her, "Muds," only in the extremities of his illness (116, 171).

If, during her 1986 visit, Kincaid ate the food cooked by her mother, when she returns during Devon's illness, she stops eating the food her mother cooks or accepting any food her mother offers her. "It was not a deliberate decision, it was not done in anger," Kincaid insists (116). Similarly, Devon in 1986, before his illness, stopped eating the food cooked by his mother just as Dalma, although he lives in the same house as his mother, has stopped speaking to her and eating the food she cooks. Reflecting on this behavior, Kincaid recalls how, when she was a child and "felt most close to and dependent on" her mother, she would not eat the food her mother cooked—a behavior she comes to see as "a sign of distancing" (118). Despite Kincaid's disclaimer, this refusal of Kincaid and her adult brothers to eat food prepared by Annie Drew also points to their intense and angry rejection of the rejecting mother, their attempt to psychically and defensively remove themselves from the powerful—and internalized—mother who threatens to overwhelm and consume them with her forceful personality and her verbally assaultive treatment of them. A woman who has a "powerful sense . . . of herself," Kincaid's mother might have altered "the shape of the world" in other circumstances (126, 127). Instead, she seems to have deformed her relationship with her adult children through her contemptuous treatment of them, openly quarreling with and cursing them and also, behind their backs, saying bad things about them to their siblings.

To be continually subjected to the verbal abuse of the contemptuous mother is to be deeply shamed and to fall into a deep hole of shame-depression, as Kincaid repeatedly shows in her fiction. The furious and shaming mother also provokes in Kincaid and her brothers a deep bitterness and a reactive shame-rage. Like Kincaid, who often quarrels with her mother and stops speaking to her, Dalma stops speaking to his mother while Devon becomes a person with "a nasty tongue when crossed" (13). And Joseph, the oldest brother, who once threw his mother to the ground, breaking her neck, directly acts out his anger in a story that Kincaid hints at early in her narrative and then elaborates on later as she actively tantalizes readers with this shameful family story. When Joseph, as Kincaid eventually explains, brought a girlfriend to the small structure where he lived, which was so close to his mother's house that she could overhear the couple, Annie Drew found their conversations and the sounds they made during sexual intercourse "an abomination." Kincaid, who takes offense at her mother's reaction, pointedly remarks, "[T]hat is the word for the feelings that roiled in her heart toward his actions, his wanting to live: abomination!" When Annie Drew first quarreled with and then threw stones at Joseph to express her disapproval—indeed her contempt-disgust, which she conveyed in her choice of words, "abomination"—he threw her to the ground in an attempt to stop her from stoning him. Despite her broken neck—"it was a break so serious that she should have died or become a quadriplegic"—Annie Drew recovered, ultimately living to bury her youngest son, Devon (189). Even as Kincaid tells this family story about Joseph and her mother, she hints that there is more to Joseph's story, remarking at one point that "his story is another big chapter and he, too, can neither speak it nor write it down" (81).

Assertively talking back, getting in the last word and telling old bad stories about her Antiguan family, the kind of stories her mother hates, Kincaid exposes her mother's contemptuous behavior to the public, returning maternal contempt with daughterly countercontempt. Becoming the daughterly antagonist of the antagonistic mother, Kincaid writes in part to settle old and fresh scores. But she also, more centrally, is determined to confront the ongoing hurts of her past and take stock of her life, which is starkly divided between her unhappy Antiguan past and her happy Vermont present, as she, in her driven way, inveighs against the mother who engaged in a lifelong campaign of humiliation against her inferiors: her children. That Annie Drew remains a formidable presence and, indeed, a lethal force in the life of her highly successful adult daughter points to the unresolved and unresolvable mother-daughter conflict that haunts Kincaid's work and life, and that continues, as we shall see in our discussion of *Mr. Potter*, even after the death of Annie Drew.

A Repressed Memory: The Burning of Kincaid's Books

As Kincaid looks to the past to understand its shaping influence on her present, she recounts her recovery of a repressed memory of her mother burning her beloved collection of books. That this memory concerns Kincaid's girlhood love of books and her creation of an idealized "bookish" world—a world her mother angrily and wantonly destroyed—points to the importance of the idealized world of books not only in Kincaid's ongoing self-narration but also in her self-fashioned writer's identity.

"Had my life stayed on the path where my mother had set it, the path of no university education, my brother would have been dead by now," Kincaid thinks when Annie Drew tells her that God will bless her for bringing Devon the AZT that prolongs his life. Remembering how her mother removed her from school before she was sixteen and before she was able to take a series of exams that might have set her on the path to a university education, Kincaid remarks, "There was no real reason for me to be removed from school, she just did it, removed me from school. My father was sick, she said, she needed me at home to help with the small children, she said" (74). To the adult Kincaid, her mother's action might have led her to the "same position" as that of her sick brother, Devon (75).

An oppressive, hostile force in the life of the adolescent Kincaid, Annie Drew actively thwarted her daughter's aspirations to pursue her education by removing her from school, and she also came to detest her daughter's reading habits. Kincaid's memory of reading a book while lying on Devon's bed during a trip to Antigua some ten years before he died provokes yet another memory that leads, inevitably, back to her troubled girlhood relation with her mother. "[T]his whole scene of me lying in bed and reading books would drive my mother to fits of anger, for she was sure it meant I was doomed to a life of slothfulness, but as it turned out, I was only doomed to write books other people might read" (44).

Expected to help care for her three brothers during her adolescence, Kincaid admits, "At thirteen, at fourteen, at fifteen, I did not like this, I did not like my mother's other children, I did not even like my mother then; I liked books, I liked reading books, I did not like anything else as much as I liked reading a book, a book of any kind" (128). When the fifteen-year-old Kincaid was left alone one day to watch Devon, she, instead of looking after him, became so absorbed in a book that she never noticed the sagging diaper of her two-year-old brother. Kincaid likens Annie Drew's fit of rage when she returned home and saw Devon's unchanged diaper to "a natural disaster, as if it had been a hurricane or an erupting volcano, or just simply the end of the world"

(132). Her mother's fury was "so fierce" that Kincaid thought her mother wanted her dead (131). In a halting passage full of digressions and parenthetical asides, Kincaid describes this pivotal shame event:

> [T]here was a moment when in a fury at me for not taking care of her mistakes (my brother with the lump of shit in his diapers, his father who was sick and could not properly support his family, who even when well had made a family that he could not properly support, her mistake in marrying a man so lacking, so lacking) she looked in every crevice of our yard, under our house, under my bed (for I did have such a thing and this was unusual, that in our family, poor, lacking a tradition of individual privacy and whether that is a good thing, whether all human beings should aspire to such a thing, privacy, their thoughts known only to them, to be debated and mulled over only by them, I do not know), and in all those places she found my books, the things that had come between me and the smooth flow of her life, her many children that she could not support, that she and her husband (the man not my own father) could not support, and in this fury, which she was conscious of then but cannot now remember, but which to her regret I can, she gathered all the books of mine she could find, and placing them on her stone heap (the one on which she bleached out the stains and smudges that had, in the ordinariness of life, appeared on our white clothes), she doused them with kerosene (oil from the kerosene lamp by the light of which I used to strain my eyes reading some of the books that I was about to lose) and then set fire to them. (133–34)

Afterward, Kincaid forgot the incident of her mother burning her books—the sole things she owned in her "then-emerging life"—only to remember it years later after her mother's 1990 visit to her Vermont home.[1] "I did not even remember that it happened at all, it had no place in the many horrible events that I could recite to friends, or the many horrible events that shaped and gave life to the thing I was to become, a writer" (134).[2] Discussing the book-burning incident in an interview, Kincaid remarks that "it must have been a source of enormous shame that made me suppress it, and when I remembered it and began to write about it, I found it very painful. But I wanted to write it. I almost feel that one's sources of humiliation should be immediately put on public display so they lose their power. Yes, it's a humiliating thing to admit, for *me* to acknowledge" (Goldfarb 98). Kincaid's difficulty in acknowledging her shame is revealed in her halting narration of this event, a form of narration often observed in the recovery of intensely shaming experiences in which the individual may struggle with the conflicting needs to "confess" and "retain" the shameful secret and in which the individual's recounting of the shaming event may contain "many pauses, repetitions, [and] false starts" (Goldberg 169, Helen Lewis, "Role of Shame" 44).

To Kincaid, books represented an idealized part of her identity. By immersing herself in the world of literature, she was able, at least temporarily, to remove herself from her family situation at a time when her family's "prospects," as she remarks, "were not more than the contents of my brother's diaper, and the contents were only shit" (131). When Annie Drew burned her daughter's books, Kincaid experienced this destructive act as an attack on—and an attempt to eradicate—her bookish, idealized identity. "Those books were my life," as Kincaid explains this scene in an interview. "I don't mean to overdramatize it, but it really did feel like an attempt at murder. My books were the only thing that connected me to a world apart from the cesspool I was in, and then they were just ashes. It felt murderous" (Goldfarb 98). That "[s]hame is a signal that the survival of one's personal identity is in jeopardy" (Goldberg 69) is evident in this governing scene of shame recounting Annie Drew's wanton destruction of the books Kincaid had used to try to repair her debilitating shame and escape from the "cesspool" of her Antiguan life by defensively separating her idealized (successful, loved) "bookish" self from her shamed (worthless, unloved) Antiguan identity.

By telling the bad old story of her mother's burning of her books in *My Brother*, Kincaid expresses her long-delayed fury at her mother's fury—a fury that Annie Drew "was conscious of then but cannot now remember, but which to her regret I can." Kincaid finds it necessary to "say the things" she is ashamed of because she cannot "bear to be subject to anything." "If you're ashamed of something, it holds you in its sway," she explains. "It can bring you to your knees" (Wachtel 64). By speaking openly of her mother's destructive fury and the "shit" of her family situation when she was growing up, Kincaid attempts to gain a sense of mastery over the pain and shame of her Antiguan past. Yet the fact that returning to Antigua to visit Devon after his AIDS diagnosis is like "falling into a deep hole" of shame and sadness reveals just how difficult it is for Kincaid to confront or attempt to work through her past.[3]

"Who Is He? How Does He Feel about Himself, What Has He Ever Wanted?": Reflecting on Devon's Wasted Life

Kincaid, as she tries to make sense of Devon's life and also his illness and dying, at once aestheticizes and provides disturbingly blunt descriptions of his failed life and diseased body. Attempting to invest his life with a kind of narrative pattern and literary meaning, she questions whether Devon's end was prefigured in his beginning. As she recalls how the infant Devon was attacked by red ants, she wonders "if it had any meaning that some small red things had almost killed him from the outside shortly after he was born and that now some small things were killing him from the inside." Adding that she does not "believe it has any meaning," she says that "this is only something a mind like mine would think about" (6). In a similar way, she tries to bind together past and present and to locate some narrative pattern and meaning in Devon's life story when she recalls how, during her 1986 visit to Antigua, she noticed the rotting roof of Devon's house. Using a well-known literary trope—the house/body metaphor—to add literary meaning to her account of Devon's physical deterioration, she remarks, "Looking up at the roof then, rotting in that drying-out way, did not suggest anything to me, certainly not that the present occupant of the house, my brother, might one day come to resemble the process of the decaying house, evaporating slowly, drying out slowly, dying and living, and in living looking as if he had died a very long time ago" (113).

Prompted by the book she is reading when she first learns that Devon is ill and then again when she is sitting next to him on the front lawn of the Antiguan hospital where he is being treated—Russell Page's *Education of a Gardener*—Kincaid thinks about Devon's love of plants and his life as a failed gardener, facts that she invests with symbolic meaning as she attempts to give narrative shape and metaphoric resonance to her brother's life story. Upon learning that her mother cut down the lemon tree that her sick brother had planted behind his small house in his mother's yard, Kincaid feels "pained" and "ashamed" at her mother's heedless act of eradication. "That lemon tree would have been one of the things left of his life. Nothing came from him; not work, not children, not love for someone else" (13). Rather than being like a "flowering," his life is "like the bud that sets but, instead of opening into a flower, turns brown and falls off at your feet" (163). When Kincaid notices that there are twelve banana plants behind Devon's house where once there was only one, she draws a connection between Devon's failed life as a gardener and the new and deadly life that has taken root within him. "Some of my brother's plants had borne fruit and were dying and were sending up new shoots. The plantsman in my brother will never be, and all the other things that he might have been in his life have died; but inside his body a death lives, flowering upon flowering, with a voraciousness that nothing seems able to satisfy and stop" (19–20).

Side by side with Kincaid's attempts to aestheticize and make a kind of narrative—and literary—sense out of Devon's life and illness are her jarringly graphic descriptions of his disease and her unsparingly honest accounts of the humiliations and failures of his wasted life. Just as Annie Drew tells "humiliating stories" about Devon (75), so Kincaid recounts over and over the "unspeakable things" he has done in his life (93–94) as she tells the kind of bad old family stories her mother detests. Explaining at one point that she has lived away from Antigua for so long that she is no longer able to readily understand the Antiguan Creole spoken by her brother, Kincaid admits that Devon sometimes laughs at her proper English, telling her that she "talk[s] funny" (8). But to Kincaid, the kind of English spoken by her brother "instantly reveals the humiliation of history, the humiliations of the past not remade into art" (108).[4] By occasionally placing the "funny" talk of Devon and her mother in parenthetical asides while providing readers with a standard English version of their speech, Kincaid subordinates Devon's and her mother's creolized speech—which to Kincaid is an inherently humiliating speech—to her own, allowing her, in effect, to talk back and indeed talk over her family as she gets in the last word.

"('Me hear you a come but me no tink you a com fo' true'),'" Devon says to Kincaid during her initial hospital visit after learning of his illness (9). Devon's condition when she first visits him in his dirty hospital room is dire: his mouth and tongue are covered with a white coat of thrush, and his lips are scarlet and covered in sores; he finds it difficult to eat and breathe; and he can barely sit up or walk. Kincaid is aware that in Antigua families are ashamed to publicly admit that a family member has AIDS—and indeed Devon, the Rastafarian seducer of women, is abandoned by his Rastafarian friends after his AIDS diagnosis—yet she announces to others this shameful family secret. Attending a lecture on AIDS given by Dr. Prince Ramsey at an AIDS workshop where she meets families of other AIDS victims, she is surprised to find "ordinary people in Antigua expressing sympathy and love for one another at a time of personal tragedy and pain, not scorn or rejection or some other form of cruelty" (37). In a similar way, she is surprised by the demeanor of Dr. Ramsey, who agrees to treat Devon, finding in the doctor what she "long ago thought impossible to find in an Antiguan with authority: he was kind, he was loving toward people who needed him, people who were less powerful than he; he was respectful" (32). Yet Kincaid's description of the slides Dr. Ramsey shows in his AIDS lecture serves to turn those suffering from sexually transmitted diseases into disgusting, grotesque spectacles. "The pictures were amazing. There were penises that looked like ladyfingers left in the oven too long and with a bite taken out of them that revealed a jam-filled center. There were labias covered with thick blue crusts, or black crusts, or crusts that were iridescent" (37).

During her visits to Devon in the final three years of his life, Kincaid struggles to understand him, repeatedly asking herself who he is, what he wants out of life, "what his life must be like for him," and how her own life would have turned out had she not been "so cold and ruthless" toward her family (68–69). When at one point the dying Devon asks Kincaid if he is the child referred to in *Lucy*'s account of the mother's repeated but failed attempts to abort her third and last male child—"('Ah me de trow'way pickney'[?])"—she insists that this abortion story is fictional, not factual. "[H]e did not tell me that he did not believe my reply and I did not tell him that he should not believe my reply," Kincaid states, confirming the truth of this novelistic account (174; see also *Lucy* 151). Unlike the Vermonters she knows, who like Kincaid are devoted "to the routine, the ordinariness of pure, hard work" (105), Devon, the throwaway child, ends up throwing away his life.

Some seven years before his diagnosis with AIDS, when Kincaid warned Devon of the need to protect himself during intercourse, he told her he would never get "such a stupid thing" as AIDS: "('Me no get dat chupidness, man')" (8). After he becomes ill, he tells Kincaid that he cannot believe he has AIDS: "('Me carn belieb me had dis chupidness')." To one of his brothers he admits that he has "made worthlessness of his life ('Me mek wutlessness ah me life, man')" (29). When the AZT Kincaid buys for Devon brings on a temporary remission of his symptoms, he tells her that he wants to change his life, and he expresses sorrow for the wastefulness of his life. Yet after he is released from the hospital, he continues to live recklessly, staying out all night on occasion, drinking beer, and seeing girls. Asked by an interviewer how she felt when she realized that her attempt to help Devon had given him an opportunity to infect others, Kincaid admitted that she "felt like an accomplice" and wondered whether she had assisted in "something murderous" (DeLombard). Adding to the complexity of Devon's story is the fact that he used his seemingly compulsive heterosexuality to cover his secret life as a homosexual, something Kincaid learned about her brother only after his death.

Stunned when the leader of the AIDS workshop suggests that she take Devon to the United States for treatment, Kincaid realizes that she cannot bring her brother—a "strange, careless person"—into the "hard-earned order" of her American life (49).[5] As Kincaid sifts through both her memories of Devon and the family stories she has heard about him, she divulges a series of scandalous episodes from his careless and unsuccessful life. Once an attractive and intelligent young man—when he was in school he took third place on an islandwide exam—Devon, despite his early promise, ends up doing "unspeakable things," things that Kincaid can "name to him" but that he cannot "name" to her (93). Involved in a crime when he was still in school in which someone was killed during the robbery of a gas station, Devon spent only a short period of time in jail because he served as a witness against the others who participated in the crime and also because Annie Drew was able to use her political connections to get him released. A man who "talked back too much," Devon lost his public works job after he insulted his supervisor during an argument: "('He cuss dem out')," as Kincaid's mother describes this incident (13). Becoming a drug user and a thief, Devon ends up stealing from his mother and brothers and would have stolen from Kincaid had her possessions not been "stored on a continent far away from where he lived" (93).

A dreamer not a doer, Devon daydreams of becoming a famous reggae singer. Using the facade of his hypersexual interest in women to cover his homosexuality, he claims that women take off their clothes when they hear him sing: "('Me nar joke, mahn, when me sing, gahl a take ahff she clothes')" (68). And he insists that he cannot go any longer than two weeks without having sex when, after the AZT causes a temporary remission of his symptoms, he engages in unprotected sex. "He was a brilliant boy, he was a brilliant man. Locked up inside him was someone who would have spoken to the world in an important way. I believe this," Kincaid asserts (59). Yet "[i]n his daydreams he became a famous singer, and women removed their clothes when they heard him sing" (60). "Who is he? I kept asking myself. Who is he? How does he feel about himself, what has he ever wanted? Girls to take off their clothes when they hear him sing? What could that mean? He doesn't make anything, no one depends on him, he is not a father to anyone, no one finds him indispensable. . . . This compulsion to express himself through his penis . . . is something I am not qualified to understand" (69–70).

Refusing to eulogize Devon or gloss over his faults or provide a sentimental account of his life, Kincaid, instead, records the humiliating facts of his failed life. Yet she also continues to try to make a kind of writerly sense out of his life. "But the feeling that his life with its metaphor of the bud of a flower firmly set, blooming, and then the blossom fading, the flower setting a seed which bore inside another set of buds, leading to flowers, and so on and so on into eternity—this feeling that his life actually should have provided such a metaphor, so ordinary an image, so common and so welcoming had it been just so, could not leave me" (167–68). Recalling Xuela's fascination with death in *The Autobiography of My Mother*, Kincaid also describes, in her compellingly frank way, her need to satisfy her own voyeuristic curiosity as she, after witnessing over the years Devon's physical suffering and prolonged dying, looks at the dead body of her brother and, Xuela-like, sees his death as a kind of humiliating defeat.

"The Indignity to Be Found in Death": Devon's Prolonged Dying and Death

"My brother died. I had expected him to, sometimes it seemed as if it would be a good thing if he were to just die. And then he did die," Kincaid remarks, recalling her confusion the moment she learned of Devon's death. "[W]hen that moment came, the moment I knew he was no longer alive, I didn't know what to think, I didn't know what to feel" (87). Kincaid, as she does in her account of her brother's wasted life, invests his prolonged dying and death with a kind of writerly meaning even as she describes her attempt to come to terms with her contradictory feelings about his death and recounts, in disturbingly graphic detail, the shameful indignities of his physical deterioration and death from AIDS, a disease that carries "a powerful social stigma" in Antigua (184). Only after her brother's death does Kincaid learn of his secret life as a homosexual, becoming aware of the sad "doubleness" of his life, his need to hide his "real self" to avoid being scorned by others (164, 165).

Determined to attach a larger meaning to Devon's death, Kincaid sees it as an individual instance of a universal—and elemental—human mystery. Devon, Kincaid remarks, was "living" in death: "Perhaps everyone is living in death, I actually do believe that, but usually it can't be seen; in his case it was a death I could see" (88). In the final stages of his disease, the AIDS-ravaged Devon exists in a liminal state. He can still speak and still breathes in and out, yet he is not "alive in a way" that Kincaid has ever seen before: he is "dead but still alive" (88, 95). "[T]o have the HIV virus is to have crossed the line between life and death. On one side, there is life, and the thin shadow of death hovers over it; and on the other, there is death with a small patch of life attached to it. This latter is the life of AIDS; this was how I saw my brother as he lay in his bed dying" (96). Kincaid tries to invest her brother's death with a universal meaning, but she also is unflinching in her account of the physical indignities of his prolonged dying. In a shameful moment of exposure, Devon shows Kincaid his penis. Recalling her earlier descriptions of the deadly flowering of his disease, Kincaid first aestheticizes but then provides a blunt account of what she sees. Devon's penis, she remarks, resembles "a bruised flower that had been cut short on the stem; it was covered with sores and on the sores was a white substance, almost creamy, almost floury, a fungus" (91).

As Devon's original symptoms return—his mouth becoming white from thrush, his lips red from fever, and his skin blackening—he hangs on to his halfway-life. "I mean he breathed and he spoke and he took in nourishment, and fluids of different textures would pass out of his anus, and these fluids did not have a fragrance, they had a smell" (150). In describing this offensive smell, Kincaid invokes the shaming discourse of dirt and defilement when she remarks that her mother's house, where Devon spends his final days, smells as if "some terrible dirty thing had gone unnoticed and was rotting away quietly" (90). A dirty, dissmelling object, the dying Devon is an object of shame. If death is often "veiled from public view" because it is "deeply vulnerable to shameful public intrusion and profaning violation" (C. Schneider 77), Kincaid unflinchingly reports the shameful facts surrounding the death of her brother, dwelling not only on Devon's deteriorating body and loss of control of his bodily functions but also on the disgusting odors he gives off.

Over time as Kincaid visits her dying brother, she distances herself from him, wishing she were not mixed up in his life and his dying. The last time she sees Devon alive—or, as she describes it, "dead really, but still breathing . . . his heart beating"—she realizes she is tired of him: "I was sick of him and wanted him to go away, and I didn't care if he got better and I didn't care if he died. . . . I only wanted him to do one or the other and then leave me alone" (107, 108). Quarreling with him during her last visit, she does not kiss or hug him goodbye or tell him that she loves him. "I did not feel strong, I felt anger, my anger was everything to me," she comments (108–09). Yet after his death, she remains haunted by the fact of his dying. "[E]ach time I remembered that he had died it was as if he had just at that moment died, and the whole experience of it would begin again; my brother had died, and I didn't love him" (148).

Writing of her trip to Antigua to attend Devon's funeral, Kincaid recalls how the airplane she flew on was blue as was the sky and the water surrounding Antigua. In her characteristic way, she tries to find some pattern or meaning in her memories only to insist that the color blue does not "run through all" her memories or experiences but instead, every scene and memory remains "itself, just itself, and sometimes a certain color might make memory more vivid and sometimes again, not so at all" (170). Curious to see what the dead Devon looks like, Kincaid asks the undertaker not to do anything to her brother's body before her arrival. "Only now . . . I wonder how I knew to say such a thing, for I am grateful (only because I would have wondered, been haunted about it, and so now my interest is satisfied, even as it raises another kind of interest, another haunting)" (177–78). His body placed in a good quality, zippered plastic bag, the dead Devon looks as if he has been "deliberately drained of all fluids, as if his flesh had been liquefied and that, too, drained out" (178). With his "wide-open" eyes and mouth, he seems to be looking at and screaming in response to "something horrifying coming toward him," his pauseless, silent scream "trailing off into eternity . . . or just trailing off into nothing" (179). In contrast, later, in his coffin with his eyes sewn shut and his mouth clamped shut, Devon looks "like an advertisement for the dead" (181). But with his seemingly fragile body "finally stilled," he also seems far away, "his farawayness so complete, so final, he shall never speak again" (190).

If, as Carl Schneider has observed, an "appropriate death is one with dignity," the dying person is also "deeply vulnerable to violation and to the degradation of his life," and death, itself, is often regarded as "an embarrassment and a humiliation" (79, 80, 87). In *My Brother*, as Kincaid focuses on the horrific symptoms of Devon's physical decline from AIDS, she exposes his shameful death to the voyeuristic gaze of her readers. In passages that recall Xuela's thoughts on death in *The Autobiography of My Mother*, Kincaid describes death as a humiliating defeat. A man who enjoyed laughing at other people's embarrassing mishaps, Devon, Kincaid insists, "would have found his death . . . funny, but only if it was happening to someone else" (180). When Kincaid and her family members look at Devon for the last time, before the coffin lid is closed, she is aware of "the indignity to be found in death" (182). In her description of the behavior of Antiguan onlookers at funerals, Kincaid generalizes from her own experiences growing up in Antigua. In her account, the suffering of the mourners evokes first pity in the onlookers and then a sense of their own superiority, "for to see someone suffer in a moment when you are not suffering can inspire such a feeling, superiority, in a place like Antigua, with its history of subjugation, leaving in its wake humiliation and inferiority; to see someone in straits worse than your own is to feel at first pity for them and soon better than them" (186).

As family members are called to take their last look at Devon, and as the coffin lid is being put in place, Kincaid is unable to summon up any tributes to her dead brother. Instead, she repeats and sums up the humiliating facts of his failed life. When Annie Drew comments that the body in the coffin does not look like Devon, Kincaid agrees with her mother but wonders to which Devon she is referring:

> Was it the baby a day old almost eaten alive by red ants, or was it the two-year-old boy who was left in my charge and whose diaper

I neglected to change as it became filled with his still-baby feces because I had become absorbed in a book; or was it the Devon who was involved in the homicide of a gas-station attendant; or the one who played cricket so well and learned to swim at Country Pond; or the one who smoked the Weed, the way she referred to his marijuana addiction; or the one who changed from a vibrant young man who had come down with a very bad case of pneumonia and then was told in an open hospital ward by a doctor accompanied by two nurses that he had the HIV virus and that shortly he would be dead?" (190–91)

Kincaid is annoyed, not comforted, when the minister, in his funeral sermon, promises that family members will be reunited in the afterlife. "I did not want to be with any of these people again in another world. I had had enough of them in this one." Yet she remains confused in her feelings about her family: "[T]hey mean everything to me and they mean nothing, and even so, I do not really know what I mean when I say this" (194). On a book tour in Chicago a week after the funeral, she experiences feelings of unexpected pain and loss. "[S]omeone I did not know I loved had died, someone I did not want to love had died, and that dying had a closed-door quality to it, a falling-off-the-horizon quality to it, the end, an end" (156). To be left behind is to experience the shock of death: "Why is it so new, why is this worn-out thing, death, someone dying, so new, so new?" (193).

Writing about Devon's Death to Save Herself

"What I am writing now is not a journal; a journal is a daily account, an immediate account. . . . For a long time after my brother died I could not write about him, I could not think about him in a purposeful way. It was really a short time between the time that he became sick and the time he died, but that time became a world," Kincaid states (91–92). When she returned to Antigua over a period of three years to visit her dying brother, Kincaid was forced to confront her painful memories of her Antiguan past. *My Brother* continues the autobiographical project begun in *Annie John*, *Lucy*, and *The Autobiography of My Mother* as it describes the horrible emotional aftereffects of Kincaid's humiliating and ruinous girlhood. As Kincaid records her thoughts about Devon's dying, trying to make a kind of writerly sense out of his life and death, she also recounts her angry and confused memories of her family, especially of her mother, intent on venting her complaints against her family and having the last word in her ongoing quarrel with her mother. Fueled by anger, Kincaid rails against her mother—the mother who once rashly burned her daughter's books—and she chides her mother for once preferring her growing sons over her adolescent daughter. Kincaid writes out of anger, but she also writes to understand herself, seeing in Devon's failed life the life she avoided or escaped. Remarking that she "just knew instinctively" that Devon's life was "parallel" to her own life, Kincaid explains, "We were both dreamers, both lived in our heads. I thought, 'This could be me'" (J. Kaufman). "I don't write about my family," she insists. "I write about myself" (Brady).

Unable to pay homage to her dead brother, who lived carelessly and left behind no lasting legacy, Kincaid instead honors the memory of her dead father-in-law, William Shawn, who, when he was editor of *The New Yorker*, discovered Kincaid's talent and continued to believe in her writing over the years after she married his son. One way she became a writer, she remarks, was by telling William Shawn things that he did not want to know about yet "was so curious about that he would listen to them anyway" (180). William Shawn was the ideal reader she wrote for over the years, for when she thought about writing something, she thought of Shawn reading it, and this made her "want to write it more" (196). Even after his death—Shawn died in 1992 at the age of eighty-five—Kincaid continues to draw strength from and take solace in Shawn's healing personality. If when she was writing about Devon's death she thought she would never again write for Shawn, she comes to recognize his continuing influence on her writing life. "The perfect reader has died, but I cannot see any reason not to write for him anyway, for I can sooner get used to never hearing from him—the perfect reader—than to not being able to write for him at all" (198).

In *My Brother* "Kincaid's elegiac self-positioning as a writer caught in a felt tension between her black Antiguan brother and her white North American father-in-law is sculpted around the quest for life in the shadow of death," remarks Sandra Paquet. "Writing and life are one and the same impulse; writing keeps death at bay" (245). Just as Kincaid wrote to save her life when she was younger, so she is compelled to write about Devon's dying, as she states in *My Brother*, so that she will not "die with him" (196). Through her writing she also seeks solace as she attempts to undo the hurts of the past and recover the books her mother burned by writing them "again and again" until they become "perfect, unscathed by fire" (198). As Kincaid tries to bring back into her life the bookish, idealized world contained in all the books her mother burned, she seeks to redeem her own idealized bookish identity, unscathed by the fires of maternal shaming and contempt. "I love working," Kincaid asserts. "I think working is the most spiritual thing in the world. . . . No one can change your idea of yourself if you've worked for what you have. I really do think work does set you free" (Shen). Kincaid writes for William Shawn, her ideal reader, and she also writes for herself. "I consider myself the reader I am writing for, and it is to make sense of something, even if to repeat to myself what has happened" (Holmstrom).

When Kincaid originally changed her name from Elaine Potter Richardson to Jamaica Kincaid, she was driven by her desire to hide her despised Antiguan identity, for she was afraid that she would fail as a writer and that her family, especially her mother, would laugh at her. Instead, she has achieved a kind of daughterly vindication as the hugely successful writer, Jamaica Kincaid. Taking pride in her writer's identity and her work, Kincaid is freed, at least temporarily, from the humiliating memories that haunt her even as she repeats to herself in her writing the "truth" of what has happened and tries, and tries yet again, to make a kind of writerly sense out of her shameful past. Kincaid, who understands that "identity, or a sense of self, is constructed by and through narrative" (N. King 2), will continue with her ongoing process of self-narration in *Mr. Potter*. Resuming her role as family historian in *Mr. Potter*, Kincaid, as we shall see in the next chapter, will once again tell the kind of bad old stories disliked by Annie Drew as she narrates the stories of Roderick Potter, her biological father, and of Elaine Cynthia Potter, her own cast-off identity as the illegitimate daughter of Mr. Potter.

❧ 8 ❧

"Like Him and His Own Father before Him, I Have a Line Drawn through Me"

Imagining the Life of the Absent Father in *Mr. Potter*

"How do I write? Why do I write? What do I write? This is what I am writing: I am writing 'Mr. Potter.' It begins in this way; this is its first sentence: 'Mr. Potter was my father, my father's name was Mr. Potter.' So much went into that one sentence; much happened before I settled on those 11 words" ("Those Words"). So Kincaid writes in a June 1999 *New York Times* "Writers on Writing" essay as she remarks on the difficult beginnings—the "many days of this and that and back and forth"—of what would eventually become *Mr. Potter*, her fictional memoir of her biological father, Roderick Nathaniel Potter. She describes her attempt to conjure up Mr. Potter's life—"He is a young man, and I am not yet born. Oh, I believe I am seeing him as a little boy"—only to find that his life remains "frozen in the vault that was his name and the vault of being only my father." As Kincaid goes about her domestic and daily routines, she continues to think about Mr. Potter, who, finally, one day is "driving a motorcar and dressing in a way imitative of men who had enormous amounts of money," but that day of writing comes with a cost, leaving Kincaid "bereft and exhausted and feeling empty" ("Those Words"). If in her description of the writing process, Kincaid seems to will Mr. Potter into a kind of imaginative and literary existence—"I look at Mr. Potter, in my own way, a way I am imagining, a way that is most certainly true and real" ("Those Words")—her essay also points to the reluctant and halting beginnings of her 2002 novel, which deals with the absent yet everpresent father

and the missing yet everpresent part of her identity: "Elaine Cynthia Potter," the daughter-narrator of *Mr. Potter*, who can readily be identified with Kincaid as she continues her ongoing process of autobiographical-fictional self-representation.

"[H]e is dead and beyond reading and writing and beyond contesting my authority to render him in my own image," Kincaid remarks in *Mr. Potter* (193), which refers not only to the death of her biological father in 1992 at the age of seventy but also to the death of her mother, Annie Drew, who died in 1999 at the age of eighty. Commenting that although the book is about her "real father," it is "not a biography," she recalls, "I didn't know him at all.[1] I only had his birth certificate, death certificate, and his parents' death certificates" *(Essence)*. But she also acknowledges her use of her family history in *Mr. Potter*, explaining, "I have always used the facts of autobiography and manipulated them with language so they are transformed into something else" (Heer). "Always I'm writing about these actual people in my past. I don't write about them to know them in any biographical way. I like to think of them in some sort of existential way" (Walker).

Even though Mr. Potter and the daughter-narrator have an "intimate connection," as Kincaid remarks, Mr. Potter is nevertheless "only a spectre"[2] in the narrator's life. Because Mr. Potter is "oral, not literate," Kincaid deliberately draws on the language of oral culture to create his world. "His world had to be made of the very thing he couldn't do, read or write. I make a world by repeating things, using bricks of language. A great deal of my imagination came about by reading things that were originally meant to be oral, such as the Bible, Homer and myths. When I was writing, I was tapping into more of the sources that formed me than any other writing I had done" (Heer). Kincaid also associates the style of *Mr. Potter*, which is heavily repetitive both in its verbal patterns and in its telling and retelling of Mr. Potter's story, with her mother's storytelling when she was growing up in Antigua. "My mother would tell me stories about herself, about me being born, about her family. That's the voice I heard, primarily. The stories she told me she told me again and again" (Heer). In her fictional memoir of her biological father, Kincaid repeats over and over something her mother said of him—that "A line runs through him," which as a girl Kincaid understood "as a curse, that he was a bad man and on top of that he was doomed" (101).

Unlike her mother, who is overpresent in her life—and memories—her father is an absence. Yet, as Kincaid's daughter-narrator remarks, "My father's absence will forever hang over my present and my present, at any given moment, will echo his absence" (192). By imagining and writing the life of her absent father, she can make him "whole and complete" and break the "silence" of the illiterate chauffeur who never "had a voice to begin with" (193, 189). Giving an oral quality to her account through her progressive and constantly repeated but also interrupted telling of Mr. Potter's story, Kincaid exposes the shameful story of her illegitimacy,[3] a heritage passed down through the paternal line. Even as Kincaid writes about her biological father in *Mr. Potter*, she also writes back to her mother. Asked how the "idea" of the novel came to her, Kincaid explained, "It came to me in thinking about my mother. The more I thought of her life, and how it was that I grew up without knowing this person that she loathed and who was my father, the more I wanted to write this book. Here was a person she absolutely detested. She never introduced me to him and he never had any interest in me" (McLarin). If in part Kincaid attempts to talk back to her mother and reverse Mr. Potter's curse—the curse of illegitimacy that he, in turn, passed down to Kincaid—she nevertheless speaks in her mother's voice as she expresses her resentment toward and contempt for her absentee father. Kincaid also re-creates the haunted world of obsessive memory in *Mr. Potter* through the refrain-like and often-repeated words of shame that come to echo in the daughter-narrator's memory and in her narrative—"I have a line drawn through me."

Recalling her characterization of Antiguans in *A Small Place* as small-minded people living small lives in a small place, Kincaid highlights the wholly unimaginative and circumscribed life of her biological father. A descendent of African slaves and a mixed-race man on whose face is written "'Africa' and 'Europe,'" Mr. Potter is "not unfamiliar with upheavals and displacements and murder and terror," for his existence in Antigua "had been made possible by such things, but he did not dwell on them and he could not dwell on them any more than he could dwell on breathing" (11, 7). In *Mr. Potter*, as she does in *My Brother*, Kincaid associates the Creole speech of Mr. Potter with a history of humiliation. When Mr. Potter says, "'Me name Potter, Potter me name,'" his voice is "so full of all that had gone wrong in the world for almost five hundred years that it could break the heart of an ordinary stone" (23). To Mr. Shoul, the Middle Eastern owner of the taxi business where Mr. Potter works, Mr. Potter is without importance, and to Dr. Weizenger, a Czechoslovakian doctor[4] who is one of Mr. Potter's passengers, Mr. Potter is a physically repulsive and worthless human being. Kincaid's daughter-narrator is sympathetic to the historical and social plight of Mr. Potter as a representative black Antiguan, but she also harshly criticizes him for his small-mindedness and narcissism: "[E]vents great or small did not enter his mind, nothing entered his mind, his mind was already filled up with Mr. Potter" (27).

Because Mr. Potter cannot read or write, he cannot "understand himself" or "make himself known to others" or "know himself" (21). "I think to be able to read is to make a crucial separation between yourself and the world," Kincaid states. The ability to read and write "is not just about some UN standard of literacy. It's really symbolic of the ability to know yourself, to separate the different parts of yourself so that you can speak to the world and yourself" (Heer). Literacy fosters the ability to separate from the world and also to appreciate its beauty, Kincaid suggests in *Mr. Potter* as she, using romanticized, literary speech, describes the quality of light in Antigua, where the sunlight is "so bright that it eventually made everything that came in contact with it transparent and then translucent" (19). If to the prosaic Mr. Potter the sun merely shines down in its "usual way," to the daughter-narrator the Antiguan sunlight is "the very definition of light . . . light that was itself and also a metaphor for all other aspiring forms of brightness" (16). When Mr. Potter is suddenly thrilled by the light—("'E ah make me trimble up inside, 'e ah make me feel funny)"—the daughter-narrator voices thoughts and feelings that her illiterate father is incapable of feeling or expressing: "[T]he light was substance itself and the light gave substance to everything else: the trees became the trees but only more so, and the ground in which they anchored themselves remained the ground but only more so, and the sky above revealed more and more of the sky and into the heavens, into eternity, and then returned to the earth" (19, 20). Mr. Potter sees the world "in that special light," but he does not think "This is Happiness itself," for he is not "separated from himself," and as he clearly sees the world and all that is in it, words fail the illiterate taxi driver (21).

Rendered by Kincaid as inarticulate—indeed, his most common expression is a series of "Eh, eh!" sounds—Mr. Potter lacks the capacity for deep thought or an emotional or aesthetic response to his Antiguan surroundings. Instead, as he drives his taxi, he is "almost in a stupor": "Mr. Potter drove along and nothing crossed his mind and the world was blank and the world remained blank" (34). An uninviting, if not unlikely, subject for a fictional memoir, Mr. Potter is presented as someone living a vacuous life-in-the-present. He lacks not only a historical and autobiographical awareness—a sense of family history and of the causal links between his childhood and adult selves—but also an interior life. Presenting her father's unstoried life as a story, Kincaid connects his past to his present and adds narrative, indeed novelistic, dimension to his empty, barren life. The absent father, thus, is given a kind of narrative presence as he is authored—and authorized by—the daughter-writer who preserves family history and transforms it into literature.

Yet even as Kincaid uses her writing to aestheticize and give a kind of verbal substance to her biological father—and to her life in his—she also vents her anger as she exposes the shameful secret of her illegitimacy. As she, in effect, elevates the life of Mr. Potter by writing his life story, she also asserts her verbal authority over him, using her writing to settle old scores against her absentee father, a shallow, unloving man who abandoned Kincaid's mother when she was seven months pregnant and rejected his daughter. Once treated in a contemptuous way by Mr. Potter, who refused to acknowledge his daughter's existence and turned his back on his four-year-old daughter the one time she approached him, ironically enough, to ask for money so she could buy writing paper, Kincaid returns paternal contempt with her own daughterly countercontempt in *Mr. Potter*.

The daughter-writer, Kincaid talks and writes back to her biological father as she continues her autobiographical project of writing stories about her family—the story of Annie Drew in *The Autobiography of My Mother*, of Devon Drew in *My Brother*, and of Roderick Nathaniel Potter in *Mr. Potter*—as a way to come to terms with her own painful Antiguan past. In *Mr. Potter*, as Kincaid ruminates over the past in her inner dialogue with her parents, she also brings into a kind of self-dialogue the two parts of her identity: that of "Elaine Cynthia Potter," the illegitimate, and thereby shamed and powerless, daughter, and "Jamaica Kincaid," the successful and powerful author. The split between "Elaine Cynthia Potter" and "Jamaica Kincaid" also looks back to Kincaid's beginnings as a writer in New York City. As Kincaid recalls her early days in New York, she comments that reading and writing gave her a "sense of self" and "self-possession," allowing her to reflect on her situation and "put into words" who she was and making her realize that she did not want to be Elaine, the powerless girl sent by her parents to the United States to work as an au pair "at their will" (Deziel). Attempting to artistically repair the rift in her identity and write over the line drawn through her, Kincaid works to give a kind of artistic and bookish legitimacy to her shameful, discarded identity as "Elaine Cynthia Potter," the illegitimate daughter of Mr. Potter who grew up with a "line drawn through" her.

Mr. Potter's Family Legacy

Explaining that she refers to her biological father as "Mr. Potter" because that is the name she "came to know him by," Kincaid's narrator slowly tells the story of Roderick Potter, a simple, unquestioning man who "did not long to know of all the Potters that he came from and how it came to be so that he came from them," and who "did not seek to interrogate the past to give meaning to the present and the future" (87, 25). The son of Nathaniel Potter, a fisherman, and Elfrida Robinson, who committed suicide by walking into the sea when her son was five years old, Mr. Potter is afraid of and hates the sea, which to him is "so much water . . . so much nothing" (12). While Mr. Potter is unaware of the cause of his hatred of the sea, readers are able to make sense of this feeling as they piece together his family history, which Kincaid places against the larger backdrop of the African diaspora.

Elaborating on a story she tells in *Annie John*,[5] Kincaid recounts the history of the narrator's grandfather, Nathaniel Potter, who, like his son, Roderick, is illiterate and unreflective: "Who am I? never entered into his thoughts . . . and Nathaniel could not read and he could not write" (57). While Nathaniel was taught by his fisherman father how to construct a fishing boat and make and mend fishing nets, he does not understand that his father was a shaping force in his life, and he cannot "give an account of himself, not even one that began with 'I was born'" (42). Unable to read or write, he is an unreflective, storyless, historyless man. "He was so much a part of the glory of the world and he could not see himself. Naked at all times, no matter what covered his body, that was Nathaniel Potter. The sun fell into the black before him; the moon rose up from the black behind him: and in between was history, all that had happened, and at its end was a man named Nathaniel Potter and who was only that, Nathaniel Potter. And he asked himself . . . What? He asked himself, not a thing" (42–43). Unloved and therefore unloving, Nathaniel does not "miss love, for it had never been part of his very being" (43).

Nathaniel's fisherman's life, which depends on the sea's bounty, becomes uncertain and indecipherable when, suddenly and inexplicably, his fish pots and fishnets come up empty day after day. Expressing his anger at what he perceives as a God-decreed fate, Nathaniel curses God and, in an irreverent act of defiance, removes his trousers, faces his bare buttocks to the sky, and angrily asks God to kiss his ass. Intoning biblical cadences and speech to describe the biblical-obeah curse that befalls the fisherman, the narrator tells of his gruesome death at the age of forty-seven in passages that recall Kincaid's earlier account in *My Brother* of the transformation of Devon's AIDS-ravaged body into a disgusting and dissmelling object. "[A] curse fell on Nathaniel Potter and this curse took the form of small boils appearing on his arms and then on his legs and then on the rest of his body and then at last covering his face. And the small boils festered and leaked a pus that had a smell like nothing that had ever lived before and all his bodily fluids were turned into the pus that leaked out of him. . . . And when he died, his body had blackened, as if he had been trapped in the harshest of fires" (47).

Nathaniel leaves behind twenty-one children—although he knows of only eleven children that he has fathered with eight different women—and not one of his children, including Roderick, can read or write. In a self-referential aside that directs attention to the daughter-narrator's—and by extension, Kincaid's—presence in the text, the narrator remarks of her grandfather, "I can read and I am also writing all of this at this very moment; at this very moment I am thinking of Nathaniel Potter and I can place my thoughts about him and all that he was and all that he could have been into words. These are all words, all of them, these words are my own" (48). The ability to "place" her thoughts in words gives Kincaid's narrator the power and authority to have the last word about the substance and meaning—or lack of meaning—of Nathaniel's life expressed in his imagined final words. "A very long 'Oooooohhhhh!!!' sighed Nathaniel Potter just before he died and many times before that and it was his only legacy to all his children and all who would come from them: this sound of helplessness combined with despair: 'Oooooohhhhh,' they all cried and cry, all who came from Nathaniel Potter" (57).

The only child of Elfrida Robinson, Roderick Nathaniel Potter is born in a one-room house in the village of English Harbour in 1922. "And Mr. Potter was not an original man, he was not made from words, his father was Nathaniel and his mother was Elfrida and neither of them could read or write; his beginning was just the way of everyone, as would be his end" (55–56). No one cares about his birth; his appearance does not make "the world pause," and he is "held with contempt" by the midwife (61, 63). One of "the despised," Mr. Potter is brought safely into the world, wrapped in a blanket, and placed next to his sixteen-year-old mother on a bed of clean rags. "[B]ut to what end? To no end at all" (67).

Yet another example of the unloving, rejecting mother that haunts Kincaid's narratives, Elfrida, after caring for Roderick for the first week of his life, tires of him and longs to rid herself of him. Leaving him alone on a bed of rags, she can hear him crying when he is hungry or lonely "and sometimes her heart broke in two when she heard his cries and sometimes her heart hardened. . . . And her breasts became parched, barren of her milky fluids (she had willed them so)" (69). An unloving mother, Elfrida is a motherless girl, as was her mother and her mother's mother, a condition reaching back to 1492—Elfrida's motherless condition, like Xuela's in *The Autobiography of My Mother*, standing as a metaphor for the African diaspora and loss of the African motherland. Passing on this legacy to her son, Elfrida, in 1927, gives away the five-year-old Roderick and then, on an ordinary day, walks into the sea, which takes her in "not with love, not with indifference, not with meaning of any kind" (76). To Roderick, who cannot recall his mother's face or name, his dead mother becomes associated with a blank space of darkness and light. Although Elfrida was a woman of no account, Kincaid's narrator cannot forget that she was the mother of her biological father, and although Elfrida was soon forgotten by Nathaniel and her son and others who knew her or knew of her, Kincaid's narrator now thinks of her.

A motherless and fatherless child handed over to people who do not care for him—the Shepherds—Roderick is a familiar Kincaidian figure: the humiliated and vulnerable child. If in rare moments of childhood playfulness he is "in harmony with his joy and is himself," he also is one of the "ordinarily degraded" (80). Calling attention to her imaginative attempt to conjure up the childhood of Roderick and give his empty life narrative dimension, the narrator directs readers to envision the hardships he endures: "See the small boy, Roderick Nathaniel Potter, asleep on a bed of old and dirty rags. . . . See the small boy, so tired, so hungry, before he falls asleep" (78). Left with Mr. Shepherd, the headmaster of the Shepherd school for wayward boys who finds the poor, hungry, and dirty boys in his school hateful—"their misfortune was a curse and to be cursed was deserving of hatred"—Roderick grows "dull and ugly, in the way of the forgotten" (96, 88).

Roderick Potter takes in Mr. Shepherd's "cruelty and ugliness with silence or indifference," and "all of it—cruelty, ugliness, silence, indifference"—becomes "a skin"; similarly, his mother's abandonment of him and his father's lack of fatherly feelings for him become "a skin," a "protective covering" without which he cannot live (93). Growing up in Mr. Shepherd's household, he is "despised for his vulnerability (his mother had abandoned him and had chosen the cold, vast vault that was the sea), held in contempt (for he could not protect himself, he could not protest when he was too tired to do one more thing that was required of him)" (94–95). Left "all alone in the world with nothing but a line drawn through him," Mr. Potter stands "before nothing, only Mr. Shepherd, the man who had been consigned to oversee his degradation in the world confirmed" (102). Despite his mistreatment at the hands of Mr. Shepherd, Roderick comes to identify with the vain and insensitive headmaster, who passes on to his charge not only "the love of contempt for all that was vulnerable and weak and in need and lost and in pain" but also a "love of self" coupled with "the love of appearing before people well dressed" (103–04).

Roderick Potter and Annie Victoria Richardson

"I was weak and vulnerable, not yet even a person, only seven months living in my mother's stomach when Mr. Potter first abandoned me; I was born in nineteen hundred and forty-nine and I never knew his face," Kincaid's narrator remarks of the abandoning Mr. Potter (104). A womanizer like his father, Mr. Potter visits many women in their one-room houses, fathering many girls who are all unloved by him—"and all of them a burden, all of them, these daughters, needing support of one kind or another: food, clothing, and then schoolbooks and above all, his love." Just when he is feeling good about himself, his daughters appear, one after another, "their forms wrapped in malice and general ill will" (119). "Who was he?" Kincaid's narrator asks. "And those daughters of his . . . those daughters of his with their cries of hunger and illness and ignorance, and their mothers who had words that were like weapons specially forged to make fatal wounds, and their sullying of his good name, for his name was good, his name was Mr. Potter, and accusing him of unfairness and betrayal of his fatherly duties and not being a good person" (119–20).

Retelling and elaborating on the story of her mother's early years in Antigua, Kincaid describes how Annie Victoria Richardson, at the age of sixteen, leaves Mahaut, Dominica, and comes to Antigua after quarreling with her father, who subsequently disinherits her.[6] A beautiful and still-young woman of twenty-five with long, black hair when she meets Mr. Potter, Annie lives in St. John's in a one-room house. "And my mother then was flames in her own fire, not waves in her own sea, she would be that later, after I was born and had become a grown woman, she would become that to me, an ocean with its unpredictable waves and undertow; she was then flames in her own fire and she was very beautiful and her beauty was mentioned sometimes with admiration and affection by others, sometimes with disapproval and scorn by some others, and it was as if her beauty was a blessing in the world sometimes, and as if her beauty was a sign of evil in the world sometimes" (135). Recalling earlier representations of the mother in Kincaid's works, Annie is described as a good/bad woman and a powerful presence, for in her passionate, unpredictable behavior, she is like a force of nature in her daughter's life.

Like Xuela in *The Autobiography of My Mother*, a character also drawn after Kincaid's mother, Annie Drew, Annie Richardson is a fierce and willful woman who repudiates motherhood. Before the age of thirty, she has four abortions, but when she tries to self-abort for the fifth time, she fails "and that failure was because of me, I could not be expelled from my mother's womb at her own will. All this my mother told me when I was forty-one years of age and had by then become the mother of two children" (136). The daughter-narrator, in an act of self-authoring, seeks the roots of her own life in the lives of her parents. Extending the bounds of the remembering self, she recounts her "memory" of her parents from the time before she was born: "I can see them breathing at the time they were being born and struggling into living and being, and I can see them passing through their lives as children and then into being the two people who came together and made me, and through all of this I see them in substantial particularity and I see them as specters, possibilities of the real, possibilities of the real as it pertains to me. And my name when I was born then was Elaine Cynthia, and Annie Richardson was my mother, and that is my substantial particularity and Mr. Potter is my specter" (137–38). In a passage that illustrates Kincaid's desire to know her characters in "some sort of existential way" (Walker), the daughter-narrator places her small life against the backdrop of the benign and violent forces of nature: "and the wind blows, and the sun shines, and the surface of the earth rises up and falls down in violent activity . . . and my mother Annie Victoria Richardson and my father Roderick Potter were, just then, at the time before I would be born, and even at the time I was born, were without interest in the world . . . and the forces that cause it to spin from one end to the other." Behind the "existential" and nihilistic awareness of the narrator lies a very personal story of Kincaid's lifelong obsession with, and inability to fully resolve, the hurts of the past: "and the sorrow I knew then, and the absence of permanent joy or spontaneous joy or frequent joy—all of this has remained unchanged from then to now, as I write this" (138).

Annie interrupts the smooth progress and certainties of Mr. Potter's life, for when she meets him, she is "already a series of beautifully poisonous eruptions . . . a whirlwind of sex and passion and female beauty and deception and pain and female humiliation and narcissism and vulnerability" (141). The narrator imagines that there is "a romance of some sort" between her parents but not any love "because my mother would not submit to anything, certainly not to love, with all its chaos, its demands, its unpredictability; and because Mr. Potter could not love anyone, not anyone who was his own" (163). The two live together, but when Annie is seven months pregnant, she quarrels with and then leaves Mr. Potter, taking all the money he has saved to buy a car so that he can become a self-employed chauffeur and thus "make of himself some semblance of a man" (142). When the daughter-narrator is born, her embattled parents hate each other with a hatred that causes Mr. Potter "to deny . . . the protection of his patrimony" (129). "[T]his hatred that existed between them became a part of my own life as I live it even today and I do not understand how this could be so, but it is true all the same" (130).

Elaine Cynthia Potter

"And my life began, absent Mr. Potter, in the dimly lit ward of the Holberton Hospital, with my mother's resentment silently beaming at him, with my mother's love for me and my mother's resentment silently beaming at me, and then I was swathed in yards of white cotton and laid to rest in the pose of the newborn which is also the pose of the dead" (146–47). Associating birth with death, Kincaid suggests, as she does elsewhere in her writings, the lethality of maternal resentment. An unwanted child born to parents who hate each other, the narrator is named "Elaine" not after a family member but after a daughter of the man Mr. Potter works for as a chauffeur, and thus the name *Elaine* becomes associated with people the mother ends up not liking or wishing well. Like Annie John, the daughter-narrator Elaine comes to know herself through her mother's stories. Elaine learns that she caused her mother, Annie, pain even before she was born—that her mother endured discomfort during her pregnancy and suffered a painful delivery—and Elaine also is told that she was such a greedy infant that her mother breastfed her until she was sucked dry, drained of her milk. Elaine learns of her essential "badness" through her mother's stories, and she comes to "remember" her one childhood encounter with Mr. Potter through a story her mother tells her.

In this story, which comes to define Elaine's girlhood and adult relation with her biological father, Mr. Potter rejects the four-year-old Elaine when she is sent by her mother to ask him for sixpence, so she can buy writing paper. Standing across the street from the garage where his taxi is kept, she waves at him and wishes him a good morning. Refusing to acknowledge her, Mr. Potter rolls his shoulders and then, turning his back on her, enters the garage. "Not only did he ignore me, he made sure that until the day he died, I did not exist at all" (126). In a subsequent retelling of this story, she remarks that Mr. Potter waved her away "as if I were an abandoned dog blocking his path, as if I were nothing to him at all and had suddenly and insanely decided to pursue an intimate relationship with him. 'Eh, eh,' said Mr. Potter" (146). If Elaine "remembers" the incident of waving to Mr. Potter because her mother has told her about it—"all of this my mother has told me, my entire life as I live it is all my mother has told me" (127)—she also comes to acknowledge the unreliability of her account. "I saw him from across the street and from across the street I asked him for money to buy books that I needed for school, but I do not remember any of this, it is only that my mother has told me so and my mother's tongue and the words that flow from it cannot be relied upon, she is now dead" (154). Retelling this story yet again, she remarks, "I have only a vague memory of him ignoring me as I passed him by in the street, of him slamming a door in my face when I was sent to ask him for money I needed to purchase my writing paper, and the full knowledge of the line drawn through me which I inherited from him" (160–61).

A "vague memory" and something she does "not remember" but was told, the story, which "cannot be relied on," nevertheless has a shaping influence on the daughter-narrator's identity, reinforcing the message of her illegitimacy and of her mother's power over her: father-less, she comes "from the female line" and belongs "only" to her mother (161). In the "vacant" look on her face captured in a photo-graph of her taken when she was seven, the narrator sees evidence of "the absence of Mr. Potter" in her childhood, an absence that contin-ues to reverberate in her adult life: "I have a line drawn through me, and that overwhelms everything that I know about myself at this moment" (145). Even though the narrator grows up entangled in her mother's life, she remains aware of the shadowy presence of Mr. Pot-ter. "And who was I then, Potter or Richardson, for though my mother wove herself around me, wound me up in a cocoon of love and bitter-ness and anger and pain, and from this cocoon I shall never emerge, . . . through those unbreakable fibers I could feel Mr. Potter, the shadow of him, . . . a shadow more important than any person I might know" (154).

Kincaid's narrator expresses her sense of loss and regret at not knowing Mr. Potter: "Mr. Potter was a man and he was my father and I never knew him at all, had never touched him, or known how he smelled . . . or the look of him after he had an ordinary experience that related to touching or smelling or seeing or hearing" (160). Yet she also expresses hostility toward the unloving Mr. Potter who fathered many girl children with different women—women who all "longed for his presence," as she imagines it. "But Mr. Potter's caresses and embraces were like a razor and each woman and girl child of his who had received one of his embraces was left with skin shredded and hanging toward the floor and blood falling down to meet the floor and bones exposed and sinew, too, and nerves" (151). An irresponsible father who spurned his illegitimate daughters, Mr. Potter eventually achieved financial success as a chauffeur, owning three cars and living in a house with many rooms. Marrying a woman who bore him a daughter and then gave birth to a boy fathered by another man, Mr. Potter loved only the boy, whom he raised as his son, of all his children.

Making and Unmaking Mr. Potter

"What am I to call you?" the thirty-three-year-old Elaine asks Mr. Potter when she finally meets him[7] during a visit he makes to the United States (168). In her enraged response to Mr. Potter, the daughter-narrator resembles her mother, Annie, whose fierce anger is likened to a destructive, natural force. "And at that moment, should anger have surged through me like a force unpredictable in nature, should I have wished my father dead, should I have gone beyond mere wishing and walked over to him and grabbed him by the throat and squeezed his neck until his body lay limp at my feet, should I have thrown him out the window . . . ? And I did wish him dead and I did want him dead and I wanted my moments past, present, and future to be absent of him" (169–70). Yet despite her murderous rage, after he leaves she feels a sense of loss and despair, which she describes as an "empty space inside" her that is small when she is not aware of it and large when she is (170).

"'Potter dead, 'e dead you know, me ah tell you, eh, eh, me ah tell you,'" Annie tells her daughter, reporting the death of the seventy-year-old Mr. Potter, who dies in 1992 (185). When Elaine later looks for Mr. Potter's unmarked burial spot in the St. John's cemetery in Antigua, the grave master tells her about the family commotion that accompanied the burial of Mr. Potter as family members quarreled, ironically enough, over who was best loved by the unloving Mr. Potter and insulted each other because Mr. Potter, despite his considerable wealth, left them nothing. Those gathered at his gravesite recounted "stories of love and hatred," including one of his daughters, who said that Mr. Potter had raped her (50). "So much suffering was attached to Mr. Potter, so much suffering consumed him, so much suffering he left behind" (52). Mr. Potter was unmourned by those who knew him: "No one cried to show sorrow over his death and no one was sorry that he had died, they were only sorry they had known him, or sorry they had loved him, for he left them nothing at all" (185).

Unlike the illiterate Mr. Potter, Elaine can read and write, so she can "make" and "unmake" Mr. Potter (158). She is the "only one" able to write "the narrative that is his life" (87). "[B]ecause I learned how to read and how to write, only so is Mr. Potter's life known, his smallness becomes large, his anonymity is stripped away, his silence broken. Mr.

Potter himself says nothing, nothing at all" (189). The man who lacked "private thoughts" or "thoughts of wonder" or "thoughts about his past, his future, and his present" (130) is given narrative and textual dimension by the daughter-writer who infuses her own rich literary sensibility into his diminished, empty existence—his lack—in her introspective and imaginative reconstruction of his life. In her existential musings on mutability and mortality, she enlarges his small life-in-the-present, giving it a kind of literary and textual depth and breadth by presenting it as an illustration of the ephemerality of human life. As she shows the connection between past and present—between Nathaniel and Elfrida's abandonment of Roderick and Roderick's abandonment of Elaine—she renders the story of Mr. Potter's life with a coherency beyond his grasp. And the narrator expresses sorrow at the death of Mr. Potter, who is unmourned by his family: "how sad never to again see the sun turn red sometimes and disappear sometimes; how sad never again to touch another person spontaneously, without thought, without reason, without justification, and to expect a similar response . . . ; how sad never again to stand in the middle of nowhere and see the world in all its brightness and brimming over with possibilities innumerable heading toward you; how sad to know that you will be alive once and never so again, no matter how you rearrange your life and your very own self" (183).

As the narrator mourns the unmourned life of Mr. Potter, she attempts to grasp the whole of his life as she "start[s] again at the beginning: Mr. Potter's appearance in the world was a combination of sadness, joy, and a chasm of silent horror for his mother (Elfrida Robinson) and indifference to his father (Nathaniel Potter), who had so many children that none of them could matter at all" (188). Even though Mr. Potter's life and death were inconsequential, his small life is given meaning and enlarged by the daughter-narrator. And through her powers as a storyteller, she gives a kind of narrative presence to the father who was an absence in her life: "Hear Mr. Potter, who was my father; hear his children and hear the women who bore those children; hear the end of life itself rushing like a predictable wave in a known ocean to engulf Mr. Potter. . . . Hear Mr. Potter! See Mr. Potter! Touch Mr. Potter!" (194–95).

The Daughter-writer

No longer the disempowered daughter, Elaine, as the daughter-writer, can gain some mastery and control over the hurts of the past not only as she reconstructs and interprets the lives of her parents but also as she represents—and experiences—them as novelistic characters. The rejected daughter with the line drawn through her, she artistically revises the past as she becomes "the central figure" in the life of the man who turned his back on her and refused to acknowledge her as his daughter (153). By giving Mr. Potter a storied, novelistic identity, she makes him whole and complete. Yet she continues to observe and judge him and, like her mother, uses storytelling as a weapon, taking her daughter's revenge as a retrospective storyteller. She also talks and writes back to her mother, Annie, who told Elaine her life. "She is now dead, she is dead now," the daughter-narrator remarks of her hated mother (127). As Elaine stands near Mr. Potter's grave, she can see her mother's grave. "Her name was Annie Victoria Richardson and she did not have a line drawn through her, and for my whole life up to then, to see my mother dead was an event I was afraid I would never witness, I had waged a battle to see my own mother dead, and from time to time I was certain I would lose." Even as she stands above the graves of her parents—in the posture of the triumphant Xuela in *The Autobiography of My Mother*, who sees death as a humiliating defeat—Elaine recognizes their continuing influence on her life: "[T]hese three things, my father, me, my mother, remain the same into eternity, remain the same now, which is a definition of eternity" (192). She remains haunted by memories of her parents and of herself as the shamed, illegitimate daughter: "My name, Elaine Cynthia Potter, crossed out by the line that was drawn through it, I first abandoned and then changed to something else altogether, so that the line drawn through me, now, cannot find me, and if it did, would not recognize me, and that line cannot see me, but I can see it, following me each day as I do some ordinary thing" (143).

In telling the story of her absentee father in *Mr. Potter*, Kincaid also tells the story of Elaine Cynthia Potter, the everpresent yet missing part of her identity. Kincaid retains her fierce anger about her past as she repeatedly and obsessively refers to the line of shame drawn through her, which she experiences as the attempted erasure of her identity. Yet even as Kincaid exposes the shame of Elaine Cynthia Potter in *Mr. Potter*, she also gives an artistic legitimacy to her cast-off identity. Like her parents, "Elaine Cynthia Potter" becomes a story authored and authorized by "Jamaica Kincaid" in her ongoing self-narration. Just as the real Elaine Cynthia Potter once sought refuge in the bookish world of novels, so Kincaid creates a bookish refuge for "Elaine Cynthia Potter" in *Mr. Potter*.

Kincaid does not claim that she can ever forget the past or heal the shame of the remembered girl with the line drawn through her. By ending her fictional memoir with the first eleven words she wrote when she began the novel—"Mr. Potter was my father, my father's name was Mr. Potter" (195)—she points to the persistence of her shame as she states the simple fact of her paternal origins. But in her self-fashioned identity as Jamaica Kincaid, she refuses to claim her inheritance or to pass her shame on to her children: "The line that is drawn through me, this line I have inherited, but I have not accepted my inheritance and so have not deeded it to anyone who shall follow me" (143). Because Kincaid cannot help but remember her Antiguan past, she remains haunted by Elaine Cynthia Potter, the shamed girl with the line drawn through her. Yet as the self-authored and thus self-possessed Jamaica Kincaid, she does find a kind of writer's solace as she gives a bookish presence and artistic legitimacy not only to her missing father but also to the missing part of her repudiated identity.

❧ 9 ❧

Conclusion:
"I Am Writing for Solace"

Seeking Solace in Writing,
Gardening, and Domestic Life

Kincaid, who began her writing career "embarked on something called self-invention," continues to find the act of writing a highly personal act: "an expression of personal growth" ("Putting" 100, Ferguson, "Interview" 169). "I'm trying to discover the secret of myself," as she comments. "[F]or me everything passes through the self" (Kennedy). Still haunted by her past, Kincaid, up to the time of her mother's death in 1999 at the age of eighty, was never able to resolve her relationship with her aging but still powerfully rejecting mother. "[I]t is an unresolved relationship, only the absence of memory resolves a relationship like that. What I have achieved astonishes and perplexes her. She doesn't seem to notice" (Drewes). Rather than voicing pride in her daughter's success as a writer, Annie Drew, even though she did come to call her "Jamaica Kincaid," communicated her contempt by seemingly not noticing what her daughter had achieved. Kincaid also suspected that her mother did not own any of the books she had written. Describing her continuing obsession with her mother, Kincaid wrote in 1996: "My mother spoke of her mother constantly, her mother never spoke of her at all; I now speak of my mother constantly, from what I am told, by my mother's other children, my mother never speaks of me at all" ("Introduction," *Generations* 11). "We're in one of our periods of not talking," Kincaid remarked in 1997 when her mother was seventy-eight. "She's just so disrespectful to her children. I thought, 'Oh no. I can't take it'" (J. Kaufman). And in 2001, Kincaid admitted that she was "still angry" and unable to forgive her mother even several years after her death. "There is a feeling that I shouldn't be having these feelings about my mother. They seem inappropriate for a woman my age. I ought to get over it, I ought to forgive her. I am not sorry she died. I have not grieved" (Conover).

Utterly rejected by her mother, who never expressed pride in her daughter or acknowledged her writerly gifts, Kincaid traces the beginnings of her writer's life to William Shawn's acceptance of her writing. She describes her years of working as a staff writer for *The New Yorker* when William Shawn was editor as a "wonderful thing" and an "incredible blessing," recalling how she felt both an "incredible sense of privilege and belonging" and a "sense of pride" in being part of "something decent, wonderful, and intelligent" (Muirhead 47, Shen). Shawn, who nourished *New Yorker* writers such as Kincaid and also became her father-in-law when she married his son, Allen, in 1979, was "our protector—he protected us from horrible people" (Kreilkamp 55). After Shawn was removed as editor of *The New Yorker*,[1] Kincaid felt she had lost her writer's home. She "exiled" herself, as she put it in 1990, from the world that had "comforted" her and had "made" her a writer (Perry, "Interview" 506). Kincaid recalls how she argued with Robert Gottlieb, Shawn's replacement, only to "miss his literary spirit" when he, in turn, was replaced in 1992 by Tina Brown, whom Kincaid accused of being "attracted to the coarse and vulgar"[2] and of turning *The New Yorker* into "a version of *People* magazine" (Garner). In 1995 when Kincaid resigned from her staff job at *The New Yorker* after almost two decades of working for the magazine—from 1976 to 1995—she very publicly denounced Brown, casting the English woman in a familiar role in Kincaid's own personal drama: that of the oppressor—both English and maternal—who threatens the inner life of the Antiguan artist/daughter. Referring to Brown as a "totalitarian, a tyrant," Kincaid stated, "The first thing a tyrant will do is to destroy the inner life of a creative person, and that is what is happening at *The New Yorker*" (Jacobs). In her public remarks, Kincaid, as is her wont, angrily talked back to Brown, referring to her as a "bully" and as "Joseph Stalin in high heels with blonde hair from England." "I didn't mind that Tina Brown was a tyrant. I wouldn't mind if she was a tyrant and smart, but she's stupid. . . . I don't like stupid people." Seeing in Brown an image of oppressors from her past, she asserted, "I want to be able to write what I think. I don't like tyrants" (Langton).

If Kincaid once compared the loss of her writer's home at *The New Yorker*—a place she had considered to be her "spiritual home" (Kennedy)—to the experience of being orphaned,[3] she has found a new kind of home at Harvard University where she began to teach as a Visiting Professor of Creative Writing in 1992. And she continues to

take deep comfort in her domestic and gardener's life in North Bennington, Vermont, starkly dividing her life into her unhappy Antiguan
past and her self-fashioned writer's life in Vermont.[4] Commenting
that she hopes she is not the "same self-serving, self-absorbed, self-
obsessed, ruthless person" she was in her twenties, Kincaid nemertheless insists that she does not "regret for one moment" how she lived
in her twenties and how she refused to sacrifice her life to help sup-
port her Antiguan family (Wachtel 63). Yet she remains a memory-
haunted woman as she continues to ruminate over her Antiguan past.
Plagued at times with what she calls "deep insomnia," something that
plunges her "into despair," she reports that she sometimes writes well
into the middle of the night (Grondahl). But she also takes deep pleasure in, and indeed finds solace in, her domestic life. "I like domestic
life. . . . I reduce everything to the domestic. If I were looking at the
great events of the world, I'd reduce them to a quarrel at the kitchen
table" (Drewes). For Kincaid, domestic life is part of her writer's life.
"I think I have to have a great deal of domestic activity to write," she
comments (Perry, "Interview" 503). "I don't consider writing a career
or a profession. . . . I think of it as part of my domestic life," she
insists (Listfield).

For Kincaid, just as domestic life is part of her writing life, so is
gardening, a passion she attributes to her mother. "When I'm in the garden, I'm actually also writing, I'm always going over the sentences—so
by the time I actually write, I've written what I'm putting down on paper
many times in my head. I don't revise my writing at all. But I do the
equivalent of revising in the garden, continuously. I never stop digging
up beds, rearranging everything" (Kreilkamp 55). In *My Garden
(Book):*—a collection of essays on gardening published in 1999, which
began as a gardening column in *The New Yorker*—Kincaid professes her
passion for gardening even as she reflects on the relationship of gardening to conquest. Recounting how her "attachment in adult life to the
garden" began in 1986 on her second Mother's Day when her husband
gave her gardening tools and flower seeds as a gift, Kincaid recalls her
slow recognition of the personal meaning attached to the odd "ungar-
denlike shapes" of her flower beds (3, 7):

> When it dawned on me that the garden I was making (and am still
> making and will always be making) resembled a map of the
> Caribbean and the sea that surrounds it, I did not tell this to the
> gardeners who had asked me to explain the thing I was doing . . . ;
> I only marveled at the way the garden is for me an exercise in
> memory, a way of remembering my own immediate past, a way of

getting to a past that is my own (the Caribbean Sea) and the past
as it is indirectly related to me (the conquest of Mexico and its surroundings). (7–8)

For Kincaid the garden is an "exercise in memory," and it also is "bound
up with words about the garden, with words themselves" (8, 7).

Like Kincaid's other works, *My Garden (Book):* draws on Kincaid's life. "I often bring autobiographical things into it," as she
remarked of her gardening column. "It's me. . . . [It's] out of my life"
(Muirhead 46). For Kincaid, the acts of remembering and representing
her experiences as a gardener are part of her ongoing self-narration and
creation of a self-authored and storied identity. As she recounts details
of her domestic and gardener's life in Vermont in the present, she continually remembers her Antiguan past, often in extended speakerly
digressions or parenthetical asides that provide a sense of immediacy
and recreate the experience of the spontaneous recall of memory. "I love
the house in which I live. Before I lived in it, before I was ever even inside
it, before I knew anything about it, I loved it," she remarks of the brown
shingled house with red shutters in which she lives, a house "at least
twenty times as big" as the one-room house in Antigua in which she was
raised (29, 37). "There isn't a room in my house now that is as small as
the house I grew up in. I can hardly believe that this is so, but it is really,
really true" (42). Living in her spacious Vermont home with its garden,
she recalls how in her Antiguan home her family lived outside and her
mother nervously presided over the yard where there was a stone heap,
which was used to wash the clothes on Monday mornings; and a latrine,
which was visited on Wednesday nights by the night-soil men; and a
soursop tree, where Kincaid was forced to eat alone when she was being
punished for bad behavior (42–44). As she considers whether or not she
should add a pond to her Vermont garden, she recalls her childhood fear
of ponds based on her belief that children had died trying to collect the
fruit of pond lilies. "[P]erhaps no such thing happened, perhaps I was
only afraid that such a thing would happen; perhaps I only thought if I
tried to reap the fruit of pond lilies I would die" (15). Acknowledging
that she knows both the proper and common names of the plants growing in her Vermont garden but does not know the names of Antiguan
plants, Kincaid thinks about her colonial upbringing in Antigua. "This
ignorance of the botany of the place I am from (and am of) really only
reflects the fact that when I lived there, I was of the conquered class and
living in a conquered place; a principle of this condition is that nothing
about you is of any interest unless the conqueror deems it so." The
botanical garden in Antigua, which contained plants from places all over

the world that were part of the British Empire and had the same climate as Antigua, reinforced how powerful the British were, for they had the ability to bring to Antiguans like the young Kincaid "the botany of the world they owned" (120).

As Kincaid reflects on the relationship between gardening and conquest, she tries to make personal sense of her own colonial history, asking, "What to call the thing that happened to me and all who look like me? Should I call it history? And if so, what should history mean to someone who looks like me? Should it be an idea; should it be an open wound?" (166). To Kincaid, the history of the dahlia is illustrative of the link between gardening and conquest. From William Prescott's book, *The Conquest of Mexico*, she learns about the extensive Aztec gardens that existed when Hernando Cortez's army invaded Mexico. The cocoxochitl flower, used by the Aztecs as animal fodder and to treat urinary-tract disorders, was taken to Europe and renamed the dahlia after the Swedish botanist, Andreas Dahl. "And so the dahlia: Who first saw it and longed for it so deeply that it was removed from the place where it had always been, and transformed (hybridized), and renamed? Hernando Cortez would not have noticed it; to him the dahlia would have been one of the details, a small detail, of something large and grim: conquest" (118).

In her contradictory way, Kincaid denounces the European habit of naming and possessing things and yet admits that botany was one of her favorite subjects in school in Antigua. She associates the botanical garden in St. John's, Antigua, with the English people's "need to isolate, name, objectify, [and] possess various parts, people, and things in the world" and yet also remembers it as an "Edenic" place where she spent Sunday afternoons as a girl and where she and her stepfather, David Drew, sat under a rubber tree during the time they were "happily (it seems to me now) sick together" (143, 144). And while Kincaid openly expresses her disdain for the English colonizers from her youth, referring to them at one point as human "parasites" (146), she has a different view of the English when she finds herself in England among exquisite flowers and in the company of pleasant people at the Chelsea Flower Show. "If you ever want to keep up a grudge against someone, don't see that person alongside beautiful flowers. I loved all the people at the Chelsea Flower Show, standing among rhododendrons in impossible shades of mauve, pink, and peach. They came streaming in . . . from all directions, as far as I could see, and they looked, not like twentieth-century citizens of a country that used to run the world but like residents of a village" (104–05). At the Chelsea Flower Show, Kincaid experiences what she imagines the "great plant appropriators" felt (102) when she sees the *Verbascum* 'Helen Johnson' and afterward spends days plotting ways to smuggle the plant back into the United States.

As Kincaid obsessively and restlessly buys plants and arranges and rearranges her Vermont garden, she understands the desire to possess plants, and for Kincaid this means to possess in abundance. "[O]nly in very rare circumstances must plants be bought in ones," she advises. "The minimum is three, preferably five, and then up from that. . . . If it is very beautiful, more of it will do" (182). Gardening is "an absolute luxury," she acknowledges. "You've eaten, you're clothed, you have a house, you look out and you rearrange the landscape. It's an aesthetic decision. It's all exaggerated, it's luxurious, it's a kind of excess" (Kreilkamp 55). At one point, as Kincaid looks at her Vermont garden, she admits, "I have joined the conquering class: who else could afford this garden—a garden in which I grow things that it would be much cheaper to buy at the store?" (123).

Only someone from the conquering class could join a group of botanists and plantspeople on a plant-hunting expedition in China. Kincaid's chronicle of her seed-hunting trip to China, where she collects the seeds of one-hundred-and-thirty different flowering plants, includes detailed reports on the seeds the members of the group collect, the places where they stay, and the food they eat. And it also contains a highly personal, and in places gossipy, account not only of the pleasures of plant hunting but also of Kincaid's moments of homesickness and sadness and anger during the trip. Admitting that she misses her Vermont family, Kincaid, after one week away from her family, begins to think she "might not be able to get back to them," and the next day, when she is about to get her period, she feels "sad" and "sick" and stays in bed (200). During the trip she not only suffers from a sprained—and then resprained—ankle, but she also has many of what she calls "nervous breakdowns," explaining that this is how she refers to her "monumentally rude and truly insulting behavior—a temporary lapse in sanity" (199–200). In her "most serious nervous breakdown," which occurs at Judian, she tells the Chinese guide, "'The rooms are the filthiest rooms I have ever been in; there is blood on the walls, there is shit on the walls, there are the remains of vomit on the walls.' Judian was the place where our guide had been born and grew up; but I did not know this when I spoke those words" (206). When John—a generally disliked member of the group characterized by one of the women in the group as "the leading candidate for asshole" (189)—tells Kincaid that "the whole experience of the unsanitariness of everything" makes their experience in China "more authentic," she thinks to herself, "Well, the last time I had such an intimate experience with anybody was with my children, changing their diapers, cleaning up their vomit when they had a flu, cooking their food . . . and I do not think all of that makes our relationship more authentic, I could have done without all of it, the vomit, the blood, the shit" (206–07). Accused by John of "always bitchin' and bitchin,'" Kincaid decides that he, in fact, is calling her a "bitch," and she is "suddenly glad" that she has "bitched and bitched" as she, in her characteristic way, turns his condemnation of her "into a badge of honor" (207–08). Only John's desire to build houses for Habitat for Humanity mitigates her "desire to slice his head off his body," she remarks, and yet when he goes off to join a group hiking in the foothills of the Himalayan Mountains, she misses him (208).

Kincaid provides an emotionally honest account of her "nervous breakdowns"—her moments of rude and insulting behavior—and also her feelings of homesickness and loss during her China trip. She also describes the happiness she feels as she collects seeds and how she is cheered by the forward-looking attitude of the botanists, who always think that the next place they visit will contain the satisfaction for which they long. Like the botanists, Kincaid brings a kind of restless energy and forward-looking attitude to her life as a Vermont gardener. "How agitated I am when I am in the garden, and how happy I am to be so agitated. How vexed I often am when I am in the garden, and how happy I am to be so vexed. What to do? Nothing works just the way I thought it would, nothing looks just the way I had imagined it, and when sometimes it does look like what I had imagined (and this, thank God, is rare) I am startled that my imagination is so ordinary" (14). If "[c]omposing with nature is in part a conquest," as Susie O'Brien remarks, it also is "in part a kind of surrender, as the garden, perhaps to a greater extent than any other work of art, is always subject to the contingency of soil, of weather, of animals; subject, in other words, to the agency of the non-human world." In *My Garden (Book):* Kincaid describes her pleasurable sense of vexation as she composes with and surrenders to the natural world in creating her Vermont garden. Over and over, she happily asks, "What to do?" with her Vermont garden—with the blue *Wisteria floribunda* that blooms out of season in late July instead of May; the white wisteria that has never bloomed; the fox and baby rabbit that appear in her garden; the young *Magnolia ashei* that blooms unexpectedly. "Oh, the deliciousness of complaining about nothing of any consequence and that such a thing should be the case in a garden: because, (again) that wisteria blooming now (or then) so close to the buddleia, which in turn is not too far from the *Phlox paniculata* 'Norh Leigh,' which is also somehow in the middle of the *Phlox paniculata* 'David,' is all pleasing to my eye, as I was looking at it then (now)" (22). Kincaid revels in the excess and profusion of her garden with its perennial peas *(Lathyrus latifolius)*, blue and pink *Platycodon grandiflorus*, monkshoods, delphiniums, hollyhocks, trumpet lilies, plume poppies, cup plants, kniphofia, dahlias, roses, and Himalayan clematis. For Kincaid, "the irritation to be found in the garden will not lead to any loss of face; it will only lead to this question: What to do? and the happiness to be found in that!" (26).

Kincaid, who dislikes the long Vermont winter, says that to look at a snow-covered landscape "is to look at despair" (60). Yet winter also has its own pleasures, for when the plant and seed catalogues begin to arrive, Kincaid looks forward to hours upon hours of enjoyable reading. On a day when the temperature is ten degrees below zero, she is cheered by the arrival of the Ronniger's Seed Potatoes catalogue[5] and spends the afternoon soaking in a bathtub of hot water drinking ginger ale and eating oranges while reading this "little treasure," which is printed on newsprint and is "plain, straightforward, humble, and comforting" (86). And she receives a psychological boost when she looks at the pictures in the "big, showy" catalogues, such as the White Flower Farm and Wayside Gardens catalogues (87). "The best catalogues for reading are not altogether unlike wonderful books; they plunge me deep into the world of the garden, the growing of the things advertised (because what are these descriptions of seeds and plants but advertisements), and that feeling of being unable to tear myself away comes over me, and there is that amazing feeling of love, and my imagination takes over as I look out at the garden, which is blanket upon blanket of white, and see it filled with the things described in the catalogue I am reading" (88). Kincaid also enjoys reading gardening books, taking special pleasure in Graham Stuart Thomas's books, finding him not only "knowledgeable" but also "deliciously authoritative and overbearing in his opinions, the way people who really know their business can't help being" (81). Similarly, she enjoys reading the "bullying" admonitions of authors such as Donald Wyman, James and Louise Bush-Brown, and the Edwardian gardener, Gertrude Jekyll, an ugly woman, as Kincaid learns when she reads a biography of Jekyll, who diverted attention from herself by making "pronouncements about correctness and beauty in the garden" (81–82, 95).

After the unbearable Vermont winter passes, Kincaid revels in the spring. "The month of May comes on suddenly and moves along swiftly, and each day pleasure after pleasure is flung before my eyes with such intensity that after the barrenness and harshness, in varying degrees, of the months before, it seems mocking, a punishment, to look out and see the bergenia, pink and white against the bleeding heart, pink and white;

the stiff pink flower of the umbrella plant . . . ; the pink and blue, white and mauve of the pulmonarias ('Mrs. Moon,' 'Janet Fisk,' 'Sissinghurst White'); the emerging green tips of the hosta . . . ; the flowering apple trees" (173–74). When her rhododendron 'Jane Grant' arrives in the mail, the plant is so beautiful that she almost weeps. "She was beautiful, all delicate and tidy; glossy, medium-green leaves with a lush indumentum . . . , and perched on top of the leaves, a generous fist of blossoms, whitish, limy green now, eventually opening, becoming a succession of pinks (as I write this, the transformation has not yet begun), all of them reminding me of something pleasurable: a girl's dress, the inside of a mouth, a moment very, very early in the morning when light from the sun itself is in doubt" (179–80). Kincaid happily declares herself in love with May. "[W]hen my turn comes to make the world, as surely it will, I shall make my May ninety days long. December, January, and February shall be allotted ten hours each; I have not finalized my plans for the other months, but none of them shall exceed May" (175). Aware that many of the plantspeople before her did not die in their own beds, Kincaid cheerfully announces, "I shall die in a nursery" (187).

In her reflections on the biblical story of the Garden of Eden, Kincaid concludes that what went wrong with Eden was that its gardener-owner and caretaker-occupants—Adam and Eve—grew tired of it. "That gardener, any gardener, is not a stable being; that gardener, any gardener, is not a model of consistency." In a self-referential description, Kincaid states that gardeners are a contradictory sort of people, for they are "so restless, so irritable, so constantly vexed, so happy with their unhappiness, so pleased that they cannot really be satisfied" (224). Gardeners, Kincaid insists, are an envious lot, coveting their neighbors' gardens. But they are also people who "only love, and they only love in the moment; when the moment has passed, they love the memory of the moment, they love the memory of that particular plant or that particular bloom, but the plant of the bloom itself they have moved on from, they have left it behind for something else" (218). Kincaid shares the gardener's restlessness, finding satisfaction in her constant search for more and more plants and new arrangements of her garden. "I shall never have the garden I have in my mind, but that for me is the joy of it," she writes (220). "I am in a state of constant discomfort and I like this state so much I would like to share it" (229).

In the garden, a place where she is in a state of constant discomfort, Kincaid finds at the same time deep contentment in the ceaseless activity and vexatious pleasures of gardening. It is also a place where she remembers her painful past as she tends to her garden. Explaining that she writes down what she is thinking, Kincaid says she is continually writing in her head. "Essentially I daydream a lot, that's what writing is to me. I'm the sort of writer who is always writing" (Drewes). "Even when I'm not writing, I'm writing—often while I'm weeding my garden" (Listfield). Haunted by her unhappy past, she is driven to remember and to write as a way of taking some control over the memories and voices— in particular the voice of the mother—that haunt her. When she writes, as she has remarked, she is "getting something" out of her head that if she did not write would drive her "absolutely insane," so for Kincaid, writing is "an act of survival" (Ferguson, "Interview" 174, 171). While the writing process is "full of pain," she continues to write about her life, stating, "This is the life I have. This is the life I write about" (Snell). She also insists that she does not "believe in healing," for if "something happened, it happened" and what is important is "knowing the truth of it." In a similar way, she does not "think there is such a thing as happiness" or believe that it is her "purpose in life to be happy," but she would like "some contentment" in her life. "And I do have some contentment. I'm often very contented. I have a wonderful family. I'm very blessed in that way. And I live in a very nice place. And that's enough" (Hansen). Being healed is not important to Kincaid. "I don't see why I should be healed. . . . I hope all the various people in the world get along, but I don't see why I should get along with myself. And I don't see why the personal afflictions I have should be healed. If they did [heal], I wouldn't have anything to write about!" (Muirhead 48).

Kincaid, even if she does not write to heal herself, does see her writing as a form of self-rescue, insisting she would "not be a healthy person without it" (Steavenson 37). "I am writing for solace," Kincaid states. "I consider myself the reader I am writing for, and it is to make sense of something, even if to repeat to myself what has happened" (Holmstrom). In shaping her garden like a map of the Caribbean and reproducing in her Vermont study the look of the stash of books she once hid as a girl under her one-room house in Antigua—books that gave her comfort and that were burned by her mother—Kincaid remembers the past but also tries to undo some of its pain. Kincaid insists that she does not believe in healing and that she cannot and will not forget. "I don't see why I should get along with myself," she remarks in her characteristic way. But in her domestic and gardener's life, which are part of her writer's life, she does find moments of contentment. And even though her creative assets are her memory, anger, and despair, she does find solace in her writing as she becomes the self-authored Jamaica Kincaid and, through her ongoing self-narration, fashions for herself a literary life and storied identity that she finds livable.

Notes

1. Introduction: "When You Think of Me, Think of My Life"

1. Eschewing identity politics, Kincaid states, "I hear people say stupid things like 'I am protecting my black identity.' I've no idea what that could mean. I can't imagine that I would invent an identity based on the color of my skin." For Kincaid, "There are so many things that make up a person and one of them is not 'an identity'" (Cryer). Instead, Kincaid believes that "one's identity should proceed from an internal structure, from one's own internal truth" (Hayden). "My husband is white, my children are half-white," as Kincaid once remarked of her marriage to Allen Shawn (the couple is now divorced). "I can really no longer speak of race, because I no longer understand what it means. I can speak with more clarity about power. I know I come from people who were slaves. I can make judgments about the past. I can see history, but I can no longer say 'white people' with any conviction. They're just a group of people behaving really abominably" (L. Jones 75).

2. See Diane Simmons 23–33; see also note 5 below.

3. Unlike recent postmodern theorists who believe that "interiority is an appearance, an effect of discourse," contemporary relational theorists hold that "a constructed interior relational world motivates behavior" (Layton 25). In this view, the self or individual subject is "a continuously evolving negotiator between relationally constructed multiple and contradictory internal and external worlds" (Layton 26). "[B]orn into families with their own histories and ways of mediating culture," individuals thus engage "in particular patterns of relating," and the internalization of these patterns, in turn, is "conditioned by the accidents of gender, race, and class and by the power differentials that structure them at a given historical moment" (Layton 26–27).

Contrary to the postmodernist claim that the notion of a "core" self is essentialist, the idea of a core self offered by relational theorists does not "assume the kind of unity . . . that silences otherness" although it does "imply something internal that recognizably persists even while it may continuously and subtly alter" (Layton 25). In this view, the multiple experiences of the self over time exist side by side with "the continuity of a self-reflective and organizing 'I,' an 'I' that creates meaning and organizes the diverse experiences and manifold self-other configurations" (Schapiro 5).

Focusing attention on the psychic processes of projection and introjection, relational theorists describe how in projection the individual puts "feelings, beliefs, or parts of [the] self" into another person or internal object while in introjection "aspects or functions of a person or object are taken into the self and come to constitute and differentiate an internal world and reshape the ego" (Chodorow, *Power* 15). Investigating the creation of mental life from a relational matrix, relational theorists describe how inner and outer reality "are continually reconstituted through projective and introjective fantasies, so that experiences of others are shaped or filtered through fantasies of inner objects and in turn reshape these inner objects" (Chodorow, *Power* 54).

4. In her insistence on the "power of feelings" and the irreducibility of the psychological, Chodorow contests the antipsychological views of contemporary cultural theorists who assert that the psychological and subjectivity are modern cultural inventions and that emotion is constituted by culture. In this view, "culture doesn't just surround or act on a bedrock of psychobiological 'emotions'; it defines, produces, and has us enact in our behavior what we are told and tell ourselves are emotions" (Pfister 19). Despite the "gripping reality" and intensity of experiences interpreted as emotional—such as giving birth or feeling anxiety about death—because the meaning of such experiences can differ within and across cultures, antipsychological theorists, as they rightly call into question the universality of emotional expression, also seem to deny the psychobiological reality of emotions (Pfister 21–22). Equally suspect to such theorists is the idea of a desiring and experiencing inner self, which is also a social creation in this view. "To conceptualize the 'inner,' not as universal, but as a social representation that comes to be experienced as natural . . . is to challenge the premise underlying the term *internalization*," as Joel Pfister comments (27–28). Thus, the psychology of interiority, while it seems self-evident and natural, is constituted through cultural representations and institutions, and indeed psychoanalysis itself can be considered as "a revealing historical symptom," giving us "a picture of the nineteenth- and twentieth-century production of 'psychological' individuals, 'psychological' families, and 'psychological' bodies" (Pfister 36). While Pfister admits that "[t]he question of the internally developed psychobiological self remains . . . debatable and open" (34), his argument focuses on the historical and cultural, at the expense of the psychological.

When cultural critics such as Pfister claim that the self and emotions are socially constructed, they ignore the kind of work being done by neurobiologists like Antonio Damasio, who provides compelling evidence of the biological underpinning of mind and self in his exploration of consciousness and emotion. "The inescapable and remarkable fact about these three phenomena—emotion, feeling, and consciousness—is their body relatedness," as Damasio explains (284). Not only is the body the "main stage for emotions," but feelings are "largely a reflection of body-state changes" (287, 288). Drawing on his work with patients with neurological disorders and also on research based on techniques such as PET and magnetic resonance imaging scans of the brain, which have allowed neurologists to observe the neural activity supporting consciousness, Damasio has concluded that "consciousness and emotion are *not* separable" and thus usually "when consciousness is impaired so is emotion" (16). Biologically determined processes laid down by a long evolutionary history, emotions are "part of the bioregulatory devices with which we come equipped to survive" (53). Emotions and feelings are "tangibly about the body": "the highly constrained ebb and flow of internal organism states, which is innately controlled by the brain and continuously signaled in the brain, constitutes the backdrop for the mind, and, more specifically, the foundation for the elusive entity we designate as self" (29, 30).

Arguing that our sense of self is generated from our mental representations of the body, Damasio explains that the idea of a sense of a bounded self comes from the body: that is, one person, one body is the root of the idea of the singularity of the self (142). "Consciousness emerges when this primordial story—the story of an object causally changing the state of the body—can be told using the universal nonverbal vocabulary of body signals. The apparent self emerges as the feeling of a feeling" (30–31). Unlike core consciousness, which provides the individual with a sense of self in the here and now, extended consciousness provides us with an elaborate sense of self and autobiographical identity. "[A]utobiographical memories," as Damasio explains, "are *objects*, and the brain treats them as such." Thus they can generate "a sense of self knowing" and so be known (196–97).

5. Several critics have focused, at least in part, on the psychodynamics of the mother-daughter relationship in Kincaid's early works. In her reading of *Annie John*, Roni Natov uses Nancy Chodorow's discussion of the "pre-oedipal longings that surface in early adolescence" alongside Julia Kristeva's notion of the "'semiotic' or the creation of meaning through pre-verbal modalities" to analyze the bond between Annie and her mother (2, 3). "Even though the intimacy between mother and daughter threatens at times to devour the newly developing spirit of the adolescent girl, it is an essential and integral source of nourishment, based as it is on connection, fluidity, and mutuality," Natov writes (14).

Diane Simmons, in her discussion of the "mother mystery" in Kincaid's work, comments, "Kincaid gives us again and again the daughter's inner turmoil, her longing, her rage, and the sense that the profundity of the loss has 'erased' her. . . . The cause of this rupture between the mutually adoring mother and daughter is never fully explained, remaining a mystery at the heart of Kincaid's work" (23). Simmons does, however, find useful Alice Miller's discussion of narcissistic mothers and Nancy Chodorow's analysis of mothers who treat their daughters as if they were "'narcissistic extensions'" (25). Simmons writes, "If the Miller and Chodorow discussions tell us something about the mother as seen in Kincaid's fiction, they may also tell us something about the daughter, showing both women to be experiencing boundary confusion, both, on some level, suffering from a failure to establish a firm sense of self, one that does not rely extensively on a relationship with the other to exist. Each is furious at the other for not being able to continue the perfect union of mother and infant past puberty and into eternity. As the mother would hold the daughter, so would the daughter hold the mother" (26–27). As the daughter approaches puberty, the mother "joins with the colonial powers in trying to turn her daughter into a version of a middle-class English girl" but the mother also provides a "model of African-based female power, that of the obeah woman" (31, 32).

For Helen Timothy, "Perhaps the most puzzling moments in Jamaica Kincaid's *At the Bottom of the River* and *Annie John* are those involving the emotional break between the mother and daughter and the violence of the daughter's response to her mother after that break. In the early stages of the narrative, Kincaid, chronicling the intense emotional bond in which they are wrapped, is at pains to detail the warmly affectionate upbringing Annie received from her mother" (233). For Timothy, Chodorow's study of the mother-daughter relationship is useful in interpreting Kincaid as it documents "the pattern of absolute dependence in a primary love relationship that links the child to the nurturing mother figure" and also as it discusses the daughter's needs to reject the mother to effect a separation from her (233–34). According to Timothy, "[E]ven in the act of rebellion Kincaid strongly shows that the break between mothers and daughters can never be final or complete, that the women are linked irrevocably to each other by ties that are finally inextricable" (242).

In the view of Louis Caton, the use of bonding theory to interpret *Annie John* is problematic. If, as psychoanalysts such as Jane Flax assert, mother-child bonding is a healthy event, and strong bonding is essential for providing the child with a "'firm base from which to differentiate,'" then "since Annie John attains an abundance of attention, love, and mothering from an early age, her movement out of the mother's orbit should happen relatively easily. The novel, however, fails to support that contention. Instead, Kincaid shows Annie's separation leading to pain, frustration, and scenes of hatred. The theoretical knowledge would seem to be at odds with the incidents that highlight emotional rebellion."

According to H. Adlai Murdoch, Annie John's "quest for identity . . . is mediated primarily by the Lacanian paradigm of the alienated subject." In Murdoch's view, Annie "identifies with the image of the other in the form of her mother in an effort to establish a coherent self." But this identification terminates when Annie, witnessing the primal scene, perceives her Dominican mother "as being both racially and culturally different" (325). "[I]t is the attempt at separation and differentiation from the mother, as well as the perception of maternal castration as viewed in and stemming from the primal scene, that initiate Annie John's rebellion against her mother" (328). Moreover, "Death and separation, repeated tropological representations of the repressed nature of Annie's desire to replace identification with the (m)other with full subjectivity, persistently . . . figure crucial points on her road to selfhood" (339).

6. Kincaid, indeed, is a Scottish surname. Information on the name and the clan Kincaid can be found at <http://www.alphalink.com.au/~kincaid/>.

7. In her analysis of the connections among memory, narrative, and identity, Nicola King describes the contrasting assumptions about memory that prevail in our culture: the idea that memory can recover buried events as they really happened or the view that the memory process involves a continuous revision of memory in light of later knowledge, so that memory is subject to a continuous process of "retranslation," making the recovery of the past impossible. For Kincaid, memory recovers the past—a past that is generally readily accessible to her, not buried or repressed—and she also continually retranslates the past in light of later knowledge. To Kincaid this process of retranslation enhances her ability to make personal sense of the past rather than suggesting the impossibility of recalling the "truth" of what happened to her in the past—in particular in her relationship with her mother.

8. In *My Brother*, Kincaid does record her recovery of a "repressed" or "forgotten" memory, her mother's burning of her books (see 128–37).

9. See also the remarks of Simmons, Timothy, and Caton included in note 5.

10. In the view of Antonia MacDonald-Smythe, "For Kincaid, the metaphoric act of inserting her mother's tongue into her own mouth functions both as a way of trammeling the power of the mother's noise and as a way of trying to understand it more fully. . . . From her mother, she learns how to knead language into a shape that adapts to the folk world that her mother continues to illuminate" (117). If "rebellion against" the maternal tongue generates "backchat," then "[t]alking back replaces back talking as a means of coming to truly liberatory speech" (109). According to MacDonald-Smythe, "Talking back reclaims womantalk. Before, the maternal tongue was seen as twisted into habits of colonial complicity. Talking back invests the maternal tongue with a new, compelling authority." In returning to memories of her mother's voice and using her mother tongue, Kincaid links "self-recovery to the 'ancient properties' of Caribbean culture, and to a recurring maternal voice which validates the oral tradition" (110).

Unlike MacDonald-Smythe, who describes talking back as a way of investing the "maternal tongue with a new compelling authority," I view the phenomenon of "talking back" in Kincaid as an act of mimicry and resistance that empowers the daughter-writer at the expense of her mother. In my analysis, I elaborate on the shame dynamics of Kincaid's continual desire to return maternal contempt with her own daughterly countercontempt and, through her writing, to get in the "last word" in her ongoing internal argument with her mother.

2. "I Had Embarked on Something Called Self-Invention": Artistic Beginnings in "Antigua Crossings" and *At the Bottom of the River*

1. Kincaid recalls being sent away to visit her Dominican grandmother when she was nine years old. "It was not an ordinary visit, I had been sent to

stay with her and my mother's sister because after nine years my mother had given birth to another child, my brother, and when he was a baby and I was nine years old, I dropped him and he landed on his head but I did not mean to do that, I only wished to do that, I did not mean to actually do that. There was a moment when I dropped him on his head and the next moment I was on a boat to Dominica to stay with my grandmother" ("Introduction," *Generations of Women* 9). In another account of this incident, Kincaid remarks that her mother sent her to Dominica "because I was so jealous of my brothers' being born that my mother was afraid I would kill them (I had dropped one brother on his head; it had been an accident)" ("Little Revenge" 68).

2. Deborah Mistron includes a chapter on obeah and Christianity in the Caribbean in her book, *Understanding Jamaica Kincaid's* Annie John (see pages 67–118). Derived from West African religions, obeah uses magic and sorcery and often involves the placement of herbs or objects in special locations to achieve desired results, such as to cure or cause illness or to poison an individual. "In the practice of Obeah," writes Mistron, "a person who wishes something to happen to someone—to have a 'fix' or a 'spell' or 'bad spirits' set on someone—visits an Obeah practitioner to describe the situation and seek out a remedy in exchange for money. Usually, the practitioner gives the client, or has the client find, certain materials, then instructs the client on how to use them. The materials could be special herbs or liquids; animal products; or items from the victim such as hair, clothing, or fingernail clippings. The instructions may include placing the materials in the victim's food or drink or in the victim's house, hanging them in a tree, or burying them in the victim's yard. If the instructions are followed, the desired effect should be achieved" (69). Obeah can also include a belief in the "spiritual survival of the dead in the form of ghosts, or 'jumbies' or 'duppies,'" as well as "bush medicine," that is, the use of herbs to cure ailments (70). After the British brought Christianity to its Caribbean colonies, a number of people either abandoned or feared and avoided obeah while others combined "their belief in Christianity with their belief in the effectiveness of Obeah" (70).

3. The devil woman, called *diablesse* in Standard French and *jablesse* in French patois, is "an extremely beautiful woman whose cloven foot betrays her demonic origin. She is usually found at crossroads, her favorite site, from which she lures susceptible males. She is said to be afraid of salt, smoke and crucifixes and in the presence of these, transforms herself into a wild animal" (MacDonald-Smythe n. 13, 139).

4. An "altered state of consciousness," dissociation, as Judith Herman writes, "might be regarded as one of nature's small mercies, a protection against unbearable pain" (43). In dissociation—a "state of detached calm, in which terror, rage, and pain dissolve"—events still "register in awareness" and yet seem "disconnected from their ordinary meanings," and similar to the hypnotic trace state, dissociation is characterized by "subjective detachment or calm, enhanced perception of imagery, altered sensation, including numbness and analgesia, and

distortion of reality, including depersonalization, derealization, and change in the sense of time" (42–43).

5. See also "The Apprentice" in *Talk Stories* 220–23.

6. Interestingly, Kincaid appears to have experienced frightening episodes of dissociation while writing *At the Bottom of the River*. She reports that she was "always somewhat frightened" while writing these stories, an experience she likened to "walking . . . on empty space." Recounting a particularly disturbing incident, she describes what happened when she was working on one section of "At the Bottom of the River." Every night as she was going to sleep, she would envision a faraway house with lights on. But then one night she "couldn't see it—and it just was horrible" because she had depended on the light "as an anchor" to reality: "I had points of reality that I had to have" (Garis).

7. The daughter's vision is derived, in part, from Kincaid's memory of the light in Antigua, which she has described as a "blinding, thick light" that made things "transparent," and the daughter's "desire for a perfect place, a perfect situation," as Kincaid explains, finds its source in British romantic poetry (Cudjoe 231, Bonetti 31). The daughter's vision of the light is also related to Kincaid's childhood fear, derived from obeah, that what she perceived as reality "was not to be trusted." In an attempt to overcome this fear, Kincaid recalls that she became obsessed with the idea that there was "one true thing" and that "there could be some light that would show the reality of a thing" (Cudjoe 230, 231). And finally, the desire for one true or real thing is associated with Kincaid's childhood exposure to English culture. As she has commented, "Within the life of an English person there was always clarity, and within an English culture there was always clarity, but within my life and culture was ambiguity. A person who is dead in England is dead. A person where I come from who is dead might not be dead. I was taught to think of ambiguity as magic, a shadiness and an illegitimacy, not the real thing of Western civilization" (Bonetti 29).

3. "The Way I Became a Writer Was That My Mother Wrote My Life for Me and Told It to Me": Living in the Shadow of the Mother in *Annie John*

1. In *Mr. Potter*, Kincaid writes that her mother was pregnant four times before she was thirty but managed each time to "force her menstruation unnaturally." But the fifth time she was pregnant, "she failed and that failure was because of me, I could not be expelled from my mother's womb at her own will. All this my mother told me when I was forty-one years of age" (136).

2. Kincaid recalls being sent to stay with a friend of her mother the night her brother Devon was born in May 1962. Not long afterward, the woman's six-year-old daughter became sick and died in Annie Drew's arms, and after that Miss Charlotte, who lived across the street, suffered a heart attack and died in

Annie Drew's arms as she tried to comfort the dying woman (*My Brother* 4–5). Kincaid also remembers spending time one summer during her school holidays with a friend of her mother who lived in "the country," which meant "a place where you could not see too many people from your own house." She writes, "There were many reasons why I came to hate this period of my young life: I was away from my mother and my family in general, I could see the graveyard from the house in which I was staying, the guinea hens were unfamiliar, the pigs were cross, the hens were unhappy, but perhaps the most lasting memory is the cotton. . . . I remember my hands aching, particularly in the area at the base of my thumbs as I tried to separate dried pod from cotton, and then the almost certainly white cotton from its certainly black seed" (*My Garden (Book):* 150–51).

During the time she spent at the woman's house, Kincaid recalls being "terrified of the darkness," which was "unrelieved by light even from other houses." She also remembers being able to see the St. John's city graveyard from the house: "[I]t seemed to me that almost every day I could see people attending a funeral. It was then I decided that only people in Antigua died, that people living in other places did not die and as soon as I could, I would move somewhere else, to those places where the people living there did not die" (*My Brother* 26–27).

3. In *My Brother* Kincaid, as she attends the funeral of her brother Devon at Straffee's funeral parlor, recalls the funeral of the hunchbacked girl. "It was in that funeral home in which he lay that I first encountered the dead. The dead then was a girl with a hunchback and I did not know her, I only saw her on the street in her school uniform, but her deformity had made her well known to other schoolchildren who were not deformed at all, and so when she died I wanted to see what she looked like. Seeing her lying in her coffin created a sense of wonder in me; seeing my brother did not, but that might have been because by the time my brother died I was so old that the idea of death seemed possible, but still only possible, something other people might decide to do" (182–83).

4. See, for example, Ferguson, *Jamaica Kincaid* 68–69, Paravisini-Gebert, 87, 109, Perry, "Initiation" 250–51, Simmons 28–29, 31–33, Timothy, 241–42, Yeoh 112–114.

5. In *At the Bottom of the River*, as we have seen, the obeah belief in the *jablesse*—the she-devil that lures people to their deaths by appearing as a beautiful woman—is associated with the mother figure, who may appear as both a beautiful and loving woman and as an angry and cruel persecutor. Kincaid recalls that obeah was an "everyday part" of her life when she was growing up: "I wore things, a little black sachet filled with things, in my undershirt. I was always having special baths. It was a complete part of my life for a very long time" (Cudjoe 229).

6. These stories are based on Kincaid's life. "[M]y mother did keep everything I ever wore," Kincaid recalls, "and basically until I was quite grown up my past was sort of a museum to me. Clearly, the way I became a writer was that

my mother wrote my life for me and told it to me" (O'Conner). Kincaid, who was considered an "adorable child," recalls that her mother would carry her in her arms and "people would reach to kiss me, and I would reach to kiss them, and when my lips met their cheek, I would bite them" (Shen; see also Kincaid's "Biography of a Dress" 94–95). Years later, when Kincaid buys the very same kind of coal pot on which her mother used to cook family meals, she remembers dancing around the coal pot as a girl and falling into the fire. "[T]o this day the scars from that burn are visible around my elbows. What did I learn about fire that I did not already know? Fire burns flesh; if you are a child you will feel it" (*My Garden (Book)*: 46).

7. Describing her extreme shame sensitivity when she was growing up, Kincaid recalls that she used to "cry a lot," a detail about her life she does not mention in *Annie John*: "If I was spoken to harshly, I would burst into tears, and it was considered a sign of my arrogance that I couldn't take criticism. I was really ashamed of being bad" (Ferguson, "Interview" 181).

8. Annie's dramatic response to the admiring praise of others when they hear her read her autobiographical essay in class reveals her extreme shame sensitivity. When Annie experiences a sudden moment of pride, her head feels "funny, as if it had swelled up to the size of, and weighed no more than, a blown-up balloon." Yet as Annie revels in a moment of pride, she also experiences shame. "Often I had been told by my mother not to feel proud of anything I had done and in the next breath that I couldn't feel enough pride about something I had done. Now I tossed from one to the other: my head bowed down to the ground, my head high up in the air" (45).

9. When Kincaid was in school, her mother was "an Anglophile, but I realize now that it was just a phase of my mother's life. She was really a stylish person; it must just have been a phase in her development" (Cudjoe 217). Describing her "middle-class English upbringing," Kincaid remarks, "I never knew we were poor: we ate well; my mother was always grand in every gesture; I was very well brought up. I could never speak bad English in her presence" (Cudjoe 220). Growing up "outside," where her mother cooked on a coal pot, Kincaid remembers how, when the family started to do things other than sleeping inside the house, "it was a sign of some pretension." Kincaid recalls being taught to set the table when the family started to eat inside, and she remembers not being allowed to touch the things inside the house that were considered valuable, such as her mother's china teacup and saucer set commemorating the coronation of "some monarch of England or another" (*My Garden (Book)*: 42).

In *Generations of Women: In Their Own Words*, which includes a photograph of Kincaid, her mother, and her daughter taken by Mariana Cook in 1996 followed by a few words from each on their relationship, Annie Drew remarked, "Growing up, Jamaica had me close to her, I would do everything and she would get the time to read. I don't know if she can still play music, but I sent her to learn to play." Responding, in turn, to her mother's remarks, Kincaid commented: "My mother would make incredibly grand gestures, but there was nothing behind them to sustain them. I remember her sending me to a certain school, but then I had no schoolbooks. I came in first anyway, by borrowing other people's books. She insists she gave me a musical education, but she did not. She sent me to a piano class, but I had no way to practice because we had no piano. I don't mind her stories being amazing, and I don't mind the facts. What I mind is their emotional dishonesty and blindness" ("Portraits: Jamaica Kincaid" 20).

10. In some remarks on the story "Girl," Kincaid states that the story captures her "mother's voice exactly." She also comments, "There are two times that I talked in my life as a child, as a powerless person. Now I talk all the time" (Ferguson, "Interview" 171). In *Annie John*, Annie talks back in this scene and later when her mother accuses her of behaving like a "slut."

11. Asked if the relationship between Annie and Gwen was meant to suggest "lesbian tendencies," Kincaid replied, "No. . . . I think I am always surprised that people interpret it so literally. The relationship between Gwen and Annie is really a practicing relationship. It's about how things work. It's like learning to walk. Always there is the sense that they would go on to lead heterosexual lives. Whatever happened between them, homosexuality would not be a serious thing because it is just practicing" (Vorda 94). Describing the real-life girl the Gwen character is based on, Kincaid remarks: "She was a brilliant, brilliant girl but nothing much happened to her. She's a supervisor somewhere. There's no question, if she and I were boys, that we would have fared much better" (Bonetti 29).

12. Around the age of nine, Kincaid was viewed as "a bookish favorite" of her teachers and as someone unable to defend herself, for she was "very weak-looking, thin, and too tall" for how thin she was. She recalls how a group of girls from her all-girls school would waylay her after school, pin her to the ground, and beat her. "There was no reason for it, I was not malicious, I was not a tattletale, I was not pretty" (*My Brother* 77). Because she was tall and thin, Kincaid was taunted by other children, who called her "Daddy Longlegs" (J. Kaufman). Once the girls at her school tried to flush Kincaid down the toilet, and on another occasion, before there were flushable toilets, they pushed her into the outhouse pot. When she was around eleven, she beat up another girl. "I remember the feeling that *I won*. I beat someone up. I won that fight. Everyone was astonished. And no one ever tried to fight with me again, and I became a kind of leader" (Ferguson, "Interview" 178).

13. Similarly, in "Antigua Crossings," when the mother says to her daughter Mignonette, "I better keep an eye on you because where there's a liar there's a thief," Mignonette starts to steal money from her mother (49). Kincaid's remark on what happened to her when she was a girl and was accused of lying—"They tried to beat it out of me, sometimes literally, by giving me a spanking—no, a beating!" (Vorda 92)—reveals once again her reluctance to talk about the physical abuse she suffered as a child. Since Kincaid's mother frequently accused

her daughter of being a "liar," one can assume that one of the individuals who tried "to beat it out" of Kincaid was her mother. This also suggests that Kincaid, yet again, is omitting the drama of maternal abuse in this scene in *Annie John* in which Mrs. John accuses her daughter of lying.

14. This description of the mother's futile search for the marbles anticipates Kincaid's account in *My Brother* (132–36) of her recovery of a "repressed" memory: Annie Drew's burning of her daughter's books, including the books Kincaid had stashed under the house. Later Kincaid would say of the book-burning incident: "[I]t must have been a source of enormous shame that made me suppress it." To her the burning of her books—books that were her "life"— felt "like an attempt at murder" (Goldfarb 98).

15. Kincaid has remarked that the story about the snake "really did happen" to her mother (Birbalsingh 147).

16. Similarly, in "Antigua Crossings," when the mother receives a letter telling her that her Dominican father is suffering from constipation, she bursts out laughing and says, "'So the great man can't shit'" (50). When asked about the "Columbus in Chains" episode in *Annie John*, Kincaid explained, "[M]y mother had really said, 'The great man can't shit.' I had written that and it wouldn't go in *The New Yorker*, so I changed it. . . . I had a long conversation with my editor at the time because *shit* was not a word that appeared in *The New Yorker* then—appropriately, I have now come to feel" (Perry, "Interview" 497).

17. Kincaid describes the cruelty of her teachers when she was growing up. "I remember having these brilliant people teach me things, and they would teach me in a way very inappropriate for a child. We would scramble to grasp as much of it as we could, and when we couldn't, we were always beaten and punished in some way. It was incredibly brutal" (Muirhead 42). In *A Small Place*, Kincaid describes the racist attitude of the Irish headmistress who told the girls "to stop behaving as if they were monkeys just out of trees" (29).

Asked whether any of her Antiguan teachers recognized her ability, Kincaid replied, "Absolutely not. Everyone thought I had a way with words, but it came out as a sharp tongue. No one expected anything from me at all. Had I just sunk in the cracks it would not have been noted." Kincaid's teachers considered her bright but difficult. "I was sullen. . . . I was always being accused of being rude, because I gave some back chat. . . . I wasn't really angry yet. I was just incredibly unhappy" (Garis).

18. Kincaid was forced to copy out verses from *Paradise Lost* as a punishment in school (see Wachtel 67, Garis, Birbalsingh 147). "I wouldn't have known my idea of justice if I hadn't read *Paradise Lost*, if I hadn't been given parts of *Paradise Lost* to memorize," Kincaid remarks. "It was given to me because I was supposed to be Satan" (Perry, "Interview" 507).

19. "The breadfruit is from the East Indies," Kincaid writes in *My Garden (Book):*. "This food, the breadfruit, has been the cause of more disagree-

ment between parents and their children than anything I can think of. No West Indian that I know has ever liked it" (135). Sent to the West Indies by the English naturalist Joseph Banks, breadfruit "was meant to be a cheap food for feeding slaves," so perhaps children refuse to eat it because they "sense intuitively the part this food has played in the history of injustice" (135–36).

20. The descriptions in *Annie John* of the mother as serpent- and crocodile-like recall the association of the mother with the *jablesse* in *At the Bottom of the River*. In "My Mother," for example, the mother transforms into a reptile-like creature.

21. In "Daytime Dancing, a Report," Kincaid recalls playing "band" during her early years at school (*Talk Stories* 28).

22. "I read *Paradise Lost* at a very early age and I did identify completely with Satan," Kincaid has remarked (Wachtel 66). In her next novel, *Lucy*, the protagonist learns that her mother's name for her—"Lucy"—is short for Lucifer. Kincaid also comes to view Lucifer as self-possessed and defiant, stating, "It is better to reign and to have self-possession in hell than to be a servant in heaven" (Vorda 94).

23. Kincaid was deeply attached to books by English authors like Charlotte Brontë when she was growing up. "My books were the only thing that connected me to a world apart from the cesspool I was in," she has remarked (Goldfarb 98). In "On Seeing England for the First Time," however, she would insist that what made her "feel like nothing" when she was growing up was the England she came to know through English literature (see 34–35). And yet she repeatedly comments on her abiding fondness for Brontë's *Jane Eyre*. "I came to know myself through these people who couldn't be more different from me. I would read *Jane Eyre*, and I imagined myself as Charlotte Brontë. That she didn't look at all like me and lived at the other end of the world a hundred years ago didn't stop me, I just thought I would be Charlotte Brontë!" (Shen). *Jane Eyre*, which Kincaid first read when she was eleven, "never ceases to be relevant. It's like the first person you fall in love with." To Kincaid, the novel seems to have particular relevance because Jane, like Kincaid, was subjected to "[a]ll sorts of cruelty," but "it never touches her soul." The novel is "very much a description of the powerful and the powerless," in Kincaid's view (Cryer). Kincaid also asserts, "I would happily sacrifice any amount of reading of any of my books for people to read *Jane Eyre*" (Balutansky 799).

24. In part, Kincaid may also be describing her self-consciousness as an adolescent about being taller than other girls. Shame theorist Benjamin Kilborne, in his discussion of fantasies of smallness or largeness, remarks, "Believing oneself to be large or small can express both feelings of helplessness and humiliation (being too small to be considered or too conspicuous to fit in) and feelings of rage, rivalry, and danger (endangering others)" (21).

25. See, for example, Natov 13–14, Perry, "Initiation" 251–53, Yeoh 112–114.

4. "As I Looked at This Sentence a Great Wave of Shame Came over Me and I Wept and Wept": The Art of Memory, Anger, and Despair in *Lucy*

1. Some of Kincaid's friends and colleagues, including her friend George Trow, were upset about her use of her experiences with the Arlen family in *Lucy*. When asked about the parallels between the Lewis character in the novel and the *New Yorker* writer Michael Arlen, George Trow commented, "I didn't like it, but that's her privilege" (Garis).

2. In particular, since Kincaid originally published the stories comprising the novel in *The New Yorker*, the readers she had in mind were the white, educated readers of the magazine (and perhaps also Michael Arlen, the real-life counterpart of the Lewis character in the novel, who became her colleague at *The New Yorker*). Although the stories comprising *Lucy* were published by *The New Yorker*, Kincaid describes having undergone "a spiritual break" with the magazine around this time (Kennedy), which was not long after William Shawn's removal from the magazine. (Shawn served as editor from 1952 to January 1987, when he was forced out and replaced by Robert Gottlieb, who served as editor from 1987 to 1992).

3. It has been argued, for example, that Lucy, as an expatriate living in the United States, must "cope with metropolitan colonizing strategies toward herself as a British 'subject'" and that she must "negotiate her way through differing representations of power" in the home of Lewis and Mariah (Ferguson, *Jamaica Kincaid* 108). In her relations with her employers and their friends, Lucy is "simultaneously fetishized and condescended to in a revamped form of old power relations between the colonizer and the colonized" by people who "pretend that the power dynamic between the haves and the have-nots does not dominate everyday life" (Ferguson, *Jamaica Kincaid* 109). In this reading, when Lewis calls Lucy the "poor Visitor," he "arbitrarily empowers himself to objectify her," and when Mariah boasts of her Indian blood in her desire for "forgiveness for colonial complicity," she "contributes to and continues the totalizing narrative of old colonial relations" by attempting to "cancel the past and reposition Lucy" (Ferguson, *Jamaica Kincaid* 110, 113). And when Mariah gives Lucy a copy of de Beauvoir's *The Second Sex*, "Lucy understands this gift as another representation of cultural imperialism that signs Mariah unmistakably as part of the colonizing project" (Ferguson, *Jamaica Kincaid* 124). Lucy, who reveals the "duplicity of the colonizing economy," represents "at a transcendent level . . . Antigua of 1967, a territory freeing itself from the colonizer, already tentatively entering an early postcolonial phase" (Ferguson, *Jamaica Kincaid* 131).

In a similar vein, critics have argued that "[t]he golden glow that permeates Mariah's being and world, from her hair and skin color to her perpetually sunny disposition, becomes, through Lucy's rereading of the seemingly 'innocent' image of the daffodil, an emblem of colonial conquest" (Mahlis 174). During the train ride to Mariah's summer home in the midwest, Mariah, argues another critic, cannot share Lucy's awareness that the passengers in the train's dining car are white and the waiters are black "because she is inscribed by the dominant colonizer's world and accepts the conqueror's status" (Oczkowicz). Describing the family photographs of Mariah, Lewis, and their children on display in their New York apartment, yet another critic states that if in these photographs "a visual culture of the happy nuclear family threatens Lucy by recreating the colonial metaphor of the family and attempting to incorporate her within it," Lucy, through her photographs of the family, reveals "the lie of domestic happiness on which the colonial metaphor depends" (Emery 268). And when Lucy, at the end of the novel, starts to write in the notebook Mariah has given to her, according to yet another critic, she is "the colonized inheriting from the colonizer the means to express herself " (Ledent 61).

4. This "embrace of hatred" also recalls veiled scenes of maternal abuse in *Annie John*, suggesting that Sylvie might also be read as a representation of the "bad" and abusive mother as well as the "bad" and defiant (but also abused) self.

5. Kincaid describes being forced to memorize Wordworth's "I Wandered Lonely as a Cloud": "Every colonial child has to do that. It's a two-edged thing because I wouldn't have known how to write and how to think if I hadn't read those things" (Perry, "Interview" 507). Later Kincaid had a reaction similar to Lucy's when she saw the white cliffs of Dover during a visit to England (see Kincaid, "On Seeing England" 40). Kincaid draws a connection between the two experiences in an interview as she recalls the "nervous breakdown" she had when she first saw the white cliffs of Dover, which she says was "quite like" Lucy's experience with the daffodils. "I had heard so much about those white cliffs. I used to sing a hymn in church that was about longing to see the White Cliffs of Dover over and over again. Things like that permeate my memory, but these things have absolutely no value to me. I hardly know the names of any flowers growing in the West Indies, except the hibiscus, but I know the names of just about all the flowers in England and I also can identify them. . . . I know the White Cliffs of Dover, and I've yearned for them. . . . So there is something wrong there, just as it would have been false for a person like Lucy to love those daffodils. Daffodils do not grow in tropical climates. I know a poem about daffodils, but I did not know a poem about hibiscus" (Vorda 102).

In *My Garden (Book):*, Kincaid states, "I do not like daffodils, but that's a legacy of the gun-to-the-head approach, for I was forced to memorize the poem by William Wordsworth when I was a child" (142). And yet in her Vermont garden, she plants the 'Mount Hood' daffodil, which she says is the "most beautiful daffodil" she has ever "seen, or rather have ever liked." "I do not like daffodils," she adds, "for a reason that is not at all aesthetic, a reason much more serious than that" (186). But when an interviewer commented in 1998 that Kincaid had transformed the daffodil into "the ultimate symbol of imperialism," she had this to say: "I hope it makes people read the poem. Wordsworth happens to be my favorite. It's not Wordsworth's fault, mind you. It was only the way in which he was used" (Balutansky 799). In a National Public Radio show in 1999, Kincaid, insisting that she no longer had an aversion to daffodils, said, "I do love daffodils now" (Penkava); and in a 2001 "In the Garden" article in *The New Yorker*, she indicated that she had planted five hundred daffodils at the foot of the lower wall of her Vermont garden ("Sowers and Reapers").

6. "When I was nine," Kincaid recalls, "I refused to stand up at the refrain of 'God Save Our King.' I hated 'Rule, Britannia'; and I used to say that we weren't Britons, we were slaves. I never had any idea why. I just thought that there was no sense to it—'Rule Britannia, Britannia rule the waves, Britons never ever shall be slaves.' I thought that we weren't Britons and that we were slaves" (Cudjoe 217).

7. Lucy's attachment to Miriam recalls Kincaid's account in 1993 of the "tremendous hold" her eight-year-old daughter, Annie, had over her. "Because I haven't known my daughter very long—she's only eight years old—I don't really know how to articulate the hold she has over me. I find it very interesting, how much I love her and how much I depend on her, on seeing her, on being near her, and how much I worship her in some way" (Wachtel 65). Drawing a connection between her childhood attachment to her mother and the "hold" her daughter had over her, Kincaid remarked, "Maybe I'm just doomed to be in awe of these two powerful women at various times of my life—first my mother and now my daughter" (Wachtel 66).

8. "The truth is, I come from a place that's very unreal," Kincaid has said of Antigua (Vorda 88). As a child, she "lived in utter fear" for a time because she was not certain that anything she saw "was itself" or whether things were "real or not" (Cudjoe 226, 227). When asked about the story of the monkey throwing a stone, Kincaid said that the story "was true," and she explained that in Dominica people were "always transforming themselves into monkeys. . . . People would turn themselves into something called a *jablesse*. You would become a *jablesse*" (Ferguson, "Interview" 181).

9. When she was working on *Lucy*, Kincaid read *The Intimate Journals of Paul Gauguin*. "It was very inspiring. You know, he's another dissenter, another rebel. Of course he died badly, of a sexual disease" (Muirhead 47). Kincaid found the *Intimate Journals* "a great comfort" because Gauguin was "so unrelenting of himself" and was "very selfish and very determined" (Vorda 103).

10. Kincaid insists that she could not have been a writer had she stayed in Antigua because she would have found it difficult to endure "the mental, the verbal, [and] the spiritual scorn" that would have been directed at her from the Antiguan community (Goldfarb 96).

11. Kincaid recalls in *My Brother* that she had been living in the United States for ten years when she learned about her stepfather's death. Because Kincaid and her mother were in one of their "periods of not speaking to each other, not on the telephone, not in letters," she learned of his death three months after he was buried, when her mother finally wrote to tell her about it (118). "[M]y

mother said that his death had left them impoverished, that she had been unable to pay for his burial, and only the charitable gifts of others had allowed him to have an ordinary burial, not the extraordinary burial of a pauper" (119). Kincaid describes her reaction to her mother's letter: "I felt condemned because I had so removed myself from my family that their suffering had gone unnoticed by me, and even as I wept over my father's death, I would not have done much to prevent it, and even as I wept over my father's death and my mother's description of emotional pain and financial deprivation, I would not do a thing to alleviate it" (120).

Lucy's account of her father's history (see 124–25) is based on the life of Kincaid's stepfather, David Drew. In *My Garden (Book):* she recalls David Drew's life. "My father: his mother left him when he was a small child, small enough for it to matter so much to him that he still spoke of it when he was over fifty years old . . . ; she went to England and he never saw her again. She once sent him a pair of shoes, but they were too big and they were put away; when he tried them on again, he had outgrown them. Perhaps at the same time, perhaps before, perhaps afterward (it was never made clear to me) his father left him and went off to build the Panama Canal" (147–48).

12. Kincaid also was an only child until age nine, and from ages nine to thirteen her life was disrupted by the birth of her three brothers. "I thought I was the only thing my mother truly loved in the world, and when it dawned on me that it wasn't so, I was devastated," she states (Listfield). By the age of fourteen she felt "already disappointed and already defeated, already hopeless, thinking and feeling that I was standing on a fragile edge and at any moment I might fall off into a narrow black hole that would amount to my entire earthly existence: I felt I hated my mother, and even worse, I felt she hated me, too" (*My Brother* 140–41). Kincaid's mother and stepfather favored their sons over her, envisioning bright futures for her brothers—"one was going to be Prime Minister, one a doctor, one a Minister, things like that"—while discounting her future. "I never heard anybody say that I was going to be anything except maybe a nurse. There was no huge future for me, nothing planned" (BBC).

13. Kincaid admits that she might owe "a lot" of her success to the "idea of feminism" and says that she does not "mind" if people place her in the feminist category, but she also refuses to proclaim herself a feminist writer. "[T]hat's just me as an individual," she explains. "I mean, I always see myself as alone. I can't bear to be in a group of any kind, or in the school of anything" (Cudjoe 221). But while refusing the label "feminist writer," she does call herself a feminist and insists, "Every woman is a feminist" (Trueheart; see also Lee).

In her essay "Islander Once, Now Voyager," Kincaid recalls how she was given two books to read—Simone de Beauvior's *The Second Sex* and Julia Child's *Mastering the Art of French Cooking*—when she was nineteen and living "as a servant" with a family in New York. "[T]he woman at the head of the household was a feminist and because of that she was not unsympathetic to my predicament in the world—I was female and poor." Kincaid describes her reaction to *The Second Sex*: "[W]hen I read it I did not feel grateful that someone

(Beauvoir or the female head of the household in which I was a servant) had made valid or confirmed the things I knew already about being female. I only became even more angry that people I had thought to be in a position superior to mine could only tell me about the misery I already knew; they could not tell me how to alleviate it." After reading the book, Kincaid put it away. But in her 2000 essay she remarks, "I recommend it to women, especially if they are at the age I was when I first read it, but I will never read it again. Not so *Mastering the Art of French Cooking*."

14. As I noted in my discussion of the autobiographical sources of *Annie John*, Kincaid was once forced to copy out verses from *Paradise Lost* at school as a punishment. "It was given to me because I was supposed to be Satan," she recalls (Perry, "Interview" 507).

15. Asked about Enid Blyton's books, Kincaid commented that Blyton's "Noddy" books were "deeply racist," for they had blond children in them and a black doll character called "Golliwog" (Muirhead 43). And yet, she admitted, "When I would read things that I now see as racist in someone like Enid Blyton, I just thought that it was an accident that the Golly who was bad was black. . . . It never occurred to me that for Blyton it meant that Black people were bad. And I loved Golly for misbehaving. I begged to have a Golliwog" (Muirhead 44).

16. This, in turn, recalls Annie John's perception of her mother's "circling hand" as death-like, revealing, again, the connection between the maternal (or lover's) hand and the hand of the abuser.

5. "Imagine the Bitterness and the Shame in Me as I Tell You This": The Political Is Personal in *A Small Place* and "On Seeing England for the First Time"

1. A personal-political essay, *A Small Place* is based on Kincaid's experiences, both as a girl and an adolescent growing up in Antigua and as an adult returning to Antigua after an almost twenty-year absence. But some critics nevertheless find it difficult to categorize *A Small Place*. For Giovanna Covi, *A Small Place* "poses a problem of genre definition: it is a political essay for its content, but it reads like fiction, while sounding like a speech delivered with the passion and rhythm of a song" (38). According to Alison Donnell, the "generic definition" of *A Small Place* "has been crucial to its reception—it has been published variously as autobiography, politics, history, sociology (but not, as far as I know, as fiction)" ("She Ties Her Tongue" 107). Susan Lanser questions the "different implications" conveyed by the different ways the book is classified: as "black studies" by the publisher and as "Antigua—Description and travel" by the Library of Congress (281). For Angelia Poon, in *A Small Place*, which was published after *Annie John*, Kincaid "leaves the realm of imaginative fiction for a more indeterminate, genre-liminal space amidst fiction, travelogue and essay from which to voice her polemic" (para. 4).

Perhaps because Kincaid, in *A Small Place*, incorporates autobiographical details familiar to readers of her fictional-autobiographical novels, some critics have described the essay as reading like fiction or occupying a genre-liminal space admist fiction and factual essay. In her many remarks in interviews on *A Small Place*, Kincaid describes it as an autobiographical work (like her fiction) in which she voices her anger not only at her colonial past but also at the governmental corruption in contemporary Antigua. While the speaker of *A Small Place* does sound like a fictional narrator or character, one can safely identify the speaker with Kincaid, the author. For in her account Kincaid incorporates details of her past, and she also makes public alleged and reported governmental scandals as she illustrates the corruption of contemporary Antiguan society and politics.

2. In an interview, Kincaid contrasts the culturally enriching experience of the white tourist who visits Vienna to the "rubbish-like" experience of the white tourist in Antigua. "I can tell you there are differences in going to Vienna and going to Antigua. If you don't go to Vienna for fun, you can also go to experience all of the cultural benefits and gain a deeper understanding of the Western world. If you go to a place like Antigua, it's to have a rubbish-like experience. You want to forget who you are for the moment. You're not interested in these people. You're not interested in their culture, except in some sort of anthropological way that offers you psychic relief. They have nothing of value you want to bring home. It's an escape, a moment to forget who you really are" (Vorda 96).

3. In describing the white tourist's cab ride from the airport to the hotel, Kincaid comments on the recklessness of the Antiguan cab driver, who also attempts to cheat the tourist. Kincaid's reckless, cheating cab driver may be a personal reference to her biological father, Roderick Potter, who worked as a cab driver in Antigua and who is the subject of her fictional memoir, *Mr. Potter*.

4. For a related discussion of the link between racial shame and the African American experience see Bouson, *Quiet as It's Kept* 12–18, n.5, 219–20, and *passim*.

5. In a 1951 article on Antigua in *Holiday Magazine*, the British author Alec Waugh described the Mill Reef Club: "Sooner or later almost certainly you will find yourself included in an invitation to Mill Reef. You will be very foolish if you do not accept it. Mill Reef is very special. It is a private club for American membership only, where a large guest house provides resort facil[...] Its members are hospitable and during the season from New Year to 15th April, stage innumerable lunch and cocktail parties. . . . There is a youthful and gay atmosphere about the Saturday night dances" (cited by Scott 977).

6. The doctor's response recalls Joel Kovel's analysis of white racism. The "nuclear experience" of "aversive" white racism, writes Kovel, "is a sense of disgust about the body of the black person based upon a very primitive fantasy: that it contains an essence—dirt—that smells and may rub off onto the body of

the racist" (84). In *Mr. Potter*, Kincaid presents a more detailed and somewhat sympathetic portrait of the Czechoslovakian "doctor," Dr. Weizenger, describing his racist attitudes but also his survival of the "ten lifetimes of [the] horror" perpetrated by the Nazis (191).

7. Recalling her excitement as a girl when new books arrived at the library in Antigua, Kincaid remarks: "God, I remember the librarian as this young, beautiful woman. It was one of the real shocks to me to see [when I returned to Antigua] that she had grown into this mature woman. . . . You know she caught me stealing books, but she would never say that" (Ferguson, "Interview" 173).

8. Questioning readings of *A Small Place* that "situate Kincaid unproblematically as an oppositional voice or a voice that renders the point of view of the 'native,'" Veronica Gregg argues that Kincaid's work "is caught within many of the assumptions it purportedly seeks to overturn." In it, "Kincaid's indictment of the historical and economic conditions that produce the tourist also reproduces Antiguans as victims or problems" (925). Moreover, Kincaid's narrator "homogenizes, reduces, fixes other Antiguans in a repetition (and extension) of the Cartesian paradigm: I think, therefore I am. They don't think, therefore, they are not quite human. . . . In the apparent decolonization of her own mind, the enlightened narrator frames herself as a unitary subject and linguistically recolonizes othered Antiguans" (927).

Interestingly, just as Kincaid talks back to her fellow Antiguans, so Jane King, a Caribbean poet from St. Lucia who describes herself as a "small-place person," talks back to Kincaid (897). "[S]o Kincaid does not like the Caribbean much, finds it dull and boring and would rather live in Vermont. There can really be no difficulty with that, but I do not see why Caribbean people should admire her for denigrating our small place in this destructively angry fashion," writes King (899). "Does Kincaid's question about whether Antiguans are children, idiots or mad people not indicate shame?" (901). "What, really is wrong with staying at home? What is the defect evidenced by all those who stay in the Caribbean? I reject the arguments that we are all corrupt, stupid or insensitive" (902).

9. "Life is hard whether you live on a Caribbean island or somewhere else," Kincaid stated in a 1991 interview. "It was hard to grow up in a place like that, in particular because it doesn't have the comforts you think a place like that has. A person living in a place like that finds the sun hard to take. They find the nice days after a while hard to take. After a while it becomes a prison. Life is just extremely hard" (Vorda 84). In another interview from 1990, Kincaid commented on how "difficult" she found it to visit her mother and brothers in Antigua. "I worry it will swallow me up and never spit me out," she remarked (Donahue).

10. In a similar way, the Amerindian narrator in Kincaid's story "Ovando" becomes "nothing" to the Spanish colonizer. A "key player in the early history of the Americas," Fray Nicolás de Ovando was an "excessive autocrat" who ruled Hispaniola from 1502 to 1508 and was "responsible for mas-

sive genocide" (Ferguson, *Jamaica Kincaid* 133, 135, 136). In the story, Kincaid's narrator makes this "charge" against Ovando: "that he loved himself so that all other selves and all other things became nothing to him. I became nothing to Ovando. My relatives became nothing to Ovando. Everything that could trace its lineage through me became nothing to Ovando. And so it came to be that Ovando loved nothing, lived in nothing and died in just that way" (83).

11. In these passages in "On Seeing England for the First Time," Kincaid indicts English literature—in particular, Victorian literature—for engendering in her a sense of inferiority. Yet, after this essay was published in 1991, Kincaid continued to remark on her love of English literature, commenting in 1996, for example, that her favorite novel was *Jane Eyre* (Cryer). And in 2000, she said that she "came to know" herself through reading works such as *Jane Eyre*. "I would read *Jane Eyre*, and I imagined myself as Charlotte Brontë. That she didn't look at all like me and lived at the other end of the world a hundred years ago didn't stop me, I just thought I would be Charlotte Brontë! Maybe George Bush's daughters want to be Charlie Parker—you don't know how the hell things are going to work" (Shen).

6. "I Would Bear Children, but I Would Never Be a Mother to Them": Writing Back to the Contemptuous Mother in *The Autobiography of My Mother*

1. Born in Mahaut, Dominica, Annie Victoria Richardson, later Annie Drew, was Carib Indian on her mother's side and of mixed Scottish and African ancestry on her father's side.

2. Kincaid discusses these obeah stories in her interviews. For the story about the *jablesse* that appeared as a monkey, see Ferguson 181; for the story about the worm crawling out of the leg of Annie Drew's brother, see Cudjoe 226; for the story about the *jablesse* that appeared as a naked woman bathing in a river, see Cudjoe 230.

3. As I discussed earlier in my analyses of *Lucy* and *A Small Place*, rage, contempt, and power scripts are used to protect against shame. Gershen Kaufman explains that rage—"[w]hether in the form of generalized hostility, fomenting bitterness, chronic hatred, or explosive eruptions"—functions to protect the self against exposure and thus defends against shame. Like rage scripts, contempt scripts protect the self, for "[t]o the degree that others are looked down upon, found lacking or seen as lesser or inferior beings, a once-wounded self becomes more securely insulated against further shame" (*Psychology* 100). Power scripts, which aim at gaining power over others, also protect the self against shame. "When power scripts combine with rage and/or contempt scripts, the seeking of revenge is a likely outcome. . . . Now the humiliated one, at long last, will humiliate the other" (*Psychology* 101).

4. While Xuela's father is in part based on Annie Drew's Dominican father (see note 10), it also seems likely that the abandoning father described in the novel is drawn from Kincaid's memories of her biological father, Roderick Potter. Kincaid met her biological father when she was in her thirties. "He's sort of typical of West Indian men: I mean, they have children, but they never seem to connect themselves with these children," she comments (Cudjoe 219). In *Mr. Potter*, Kincaid tells the story of her biological father in yet another invented memoir.

5. This recalls the image of the biting child in *Annie John*, which, in turn, is based on Kincaid's life (see Shen).

6. Discussing the role of language in the novel, Giselle Anatol remarks that if Xuela's "vehement anti-colonial attitude appears incompatible with the fact that when she enters the realm of orality, she employs the English language," the fact that she associates "pain and English . . . is clearly anti-colonial," and she "enters into the 'master' discourse to condemn her colonizer" (941). In Anatol's view, Xuela's "failure to speak Creole seems to ride on Kincaid's teasing out a very literal interpretation of the phrase 'mother tongue'" since Xuela's "alienation from her biological mother results in her rejection of, or alienation from, her 'true' mother tongue" (942). Aware that her father, Alfred Richardson, speaks Creole only with members of his family and with others who have known him since his childhood, Xuela comes to associate her father's Creole speech "with expressions of his 'real self '"—an African Caribbean self that he finds embarrassing—and she also becomes suspicious of his "Eurocentric manipulation of English in order to garner respect and power" (943). But the novel also warns against the "romanticization of Creole" as the mother tongue found in the English/Creole, "father tongue"/"mother tongue" binary. Although Xuela's "standard"-English-speaking father can speak Creole, "he in no way identifies with the majority of people who also speak this Nation Language. Nothing suggests that Richardson's 'African-Caribbeanness' is 'real' or substantial simply because he can speak Creole. Arguing for an 'authentic' Caribbean subjectivity based upon language leads one into dangerous territory" (945–46).

7. Kincaid remembers being "set free by writing" when she was around nine or ten years old. "My mother had sent me to live with her family, and I missed my mother and wrote her letters which I never posted, and I said I was being very badly treated, which was not true. And they were found. Her family were so upset they sent me back. That was the first time I wrote something that changed my life. It changed my situation anyway" (Muirhead 42–43).

8. In a similar way, Lucy is betrayed by her mother, who loves her sons and envisions important futures for them but not for her daughter. As I noted in my discussion of the autobiographical sources of *Lucy*, Lucy's "betrayal" is based on Kincaid's life, for Kincaid's mother and stepfather planned important futures for their sons but not for their daughter (see, e.g., BBC).

9. Xuela's relationship with her stepmother recalls Kincaid's relationship with her mother, Annie Drew. In *My Brother*, Kincaid writes about learning of

her stepfather's death some three months after he died because she and her mother "were in one of our periods of not speaking to each other." Kincaid had "terrible feelings" for her mother, who, in turn, had "terrible feelings" for her daughter (118). "She did not like me, I did not like her; I believe she wanted me dead, though not actually; I believe I wanted her dead, though not really" (119).

10. Xuela's father is in part based on Annie Drew's Dominican father, who was of mixed Scottish and African ancestry. "He was a policeman, but then he became rather pious. He owned some land and was a lay preacher," Kincaid recalls (Cudjoe 225).

11. Kincaid's mother told this story about her encounter with a *jablesse*: "They were going to school and saw a beautiful woman bathing in the river— Dominica has so many rivers. In those days they didn't have many bridges, so they had to cross this river—which was particularly full because it had rained a lot. At the mouth of this river they saw a woman, a beautiful woman, surrounded by these mangoes, wonderful mangoes. In fact, my mother has shown me the mango trees and the place where this happened. Well, they were about to swim to her, but some people realized that this was not real—it was too beautiful, the mangoes were too beautiful. One boy swam to her, and he drowned. His body was never found. He vanished; everything vanished. My mother didn't tell me that story as a folktale; that was an illustration to me of not believing what I saw, of really not being deceived by appearances, of really being able to tell that it was really a woman and not someone who would drown you" (Cudjoe 230). See Cobham for a discussion of the African sources of this story about the river goddess—a figure that is "immediately recognizable from her description as the West African Mammywata, known in Jamaica as 'River Mumma'" (871).

12. When Kincaid was forty-one years old, her mother told her that she had had four abortions before the age of thirty. "Four times this thickening of fluids gathered in her womb, four times before she was thirty years of age she managed to throw it out. . . . And when my mother tried to force her menstruation unnaturally for the fifth time, she failed and that failure was because of me, I could not be expelled from my mother's womb at her own will" (*Mr. Potter* 136).

13. Alfred John Richardson was the name of Kincaid's maternal grandfather, and both he and his son were named after King Alfred (see Kincaid, "On Seeing England for the First Time" 34).

14. John, the brother of Kincaid's mother, "was possessed, and something was set on him," Kincaid recalls. He died "from *obeah* things. He had a worm crawl out of his leg. Now, this sounds odd, but it did happen" (Cudjoe 226).

15. Kincaid's mother left Dominica when she was sixteen after a quarrel with her father—a quarrel that led him to disinherit her. After moving to Antigua, the birthplace of her father, Annie worked for a while as a housekeeper;

then she worked for a St. John's doctor, who was one of her father's friends; and then, after the doctor left St. John's, she worked for Dr. Weizenger, a dentist from Czechoslovakia who also claimed he was a doctor.

16. This description of Xuela's shame because she did not know her father can be read as a veiled reference to Kincaid's shame because she did not know her biological father, Roderick Nathaniel Potter, and he, in turn, did not know his father, Nathaniel Potter, a fisherman. In *Mr. Potter*, Kincaid writes, "A line runs through Mr. Potter's very own self: I hold in my hand a document that certifies the day of his birth, the name of his mother . . . and there is an empty space with a line drawn through it where the name of his father, Nathaniel Potter, ought to have been." In a similar way, Kincaid's birth certificate has "an empty space with a line drawn through it where the name of my father, Roderick Nathaniel Potter, ought to be" (100).

17. Kincaid, as noted above, explains that Xuela's loss of her mother can be read as a metaphor for the African diaspora and the loss the motherland, Africa: "For Africans, Africa died the minute they were born into the new world" (Jaggi). Since Xuela's mother is part of the extinct Carib people, Xuela's loss includes not only her African but also her Carib Indian roots.

7. "I Shall Never Forget Him Because His Life Is the One I Did Not Have": Remembering Her Brother's Failed Life in *My Brother*

1. The ability of Kincaid's mother to continue to cause pain in her adult daughter is evident in the account in *My Brother* of Annie Drew's 1990 visit to Kincaid's Vermont home. During the visit, Kincaid and her mother had an enormous quarrel, and Kincaid asked her mother to apologize for all the suffering she had caused her, but to no avail. Instead, her mother proclaimed the rightness of her actions, saying, "'I am never wrong, I have nothing to apologize for, everything I did at the time, I did for a good reason'" (27). Justifying her actions to one of Kincaid's friends, as Kincaid later learned, Annie Drew confided that Kincaid disliked her because she had been a strict mother, but had she not been, Kincaid would have ended up having ten children by ten different men. Illustrating her strictness, she told Kincaid's friend that her daughter, who loved books and reading, used to lend her books to a boy and that one day Annie Drew told the boy, whom she believed was hiding his true intentions by borrowing books, to stop coming to the house, telling him that it was not a lending library. Annie Drew's remark to Kincaid's friend ultimately led to Kincaid's recovery of the repressed memory of her mother's burning of her girlhood collection of books.

2. Despite her enduring memory of the "horrible events" of her past, Kincaid "forgot"—that is, repressed—her memory of this incident, and yet, as one critic has astutely observed, Kincaid does seem to approach this troubling memory in the scene in *Annie John* in which the mother, in a rage, searches under the

house for Annie's hidden stash of marbles. But in the earlier account, the mother fails to find the marbles, giving Annie a "second chance" (see Rice 30–31). If the slow and digressive narration of the book-burning incident suggests the delaying tactics "typical of trauma recovery" in which the trauma victim defers confronting her painful memory (Rice 27–28), then this account of the mother's burning of her daughter's books may also include an omitted narrative suggested in Kincaid's remark that she believed her mother wanted her dead—that of the mother's physical assault on her daughter.

3. "That period of my life, just before I was sent away, seemed both incredibly narrow and cannonlike and dark as a tunnel, and yet exceptionally lit up," Kincaid recalls. "I do remember the flames and the incredible anger at my desire to contextualize myself from the world I was in, with the books, and the burning. . . . It was astonishing, and I didn't see how I would ever come out of that. That seemed to be my life. And I don't know if Devon had such a moment in which his life really was stilled. By the time he died many years later, he had long been dead. I felt that I had died then. It was just sheer luck, it was just sheer, what? . . . I don't know . . . blessing, that got me out of that. I have not much doubt that I would not have lived very long" (B. Schneider 8).

4. Noting that Kincaid "brings more of the Antiguan creole into *My Brother* than she has done in her other works," Maria Lima remarks, "This move from Standard English to Creole speech is meant not only to underscore the class differences between Kincaid and her family of origin, but it also makes manifest, as François Lionnet writes of Michelle Cliff, 'the double consciousness of the post-colonial, bilingual, and bicultural writer who lives and writes across the margins of different traditions and cultural universes.' . . . What is different in Kincaid's use is the way she seems to devalue the Creole form by calling it 'the English that instantly reveals the humiliation of history, the humiliation of the past not remade into art.' Can readers therefore consider Kincaid's autobiographical fiction to this date—her continuing bildungsroman—an effort to remake the humiliation of the past into art? I am, of course, assuming here that Kincaid means not only the individual humiliation of growing up undervalued and with little hope, but the collective humiliation of history that she describes in *A Small Place*. If her ongoing bildungsroman is indeed her effort to remake the humiliation of the past into art, who is she really writing for?" (858).

5. "Certainly, the asymmetrical relation between Antigua and the United States, allegorized here in the brother-sister relationship, is exemplified by the epidemiology of HIV/AIDS in the Caribbean," writes Sarah Brophy. "According to the Joint United Nations Programme on HIV/AIDS, the incidence of HIV in the Caribbean is almost four times that in North America, making the rate of HIV infection in the region second only to that in sub-Saharan Africa" (266). In Brophy's view, Devon emerges as Kincaid's political unconscious: "Devon embodies her political unconscious in that he represents an extreme example of the vulnerability of those who remain in the place that Kincaid has left, a vulnerability that remains profound even when it is masked by a performance of

masculine bravado and indifference. Devon's presence and voice haunt his sister's text, compelling her to evaluate her complicity, from a distance, in his suffering and motivating her to criticize his ignorance and the social and economic conditions that have produced it" (268). While Devon is viewed as a victim of "neocolonial economic and social factors" in *My Brother*, as Brophy comments (266), Kincaid also, as is her wont, places emphasis on the destructive powers of Annie Drew, describing Devon and his two brothers as victims of their mother.

8. "Like Him and His Own Father before Him, I Have a Line Drawn through Me": Imagining the Life of the Absent Father in *Mr. Potter*

1. Kincaid recalls how a man once approached her and her mother and identified himself to Annie Drew as "'Walker, Potter's brother,'" leading Kincaid to wonder who "Potter" was. "They wouldn't explain," Kincaid recalls. "What's untypical is I didn't accept [their silence]. I should have said, 'Oh, yes' and just joined the parade. I said 'No.' I'm really not interested in a constant attempt to . . . make you think there wasn't a yesterday" (V. Jones). Commenting that *Mr. Potter* was "not meant" to be about her and her relationship with her "real father," Kincaid explains, "When I was writing it, I wasn't writing it to explore the fact that my father abandoned me, I was writing to explore what it means to be abandoned or what it means to live with someone who you would never know. The narrator may be 50-per-cent Mr. Potter, but she will never know him, and the only way he recognizes her is through the shape of her nose" (Macgowan).

2. Kincaid has described her biological father as "sort of typical of West Indian men: I mean, they have children, but they never seem to connect themselves with these children" (Cudjoe 219). When an interviewer asked Kincaid about her biological father in 1996, she remarked, tellingly, "He was as real to me as you. Yes, you'll go and I'll think, was there someone here?" (Jacobs).

3. Deborah Mistron's *Understanding Jamaica Kincaid's* Annie John includes information on social attitudes toward illegitimacy in Antigua during Kincaid's formative years. "Despite the fact that illegitimacy and mother-centered homes are accepted by the people, until quite recently (1986), and during the time that Annie John was growing up, illegitimate children were often discriminated against. Legitimate children often had more advantages, a higher social status, and more educational opportunities. Legitimate children were baptized on Sundays, at a church service; illegitimate ones were baptized separately during the week. Illegitimate children were often denied entrance to the better schools on the island and thus had fewer educational and vocational opportunities. . . . In 1986, a law was passed in Antigua that prohibited discrimination against illegitimate children; it also gave them equal rights to inherit property from their fathers, even if the father had died without a will" (159). Mistron's analysis of Annie John's family situation is telling, pointing as it does to Kincaid's avoidance of the issue of her own illegitimacy in her early works. Mistron

comments that Annie John's "father, typically, is older, with several previous relationships and children, but married to her mother, which gives Annie and her mother increased social status" (159).

Insight into the causes of illegitimacy in Antigua is found in an article Mistron includes by Mindie Lazarus-Black entitled "Bastardy, Gender Hierarchy, and the State: The Politics of Family Law Reform in Antigua and Barbuda" (originally published in *Law and Society Review* [Winter 1992]: 863–99). Remarking on Antigua's low marriage rate and high rate of illegitimacy, Lazarus-Black states: "In the early 1980s . . . the marriage rate per one thousand persons was less than three, while the illegitimacy rate at birth averaged 80%. A variety of reasons account for these continued rates, including the legacy of laws that discouraged marriage and prohibited divorce, individuals' reluctance to marry until they have established a home and some financial security, an unwillingness on the part of men to wed until they feel they have 'sown their wild oats,' the critical relationship between marriage and individual religious salvation which becomes especially important in one's later years, and individuals' outright resistance to this form of state intervention in their personal lives. Visiting 'friends' and long-term, nonlegal relationships are common and prevail alongside formalized unions. Although both men and women say marriage is an ideal to which they aspire 'some day,' parenting outside of marriage is also highly valued. Within marriage, husbands and wives have segregated roles. . . . Both sexes believe firmly that a wife should defer to her husband when the couple faces important decisions. . . . A cultural prescriptive, common throughout the region, holds that men 'by nature' love to love more than one woman and ensures that many men will father 'outside' children even after they are wed" (180).

4. See *A Small Place* 28–29, 34.

5. See *Annie John* 121–22.

6. Kincaid recalls that when her mother's father died a wealthy man, he left his money to his other daughter who, in turn, left the family fortune to the illegitimate daughter of her husband. When Kincaid asked her mother, who had been disinherited after quarreling with her father, if she was "sorry" about what had happened, her mother replied, "'No, I was born with nothing, and I will die with nothing.' Something happened between her father and her, and she wouldn't compromise" (Ferguson, "Interview" 166). In another interview, Kincaid commented that her mother was disinherited because she married against her father's wishes (see Steavenson 37). See also *Annie John* 19–20.

7. In an interview, Kincaid describes this encounter with her biological father when he visited her in New York City in 1982. "He said he was my father, and I thought, 'How interesting,'" she recalls. "Then he actually began to make a claim of being my father, an emotional claim." When she asked him what she should call him and he answered "'Oh, why, Dad,'" the conversation ended, and they "never spoke again." "What I would have wanted him to say—how sorry he had been, how wrong he had been—he didn't say it. Then I didn't want to participate anymore," Kincaid explains. She also voices her anger at her father.

"'You weren't my father when I was a year old, and you're my father now?' . . . What do we do with the years in between? Do we just forget them? My tradition says 'Yes.' I say 'No'" (V. Jones). In another interview, Kincaid describes the aftermath of this encounter. "When he found me not interested in the idea of his being my dad, he actually disinherited me. It's in his will" (McLarin).

9. Conclusion: "I Am Writing for Solace": Seeking Solace in Writing, Gardening, and Domestic Life

1. "Mr. Shawn used to protect us, used to try to get us enough money at the magazine, and to make sure we did the best kind of writing we could," Kincaid recalls. Discussing Shawn's removal from the magazine, she states, "It was sort of a tragedy for American literature when he was removed from the *New Yorker*, and it killed him, I think. He was treated very brutally. I think American literature is really changed for it. A lot of us got hurt when the *New Yorker* fell apart" (Kreilkamp 55). Shawn, who was removed as *New Yorker* editor in 1987, died in 1992 at the age of eighty-five.

2. Kincaid was incensed when she learned that Tina Brown was planning to invite comedienne Roseanne Barr to guest-edit a special issue of *The New Yorker* on women (Barr ended up being one of several consultants on the issue). "I found the situation there intolerable," she remarked. "I needed to separate myself from the Las Vegas showgirls with ornate nipples in the magazine. I don't blame Tina Brown. She's just scared like anyone else working for the Conde Nast empire" (Grondahl). Under Tina Brown, writers were not encouraged to pursue their own ideas. Kincaid described the editorial policy in this way: "'You have an idea? . . . And who will be paying you for your idea? No, here is *our* idea, and we pay you for doing *our* idea.' I mean, it was brutal" (Shen). Tina Brown was editor of *The New Yorker* from 1992 to 1998; in 1998 David Remnick became editor of the magazine.

3. Kincaid, did, nevertheless, start publishing in the magazine again in 2001, several years after Tina Brown's departure.

4. Kincaid, who is now divorced, was determined to protect the privacy of her marriage and family life during the years of her marriage to Allen Shawn, a composer who teaches at Bennington College in Bennington, Vermont, and she was also reticent about her 1993 conversion to Judaism, the faith of Allen Shawn. "He's a very nice man who seems to love me very much," Kincaid once said of her husband. "But he doesn't like to read about our private life. He was a wonderful unexpected thing in my life, I never thought I'd be married. I knew from the beginning that I was a very difficult person and very shy. Who would I marry? Now I wouldn't know how to live without this person" (Drewes). Respecting her husband's wishes, Kincaid disclosed little about her family, but she did offer a few tantalizing glimpses into her private life, describing her husband as a "great companion" and someone "very interested" in her, who read

her work daily. "Probably I couldn't be a writer without Allen. . . . I really depend on him as a reader," as she once remarked (Perry, "Interview" 505).

In 1990, a reporter said this of Kincaid and her husband: "In every physical aspect they are opposites. He is small and pale; she is tall and dark. His nose is thin; hers is wide. His hair is sparse; hers is thick. They have in common an extreme gentleness of manner. He looks up a long distance at her from under the tops of his wire glasses, and she looks down from her dark-rimmed eyes, and such an expression passes between them of benevolence and devotion that you wonder why it isn't common knowledge that the ideal couple is in fact a tall black woman and a short white man" (Garis). Another glimpse of the marriage was provided by a reporter in 1997 who, in discussing Kincaid's "straight talk," remarked, "Even her husband sometimes admonishes her: 'Dear, please do mince words'" (J. Kaufman). Kincaid married Allen Shawn in 1979; in April 2003, an interviewer reported that the couple had "recently" divorced (McKenna).

Describing her relationship with her two growing children in comments made in 1993—Annie was eight at the time and Harold five—Kincaid stated that while Annie had "a tremendous hold" over her and she felt she knew her daughter "very well," Harold had a different kind of "hold" over her, for he was "more mysterious" to her. "I don't understand men, really, or masculinity. I often look at him with a kind of curiosity that I don't feel with my daughter at all." Attempting to make sense of her deep attachment to her daughter, she explained, "I find it very interesting, how much I love her and how much I depend on her, on seeing her, on being near her, and how much I worship her in some way. I think that it will be a very absorbing thing for me to see how that kind of hold develops. I think it may be quite difficult for me. . . . Maybe I'm just doomed to be in awe of these two powerful women at various times of my life—first my mother and now my daughter" (Wachtel 65–66). If, as Kincaid's comments suggest, she was "doomed" to relive her childhood relationship with her idealized mother in her relation with her young daughter, she was not caught up in a blind repetition of the past. For she was acutely aware of the "hold" her daughter had on her and, indeed, seemed intent on finding a way to articulate and make writerly sense out of her deep attachment to and identification with her growing daughter. She also was determined not to force her will on her children. "[T]hey don't feel they have to be anything," as she later remarked of her children in 1997. "I see that they will be different from me. I don't have expectations of them living for me. I feel I serve them and it may not be good service. They do have the final word on that" (J. Kaufman).

In 1996, when Kincaid, her mother, Annie Drew, and her daughter, Annie Shawn, were photographed for Mariana Cook's *Generations of Women: In Their Own Words*, each said a few words about their relationship. In her remarks, Annie Shawn said that she and her mother loved each other "very much" and that she was "similar to" her mother but was "more forgiving." "[W]hen I'm being mean my mom says, 'Oh, you're just like Grandma Annie,' but I don't think I am. Sometimes my mother acts like my grandmother a little bit. I think my mom's going to look like her mother when she gets old." Annie

Shawn also said that her mother was not like any of the mothers of her friends: "[T]hey're all normal, not very interesting. Everyone says my mom's the coolest mom and I agree. At my parties she dances and teaches everyone weird dances" ("Portraits: Jamaica Kincaid, Annie Shawn, and Annie Drew" 20).

In a *People* magazine interview in 1997, Kincaid was reluctant to talk about her conversion four years before to Judaism. "I don't know why," she commented, "but I do feel that God is a private issue." Beth El's rabbi, Howard Cohen, said this of Kincaid, who was serving as the president of the congregation: "Jamaica will show up at a business meeting in overalls with garden dirt under her nails. She is able to win the respect of CEOs and persuade them to commit time and money to the synagogue." Cohen also remarked of Kincaid, "There is something of the prophet in her writing. . . . She writes a lot about oppression and makes people uncomfortable, which is what the prophets did" (J. Kaufman).

5. In a *New Yorker* essay published in 2001, Kincaid remarked: "I see that my favorite catalogue in the world, Ronninger's Seed & Potato Company, has been absorbed into something called Irish Eyes & Garden City Seeds. The old catalogue by Mr. Ronninger (I assume it is a Mr.; I do not know for sure) seemed to regard the potato as the staff of life itself, as if it were something holy, requiring a special brand of attention. . . . Also, the writing in the catalogue was the same every year, and every year I read it as if it were completely unfamiliar to me. Mr. Ronninger lived somewhere in Idaho I had never heard of, and perhaps he grew tired of his reverence for the potato, because one year, quite unexpectedly, the Ronninger's Seed & Potato catalogue disappeared, only to reappear inside this not at all appealing thing called Irish Eyes & Garden City Seeds" ("Days of Ice and Roses").

Works Cited

Primary Sources—Works of Jamaica Kincaid

Fiction and Nonfiction Books

Annie John. New York: Farrar, Straus, and Giroux, 1985.

At the Bottom of the River. 1983. New York: Plume-Penguin, 1992.

The Autobiography of My Mother. 1996. New York: Plume-Penguin, 1997.

Lucy. 1990. New York: Plume-Penguin, 1991.

Mr. Potter. New York: Farrar, Straus, and Giroux, 2002.

My Brother. 1997. New York: Noonday-Farrar, Straus, and Giroux, 1998.

My Garden (Book):. New York: Farrar, Straus, and Giroux, 1999.

A Small Place. 1988. New York: Plume-Penguin, 1989.

Talk Stories. New York: Farrar, Straus, and Giroux. 2001.

Uncollected Short Stories, Essays, and Other Nonfiction Works

"Antigua Crossings." *Rolling Stone* 29 June 1978: 48–50.

"Biography of a Dress." *Grand Street* 43 11.3 (Fall 1992): 93–100.

"Days of Ice and Roses." *The New Yorker* 77.3 (12 Mar. 2001): 59–63. Lexis-Nexis Academic Universe. 15 November 2002 <http://web.lexis-nexis.com/>.

"Introduction." *Generations of Women in Their Own Words.* Photographs by Mariana Cook. San Francisco: Chronicle Books, 1998. 9–11.

"Introduction." *Talk Stories,* 3–14.

"Islander Once, Now Voyager." *New York Times* 22 Sept. 2000: B 27, B 38. 22 Sept. 2000 <http://www.nytimes.com./2000/09/22/arts/22KINC.html>.

"The Little Revenge from the Periphery." *Transition* 73 (1997): 68–73.

"On Seeing England for the First Time." *Transition* 51 (1991): 32–40.

"Ovando." *Conjunctions* 14 (1989): 75–83.

"Putting Myself Together." *The New Yorker* 71.1 (20 and 27 Feb. 1995): 93–94, 98, 100–01.

"Sowers and Reapers." *The New Yorker* 76.43 (22 Jan. 2001): 41–45. Lexis-Nexis Academic Universe. 15 Nov. 2002 <http://web.lexis-nexis.com/>.

"Those Words That Echo . . . Echo . . . Echo through Life." *New York Times* 7 June 1999: E1. 22 June 2000 <wysiwyg://61/http://www.nytimes.co...y/books/060799kincaid-writing.html>.

Kincaid's Interviews

Balutansky, Kathleen. "On Gardening: An Interview with Jamaica Kincaid." *Callaloo* 25.3 (2002): 790–800. 1 Nov. 2002 <http://muse.jhu.edu/journals/callaloo/v025/25.3balutansky.html>.

BBC World Service. "Her Story: Jamaica Kincaid." 11 Nov. 2001 <http://www.bbc.co.uk/worldservice/arts/features/womenwriters/kincaid_life.shtml>.

Birbalsingh, Frank. "Jamaica Kincaid: From Antigua to America." *Frontiers of Caribbean Literature in English*. Ed. Frank Birbalsingh. New York: St. Martin's, 1996. 138–51.

Bonetti, Kay. "Jamaica Kincaid." *Conversations with American Novelists: The Best Interviews from the* Missouri Review *and the American Audio Prose Library*. Ed. Kay Bonetti et al. Columbia: University of Missouri Press, 1997. 26–38.

Brady, Thomas. "Talking with Jamaica Kincaid: From Her Books Comes the Story of Her Life." *The Philadelphia Inquirer* 30 Nov. 1997: Q2. 2 Jan. 2002 <http://www.philly.com/packages/history/arts/literature/kincaid.asp>.

Conover, Patricia. "For Jamaica Kincaid, All Literary Roads Lead Home." *Portland Oregonian*, 22 April 2001: F9. Dow Jones Interactive—Library Publications. 9 Feb. 2002 <http://ptg.djnr.com/>.

Cryer, Dan. "The Unlikely Success of Jamaica Kincaid." *Newsday* 8 Jan. 1996: B4. Dow Jones Interactive—Library Publications. 9 Feb. 2002 <http://ptg.djnr.com/>.

Cudjoe, Selwyn. "Jamaica Kincaid and the Modernist Project: An Interview." *Caribbean Women Writers: Essays from the First International Conference*. Ed. Selwyn Cudjoe. Wellesley, Mass: Calaloux, 1990. 215–32.

DeLombard, Jeannine. "My Brother's Keeper: An Interview with Jamaica Kincaid." *Lambda Book Report* 6.10 (May 1998): 14. EBSCO: Academic Search Elite. 29 Aug. 2002 <http://web5.epnet.com/>.

Deziel, Shanda. "Fact, Fiction, Frappuccino." *Maclean's* 115.22 (June 3, 2002): 35. EBSCO: Academic Search Elite. 5 June 2002 <http://ehostvgw11.epnet.com/>.

Dilger, Gerhard. "I Use a Cut and Slash Policy of Writing: Jamaica Kincaid Talks to Gerhard Dilger." *Wasafiri* 16 (Autumn 1992): 21–25.

Donahue, Deirdre. "Kincaid Calls on Antigua's Influence." *USA Today* 8 Nov. 1990: 5D. Dow Jones Interactive—Library Publications. 9 Feb. 2002 <http://ptg.djnr. com/>.

Drewes, Caroline. "Jamaica Kincaid Rages On: Settled, Successful, She Taps into the Past for Her Books." *San Francisco Examiner* 15 Oct. 1990: C1. Dow Jones Interactive—Library Publications. 9 Feb. 2002 <http://ptg.djnr.com/>.

Essence. "First Person Singular." *Essence* 33.1 (May 2002): 108. EBSCO: Academic Search Elite. 5 June 2002 <http://ehostvgw11.epnet.com/>.

Ferguson, Moira. "A Lot of Memory: An Interview with Jamaica Kincaid." *The Kenyon Review* 16.1 (Winter 1994): 163–88.

Garis, Leslie. "Through West Indian Eyes." *New York Times Magazine* 7 Oct. 1990: Sect. 6, pp. 42–44, 70, 78, 80, 91. 22 June 2000 <http://www.nytimes.com/books/97/10/19/home/kincaid-eyes.html>.

Garner, Dwight. "Jamaica Kincaid: The Salon Interview." 13 Jan. 1996. 22 June 2000 <http://www.salon.com/05/features/kincaid.html>.

Goldfarb, Brad. "Writing=Life: An Interview with Jamaica Kincaid." *Interview* 27.10 (October 1997): 94–99.

Grondahl, Paul. "Pouring Her Soul into Her Words." *Albany Times Union* 13 Feb. 1996: C1. 26 Nov. 2001 <http://www.albany.edu/writers-inst/timesjk.html>.

Hansen, Liane. "Jamaica Kincaid: Liane Speaks to Writer Jamaica Kincaid about the Death of Her Brother from AIDS." National Public Radio's Weekend Edition 23 November 1997. Dow Jones Interactive—Library Publications. 9 Feb. 2002 <http://ptg.djnr.com/>.

Hayden, Chris. "Jamaica Kincaid Writes out of Deep Desire." *St. Louis Post-Dispatch* 31 Oct. 1997: 1E. LexisNexis Academic Universe. 6 Sept. 2002 <http://web.lexis-nexis.com/>.

Heer, Jeet. "What's Found in Translation: Jamaica Kincaid Bridges Oral and Written Traditions in Her Latest Novel." *National Post Online.* 27 May 2002.

5 June 2002 <http://www.nationalpost.com/search/story.html?f=/stories/ 20020527/351057.html>.

Holmstrom, David. "Jamaica Kincaid: Writing for Solace, for Herself." *Christian Science Monitor* 88. 35 (17 January 1996): 14. EBSCO: Academic Search Elite. 29 Aug. 2002 <http://web5.epnet.com/>.

Jackson, Charles. "'A Painful Loss': Kincaid Says 'People Cannot Recover Africa.'" *Syracuse Herald-Journal* 8 May 1996: C4. Dow Jones Interactive—Library Publications. 9 Feb. 2002 <http://ptg.djnr.com/>.

Jacobs, Sally. "Don't Mess with Jamaica Kincaid: Author and Gardener, She Withers as Well as Creates." *The Boston Globe* 20 June 1996: Living Section 57. LexisNexis Academic Universe. 6 Sept. 2002 <http://web. lexis-nexis.com/>.

Jaggi, Maya. "Kincaid in Revolt." 5 Nov. 1997. *Mail and Guardian Online.* 2 Jan. 2002 <http://www.mg.co.za/mg/books/kincaid.htm>.

Jones, Lisa. "Some Nerve: Writer Jamaica Kincaid Has a Few Choice Words with Lisa Jones about Race, Class, Power, Mother Love . . ." *Mirabella* (November 1990): 74–75.

Jones, Vanessa. "Jamaica Kincaid Explores a Father of Her Own Invention: Kincaid Writes Her Own Truth in *Mr. Potter*." *The Boston Globe* 20 June 2002: D1. Dow Jones Interactive—Library Publications. 28 June 2002 <http://ptg.djnr.com/>.

Kaufman, Joanne. "Jamaica Kincaid: An Author's Unsparing Judgments Earn Her an Unwanted Reputation for Anger." *People Magazine* 48.24 (15 December 1997): 109–14. Dow Jones Interactive—Library Publications. 9 Feb. 2002 <http://ptg.djnr.com/>.

Kennedy, Louise. "A Writer Retraces Her Steps: Jamaica Kincaid Finds Herself in Her Words." *The Boston Globe* 7 November 1990: Living Section 85. LexisNexis Academic Universe. 6 Sept. 2002 <http://web.lexis-nexis.com/>.

Kreilkamp, Ivan. "Jamaica Kincaid: Daring to Discomfort." *Publishers Weekly* 243.1 (1 Jan. 1996): 54–55.

Langton, James. "Women at War: A 'Falling Out' Is How the Writer Jamaica Kincaid Refers to Her Row with the Formidable Tina Brown, Editor of *The New Yorker*." *The Sunday Telegraph London* 13 Oct. 1996: 6. Dow Jones Interactive—Library Publications. 9 Feb. 2002 <http://ptg. djnr.com/>.

Lee, Felicia. "It's a Time of Change for Ex-*New Yorker* Writer Kincaid." *Atlanta Journal and Constitution* 20 Feb. 1996: D3. Dow Jones Interactive— Library Publications. 9 Feb. 2002 <http://ptg.djnr.com/>.

Listfield, Emily. "Straight from the Heart." *Harper's Bazaar* 123 (October 1990): 82.

Macgowan, James. "Me Myself and My Narrator." *The Ottawa Citizen* 2 June 2002: C10. LexisNexis Academic Universe. 18 Sept. 2003 <http://web.lexis-nexis.com/>.

McKenna, Sheila. "Kincaid Has Authored a Real Success Story." *Newsday* 4 April 2003: A55. LexisNexis Academic Universe. 18 Sept. 2003 <http://web.lexis-nexis.com/>.

McLarin, Kim. "BIBR Talks with Jamaica Kincaid." *Black Issues Book Review* 4.4 (Jul.–Aug. 2002). EBSCO: Academic Search Elite. 29 Aug. 2002 <http://web5.epnet.com/>.

Mehren, Elizabeth. "Cruelty and Loneliness in an Island Paradise: Jamaica Kincaid's Books Turn to Her Troubled Past." *Los Angeles Times* 28 Nov. 1997: E1. LexisNexis Academic Universe. 6 Sept. 2002 <http://web.lexis-nexis.com/>.

Mendelsohn, Jane. "Leaving Home: Jamaica Kincaid's Voyage round Her Mother." *Village Voice Literary Supplement* 89 (October 1990): 21.

Muirhead, Pamela. "An Interview with Jamaica Kincaid." *Clockwatch Review* 9 (1994–1995): 39–48.

Nurse, Donna. "Jamaica Kincaid Tends Her Garden." *The Globe and Mail* 2 Dec. 1997: D3.

O'Conner, Patricia. "My Mother Wrote My Life." *New York Times Book Review* 7 April 1985: 6.

Penkava, Melinda. "How Did the Old Nursery Rhyme Go?" National Public Radio: Talk of the Nation, November 15, 1999. Dow Jones Interactive—Library Publications. 9 Feb. 2002 <http://ptg.djnr.com/>.

Perry, Donna. "An Interview with Jamaica Kincaid." *Reading Black, Reading Feminist: A Critical Anthology.* Ed. Henry Louis Gates. New York: Meridian-Penguin, 1990. 492–509.

"Portraits: Jamaica Kincaid, Annie Shawn, and Annie Drew." *Generations of Women in Their Own Words.* Photographs by Mariana Cook. Introduction by Jamaica Kincaid. San Francisco: Chronicle Books, 1998. 20.

Schneider, Bart. "Geography Lessons: An Interview with Jamaica Kincaid." *Hungry Mind Review* (Winter 1997–1998): 8–9.

Shen, Andrea. "Tending Her Gardens." *Harvard University Gazette* 16 Mar. 2000. 17 Dec. 2001 <http://www.news.harvard.edu/gazette/2000/03.16/kincaid.html>.

Snell, Marilyn. "Jamaica Kincaid Hates Happy Endings." *Mother Jones* 22.5 (Sept.–Oct. 1997): 28–31. 22 June 2000 <http://www.motherjones. com/mother_jones/SO97/snell.html>.

Steavenson, Wendell. "Mercurial Maternalism." *San Francisco Review* 21.3 (May–June 1996): 36–37.

Trueheart, Charles. "The Writer's Lessons from Literature and Life: Jamaica Kincaid Meets with Students at Dunbar High." *Washington Post* 2 Nov. 1991: G1. Dow Jones Interactive—Library Publications. 9 Feb. 2002 <http://ptg.djnr.com/>.

Vorda, Allan. "I Come from a Place That's Very Unreal: An Interview with Jamaica Kincaid." *Face to Face: Interviews with Contemporary Novelists*. Ed. Allan Vorda. Houston: Rice University Press, 1993. 77–105.

Wachtel, Eleanor. "Eleanor Wachtel with Jamaica Kincaid: Interview." *Malahat Review* 116 (Fall 1996): 55–71.

Walker, Susan. "Jamaica Kincaid, Master Storyteller." *The Toronto Star* 27 May 2002: E4. LexisNexis Academic Universe. 6 Sept. 2002 <http://web. lexis-nexis.com/>.

Secondary Sources

Anatol, Giselle. "Speaking in (M)other Tongues: The Role of Language in Jamaica Kincaid's *The Autobiography of My Mother*." *Callaloo* 25.3 (2002): 938–53. Project Muse. 8 Nov. 2002 <http://muse.jhu.edu/journals/callaloo/v025/25.3anatol.html>.

Benjamin, Jessica. *The Bonds of Love: Psychoanalysis, Feminism, and the Problem of Domination*. New York: Pantheon, 1988.

Berke, Joseph. "Shame and Envy." Nathanson, *Many Faces of Shame*, 318–34.

Bernard, Louise. "Countermemory and Return: Reclamation of the (Postmodern) Self in Jamaica Kincaid's *The Autobiography of My Mother* and *My Brother*." *Modern Fiction Studies* 48.1 (2002): 113–38. Project Muse. 11 Nov. 2002 <http://muse.jhu.edu/journals/modern_fiction_studies/v048/48.1bernard.html>.

Bouson, J. Brooks. *Quiet as It's Kept: Shame, Trauma and Race in the Novels of Toni Morrison*. Albany: State University of New York Press, 2000.

Brophy, Sarah. "Angels in Antigua: The Diasporic of Melancholy in Jamaica Kincaid's *My Brother*." *PMLA* 117.2 (March 2002): 265–77.

Broucek, Francis. *Shame and the Self*. New York: Guilford, 1991.

Caton, Louis. "Romantic Struggles: The Bildungsroman and Mother-Daughter Bonding in Jamaica Kincaid's *Annie John*." *MELUS* 21.3 (Fall 1996): 125–42. OCLC FirstSearch. 29 June 2000 <http://newfirstsearch.oclc.org>.

Chodorow, Nancy. *The Power of Feelings: Personal Meaning in Psychoanalysis, Gender, and Culture.* New Haven: Yale University Press, 1999.

——. *The Reproduction of Mothering: Psychoanalysis and the Sociology of Gender.* Berkeley: University of California Press, 1978.

Cobham, Rhonda. "Mwen na rien, Msieu": Jamaica Kincaid and the Problem of Creole Gnosis." *Callaloo* 25.3 (2002): 868–84. Project Muse. 8 Nov. 2002 <http://muse.jhu.edu/journals/callaloo/v025/25.3cobham.html>.

Covi, Giovanna. "Jamaica Kincaid's Prismatic Self and the Decolonialisation of Language and Thought." *Framing the Word: Gender and Genre in Caribbean Women's Writing.* Ed. Joan Anim-Addo. London: Whiting and Birch, 1996. 37–67.

Curry, Renee. "'I Ain't No Friggin' Little Wimp': The Girl 'I' Narrator in Contemporary Fiction." *The Girl: Constructions of the Girl in Contemporary Fiction by Women.* Ed. Ruth Saxton. New York: St. Martin's, 1998. 95–105.

Damasio, Antonio. *The Feeling of What Happens: Body and Emotion in the Making of Consciousness.* New York: Harcourt Brace, 1999.

de Abruna, Laura Niesen. "Jamaica Kincaid's Writing and the Maternal-Colonial Matrix." *Caribbean Women Writers: Fiction in English.* Ed. Mary Condé and Thorunn Lonsdale. New York: St. Martin's, 1999. 172–83.

Donnell, Alison. "Dreaming of Daffodils: Cultural Resistance in the Narratives of Theory." *Kunapipi* 14.2 (1992): 45–52.

——. "She Ties Her Tongue: The Problems of Cultural Paralysis in Postcolonial Criticism." *Ariel: A Review of International English Literature* 26.1 (January 1995): 101–16.

——. "When Writing the Other Is Being True to the Self: Jamaica Kincaid's *The Autobiography of My Mother.*" *Women's Lives into Print: The Theory, Practice and Writing of Feminist Auto/Biography.* Ed. Pauline Polkey. New York: St. Martin's-Macmillan, 1999. 123–36.

Eakin, Paul John. *How Our Lives Become Stories: Making Selves.* Ithaca: Cornell University Press, 1999.

Emery, Mary Lou. "Refiguring the Postcolonial Imagination: Tropes of Visuality in Writing by Rhys, Kincaid, and Cliff." *Tulsa Studies in Women's Literature* 16.2 (Fall 1997): 259–80.

Fanon, Frantz. *Black Skin, White Masks.* Trans. Charles Markmann. New York: Grove, 1967.

Ferguson, Moira. *Jamaica Kincaid: Where the Land Meets the Body.* Charlottesville: University Press of Virginia, 1994.

Fox, Pamela. *Class Fictions: Shame and Resistance in the British Working-Class Novel, 1890–1945*. Durham: Duke University Press, 1994.

Gilmore, Leigh. *The Limits of Autobiography: Trauma and Testimony*. Ithaca: Cornell University Press, 2001.

Goldberg, Carl. *Understanding Shame*. Northvale, NJ: Jason Aronson, 1991.

Gregg, Veronica. "How Jamaica Kincaid Writes the Autobiography of Her Mother." *Callaloo* 25.3 (2002): 920–37. Project Muse. 8 Nov. 2002 <http://muse.jhu.edu/journals/callaloo/v025/25.3gregg.html>.

Herman, Judith Lewis. *Trauma and Recovery*. New York: BasicBooks-HarperCollins, 1992.

Hodge, Merle. "Caribbean Writers and Caribbean Language: A Study of Jamaica Kincaid's *Annie John*." *Winds of Change: The Transforming Voices of Caribbean Women Writers and Scholars*. Ed. Adele Newson and Linda Strong-Leek. New York: Peter Lang, 1998. 47–53.

Kaufman, Gershen. *The Psychology of Shame: Theory and Treatment of Shame-Based Syndromes*. New York: Springer, 1989.

———. *Shame: The Power of Caring*. 1980, 1985. 3rd ed. Rochester, VT: Schenkman Books, 1992.

Kilborne, Benjamin. *Disappearing Persons: Shame and Appearance*. Albany: State University of New York Press, 2002.

King, Jane. "A Small Place Writes Back." *Callaloo* 25.3 (2002): 885–909. Project Muse 8 Nov. 2002 <http://muse.jhu.edu/journals/callaloo/v025/25.3king.html>.

King, Nicola. *Memory, Narrative, Identity: Remembering the Self*. Edinburgh: Edinburgh University Press, 2000.

Kovel, Joel. *White Racism: A Psychohistory*. 1970. New York: Columbia University Press, 1984.

Lanser, Susan. "Compared to What? Global Feminism, Comparatism, and the Master's Tools." *Borderwork: Feminist Engagements with Comparative Literature*. Ed. Margaret Higonnet. Ithaca: Cornell University Press, 1994. 280–300.

Layton, Lynne. *Who's That Girl? Who's That Boy? Clinical Practice Meets Postmodern Gender Theory*. Northvale, NJ: Jason Aronson, 1998.

Ledent, Bénédicte. "Voyages into Otherness: *Cambridge* and *Lucy*." *Kunapipi* 14.2 (1992): 53–63.

Lewis, Helen Block. "Introduction: Shame—The 'Sleeper' in Psychopathology." Helen Lewis, *Role of Shame* 1–28.

———. "The Role of Shame in Depression Over the Life Span." Helen Lewis, *Role of Shame*, 29–50.

——— (ed). *The Role of Shame in Symptom Formation*. Hillsdale, NJ: Lawrence Erlbaum, 1987.

Lewis, Michael. *Shame: The Exposed Self*. 1992. New York: Free Press-Simon and Schuster, 1995.

Lima, Maria. "Imaginary Homelands in Jamaica Kincaid's Narratives of Development." *Callaloo* 25.3 (2002): 857–67. Project Muse. 8 Nov. 2002 <http://muse.jhu.edu/journals/callaloo/v025/25.3lima.html>.

MacDonald-Smythe, Antonia. *Making Homes in the West/Indies: Constructions of Subjectivity in the Writings of Michelle Cliff and Jamaica Kincaid*. New York: Garland, 2001.

Mahler, Margaret, Fred Pine, and Anni Bergman. *The Psychological Birth of the Human Infant: Symbiosis and Individuation*. New York: Basic Books, 1975.

Mahlis, Kristen. "Gender and Exile: Jamaica Kincaid's *Lucy*." *Modern Fiction Studies* 44.1 (1998): 164–83. 29 June 2000. <http://muse.jhu.edu/journals/modern_fiction_studies/v044/44.1mahlis.html>.

Miller, Alice. *For Your Own Good: Hidden Cruelty in Child-rearing and the Roots of Violence*. 1983. Trans. Hildegarde and Hunter Hannum. New York: Noonday-Farrar, Straus, and Giroux, 1990.

———. *Prisoners of Childhood: The Drama of the Gifted Child and the Search for the True Self*. Trans. Ruth Ward. New York: Basic Books, 1981.

Mistron, Deborah. *Understanding Jamaica Kincaid's* Annie John: *A Student Casebook to Issues, Sources, and Historical Documents*. Westport, CT: Greenwood, 1999.

Morrison, Andrew. *The Culture of Shame*. New York: Ballantine-Random House, 1996.

———. *Shame: The Underside of Narcissism*. Hillsdale, NJ: Analytic, 1989.

Murdoch, H. Adlai. "Severing the (M)other Connection: The Representation of Cultural Identity in Jamaica Kincaid's *Annie John*." *Callaloo* 13.2 (Spring 1990): 325–40.

Nathanson, Donald. *Shame and Pride: Affect, Sex, and the Birth of the Self*. 1992. New York: Norton, 1994.

Nathanson, Donald (ed). *The Many Faces of Shame*. New York: Guilford, 1987.

Natov, Roni. "Mothers and Daughters: Jamaica Kincaid's Pre-Oedipal Narrative." *Children's Literature: Annual of the Modern Language Association Division on Children's Literature* 18 (1990): 1–16.

O'Brien, Susie. "The Garden and the World: Jamaica Kincaid and the Cultural Borders of Ecocriticism." *Mosaic* 35.2 (June 2002): 167–84. 15 Nov. 2002 <http://infotrac.galegroup.com>.

Oczkowicz, Edyta. "Jamaica Kincaid's *Lucy*: Cultural 'Translation' as a Case of Creative Exploration of the Past." *MELUS* 21.3 (Fall 1996): 143–57. OCLC First Search. 29 June 2000. <http://NewFirstSearch.oclc.org>.

Paquet, Sandra Pouchet. *Caribbean Autobiography: Cultural Identity and Self-Representation*. Madison: University of Wisconsin Press, 2002.

Paravisini-Gebert, Lizabeth. *Jamaica Kincaid: A Critical Companion*. Westport, CT: Greenwood, 1999.

Perry, Donna. "Initiation in Jamaica Kincaid's *Annie John*." *Caribbean Women Writers: Essays from the First International Conference*. Ed. Selwyn Cudjoe. Wellesley, MA: Calaloux, 1990. 245–53. (Rpt. in *Contemporary American Women Writers: Gender, Class, Ethnicity*. Ed. Lois Zamora. New York: Longman, 1998. 128–37.)

Pfister, Joel. "On Conceptualizing the Cultural History of Emotional and Psychological Life in America." *Inventing the Psychological: Toward a Cultural History of Emotional Life in America*. Ed. Joel Pfister and Nancy Schnog. New Haven: Yale University Press, 1997. 17–59.

Poon, Angelia. "Re-writing the Male Text: Mapping Cultural Spaces in Edwidge Danticat's *Krik?Krak!* and Jamaica Kincaid's *A Small Place*." *Jouvert: A Journal of Postcolonial Studies* 4.2 (Winter 2000): 30 paras. 23 May 2001 <http://social.chass.ncsu.edu/jouvert/v4i2/anpoon.htm>.

Rice, Anne P. "Burning Connections: Maternal Betrayal in Jamaica Kincaid's *My Brother*." *A/B: Auto/Biography Studies* 14. 1 (Summer 1999): 23–37.

Rich, Adrienne. *Of Woman Born: Motherhood as Experience and Institution*. New York: Norton, 1976.

Rozin, Paul, Jonathan Haidt, Clark McCauley. "Disgust." *Handbook of Emotions*. Ed. Michael Lewis and Jeannette Haviland. New York: Guilford, 1993. 575–94.

St. Clair, Michael. *Object Relations and Self Psychology: An Introduction*. Monterey, CA: Brooks/Cole, 1986.

Schapiro, Barbara. *D. H. Lawrence and the Paradoxes of Psychic Life*. Albany: State University of New York Press, 1999.

Scheff, Thomas. "The Shame-Rage Spiral: A Case Study of an Interminable Quarrel." Helen Lewis, *Role of Shame*, 109–49.

Scheff, Thomas, and Suzanne Retzinger. *Emotions and Violence: Shame and Rage in Destructive Conflicts*. Lexington, MA: Lexington Books-D.C. Heath, 1991.

Schneider, Carl. *Shame, Exposure, and Privacy.* 1977. New York: Norton, 1992.

❦Scott, Helen. "'Dem Tief, Dem a Dam Tief ': Jamaica Kincaid's Literature of Protest." *Callaloo* 25.3 (2002): 977–89. Project Muse. 8 Nov. 2002 <http://muse.jhu.edu/journals/callaloo/v025/25.3scott01.html>.

Simmons, Diane. *Jamaica Kincaid.* New York: Twayne-Macmillan, 1994.

Steinberg, Marlene. "Systematizing Dissociation: Symptomatology and Diagnostic Assessment." *Dissociation: Culture, Mind, and Body.* Ed. David Spiegel. Washington: American Psychiatric, 1994. 59–88.

Timothy, Helen. "Adolescent Rebellion and Gender Relations in *At the Bottom of the River* and *Annie John.*" *Caribbean Women Writers: Essays from the First International Conference.* Ed. Selwyn Cudjoe. Wellesley, MA: Calaloux, 1990. 233–42.

Waites, Elizabeth. *Trauma and Survival: Post-Traumatic and Dissociative Disorders in Women.* New York: Norton, 1993.

Wurmser, Léon. *The Mask of Shame.* 1981. Northvale, NJ: Jason Aronson, 1994.

———. "Shame: The Veiled Companion of Narcissism." Nathanson, *Many Faces of Shame,* 64–92.

Yeoh, Gilbert. "From Caliban to Sycorax: Revisions of *The Tempest* in Jamaica Kincaid's *Annie John.*" *World Literature Written in English* 33.2 & 34.1 (1993–94): 103–16.

Index

Anatol, Giselle, 211n6

Annie John: 2, 13–14; abuse, trauma specialists on, 40–41, 42, 45; Annie Drew in, 40, 58, 64, 197–98n2, 198–99n6, 199–200n9, 200–201n13, 201nn15–16; autobiographical sources of, 37–40, 61, 65–66, 197–98nn1–3, 198–99nn5–7, 199–202nn9–19, 202nn21–23; and "Biography of a Dress," abused daughter in, 43–44; childhood abuse in, 39–40, 44–45, 47, 50, 52, 57, 58, 61–62, 63–64, 200–201n13; childhood shaming in, 40, 42; closure, Kincaid on, 64; as coming-of-age novel, 37; Kincaid on, 37–38, 64; mother as oppressive, Kincaid on, 38; mother enigma, critics on, 39, 40, 63; narrative withholding and avoidance in, 42; shadow trauma story in, 39–40, 44–45, 47, 50, 52, 57, 58, 61–62, 63–64; shaming, effects of, psychologists on, 41–42, 47, 48, 49, 56, 59, 60, 61, 62; writing as act of self-rescue, Kincaid on, 38
—Annie John: abusive play of, 45, 52; adolescent depression of, 58–59, 61–63; autobiographical writing of, 48; as beloved and abused child, 44–47; breakdown and recovery of, 61–63; colonial education, identification with and resistance to, 53–56; dead children and maternal abuse, secret of, 44–45; dependency needs and abandonment fears of, 44, 45, 47–49, 57; dissociative experiences of, 57, 58, 61–62, 64; dysphoria of, 64–65; English culture, defiance toward, 49, 54–55, 56; feminine roles, rebellion against, 56, 57; good/bad identities of, 46, 49–50, 51–53, 54, 58, 59; leavetaking of, 64–65; as liar and thief, 52; Lucifer, identification with, 59; maternal contempt, response to, 49, 50, 58–59, 60–61, 62, 63, 64; maternal rejection, sensitivity to, 45, 47–50, 52, 55–56, 60–61; maturing body, shame-anxiety about, 56–57; mother, idealization of, 46, 47, 48, 50; mother's sexual shaming of, 60; obeah, fear of, 45–46; shame of, 45, 47, 48–49, 50–51, 51–52, 56–57, 59–63, 64; shame defenses of, 48–49, 49–50, 51–52, 54–55, 56, 57, 59, 60, 63, 64; talks back to the mother, account of, 50, 60; unladylike behavior of, 49, 56–57
—Gwen: Annie's idealization of, 51; Annie's rejection of, 57; as idealized "good" self, 51